GLOBAL GOOD NEWS

MISSION IN A NEW CONTEXT

Edited by Howard A. Snyder

ABINGDON PRESS / Nashville

GLOBAL GOOD NEWS: MISSION IN A NEW CONTEXT

Copyright © 2001 by Abingdon Press

This book is printed on recycled, acid-free, elemental-chlorine–free paper.

Library of Congress Cataloging-in-Publication Data

Global good news: mission in a new context / edited by Howard A. Snyder.
    p. cm.
Includes bibliographical references and index.
ISBN 0-687-01586-3 (alk. paper)
    1. Missions—Theory. 2. Postmodernism—Religious aspects—Christianity.
I. Snyder, Howard A.

BV2063 .G55 2001
266'.001—dc21

2001022578

CONTENTS

SHARING GOOD NEWS

INTRODUCTION

THE NEW SHAPE OF GLOBAL WITNESS

Three facts are indisputable:
- Global society is becoming highly interconnected.
- Despite technical progress, the world is full of pain, suffering, and violence.
- Christians have a mission to share the message of Jesus Christ with the whole world.

Hard evidence supports each of these claims. These are not primarily faith statements; they are public truths. A Hindu or atheist or secularist could agree with them. The evidence of our fractured but connected globe is broadcast daily. And even non-Christians can see, if they look at the Bible, that Christians have a world mission. Whether they see this as good news or bad news is another question.

This book argues that the Christian mission is good news. In fact, *the* good news. The contributors recognize, and at times insist, that the Christian church has often twisted the good news into bad news. Too often it has talked about Jesus but acted like the devil.

Nonetheless, we make the claim that the gospel really is good news. Here also we would take Jesus as our model, for he told the would-be gospelers of his day, "For the sake of your tradition, you make void the word of God" (Matt. 15:6). In other words, you say one thing and do another. You tell people what to do but practice injustice yourself. You talk about love in an unloving way. You turn good news into bad news.

And yet there *is* good news. Jesus Christ is good news, however the message may at times be distorted. It is good news when someone discovers a cure for a dread disease, and those who know about it bear an awesome responsibility.

According to the New Testament writers, if the gospel is good news for any, it is good news for all. It is global good news. That is, it is a message and a life for the whole human family. Of course, some may hear it as bad news. Word of a cure for a dread disease sounds like bad news to people who don't want to be well, or to people who profit from keeping people sick. And it may seem irrelevant to those who don't realize they have the disease.

What does it mean, in our kind of world, to say the gospel is global good news? This book explores that question. The contributors, men and women of diverse backgrounds, share the conviction that, properly understood, the gospel *really is* good news for *everyone*. As the reader will see, the contributors don't all agree as to what the gospel "properly understood" really means. In some ways this book is a debate as well as a search for answers. All the contributors, however, have wrestled with the global meaning of the Christian message and bring keen insight to the task at hand. The goal is to inform concerning the critical challenges facing Christian witness today, to draw connecting lines between these challenges and the story of Jesus Christ, and to show some of the important ways in which the gospel really is global good news. The result is a remarkable collection of essays exploring the most important questions in Christian mission for the coming decades. The very points of tension or disagreement in the book provide insight into the contemporary discussion about the meaning of mission and evangelism.

This book had its genesis in a series of lectures presented at United Theological Seminary in Dayton, Ohio, in October 1992. At that time, United's Heisel Chair of Evangelization and Church Renewal was inaugurated. To mark this historic event, United hosted a Consultation on Evangelization in the Postmodern World. Most of the chapters in the book are based on lectures given at that consultation. Other chapters have been added to round out the topics addressed at that time. The book has grown and changed as events since 1992 have given us opportunity to think more deeply about global good news in our day.

The book explores several critical issues of global evangelization. It is not one sustained argument but an inquiry into key questions from varying perspectives. Some of the essays focus mainly on the practice of mission and evangelism; others probe deeply into fundamental issues of mission theology, offering new, cutting-edge analysis. This volume is thus a substantial contribution at both the theoretical and practical levels—and, in fact, seeks to bridge that divide. The authors represent the encounter and experience of the Christian faith in many lands, including Argentina, Brazil, England, Ghana, Indonesia, Myanmar, Bolivia, South Africa, the United States, and Zimbabwe. Along the way, the book tells a number of remarkable stories of the transforming power of the gospel in very diverse cultural contexts—in their own way showing that the gospel is global good news.

While I have not attempted to harmonize or mask points of disagreement among the contributors, in my own concluding chapter I have out-lined what I believe is a consistent, biblically faithful presentation of the good news. The final chapter does in fact draw together a number of key themes that run throughout the book—particularly those relating to Christology, ecclesiology, missiology, soteriology, and "religiology."

The first half of the book explores our emerging global context and the challenges it presents for Christian mission. The second half attempts to show what it means to share the good news of Jesus Christ in this emerging world. Three critical issues facing world Christian witness are the emergence of postmodernity, the new cutting edges of science, and increasing contact between the world's great religions. William O'Brien, David Lowes Watson, and Norman Thomas deal insightfully with these issues. Then Mortimer Arias, Gregory Leffel, and George Hunter draw out some of the implications for church and mission, in various ways calling for a substantial rethinking of our models of the church-in-mission.

In the second half of the book, Andrew Kirk, Luís Wesley de Souza, Seth Asare, and Priscilla Pope-Levison dig deeply into the question of mission theology. Robert Tuttle and Yishey Latt examine issues of cul-ture, asking how the gospel can be both culturally sensitive and biblical-ly faithful. Finally, Neuza Itioka and Howard Snyder make the case for a contemporary evangelization that takes seriously the challenges of evil and of pluralism yet remains centered in Jesus Christ and the power of the Spirit.

Howard A. Snyder

THE NEW GLOBAL CONTEXT

"Mission is the DNA of the church," says William R. O'Brien. Mission draws the church to fulfill its intended purpose. Surveying the global situation today, O'Brien argues that global Christian mission has "already phased into a new paradigm" that will mark the third millennium. Decreasing denominational "brand loyalty" and other factors mean that "the old vertical Catholic/Protestant divide" is being superseded by a new horizontal axis that cuts through all our ecclesiastical groupings. But is the church encumbered by too much old baggage to move with the new paradigm?

CHAPTER ONE

MISSION IN THE VALLEY OF POSTMODERNITY
William R. O'Brien

A.D. *2025: Missions Scenario*

Background/Context

USA: Baby boomers are approaching retirement (normal retirement age ranging between seventy and seventy-five years of age). Multiple transitions during the working years of baby boomers have included:

- from hierarchical organization to networking;
- from industrial society to knowledge society;
- from broadcasting to narrowcasting;
- from bureaucratic processes to entrepreneurial projects; and
- from unlimited growth to survival.

EUROPE: The maturing of United Europe and Confederated Russoslavia. A pragmatic Pope and charismatic Archbishop of Canterbury lead their confessions to a "ground of unity."

MIDDLE EAST: Struggling with the aftermath and consequences of limited nuclear warfare over water rights, the vastly diminished Orthodox Church takes the lead in reconciliation through its Magi Peace Force.

AFRICA: Still in a catch-up mode, it is mired in a twentieth-century-type ideological and religious conflict between Afro-Marxism, Islam, and Christianity. All are competing for allegiances in dealing with consequences of AIDS, poverty, mismanagement, and environmental disasters.

LATIN AMERICA: Brazil and Argentina create a binary market with common currency called the *pezado,* joining three other global interchangeable currencies: the Dollar, the Euro, and the YuAsia.

ASIA: After the near collapse of the Nikkei stock market, the free-fall of the yen, and the restructuring of the Asian Market, the Pacific Rim takes on a new identity as one of the four major economic blocs in the world, with the new YuAsia based on Singapore's stackpole currency for the Association of Southeast Asian Nations, and the strong Yuan in China.

A.D. 2025: GIVENS AFFECTING MISSION STRATEGIES

1. The information society/technological revolution means instant voice contact anywhere in the world.

2. Global poverty: 50 percent of the entire world population now lives in absolute poverty.

3. Human-produced ecological disasters in the late twentieth and early twenty-first centuries (Aral Sea, Amazon rain forests, North African desertification encroaching deep into the south) call into question the whole issue of earth stewardship. New transnational businesses are formed to deal with disasters.

4. Energy alternatives for daily life also create innovations affecting mission strategies in difficult places—for example, solar-powered one-eye burners for nomadic cooking in deserts and other remote areas and solar-powered "credit card" radios with pretuned frequencies.

5. Redrawn national boundaries further encourage emphasis on peoples rather than nation-states.

6. Rapid global transit (two hours from New York to Tokyo).

7. Pan-confessional approach to worship/*koinonia* resulting in both Protestant and Catholic orders for more entrepreneurial and transnational approaches to missions.

Narrative

Back in A.D. 2008 a trans-Christian Global Missions Commission emerged. Under that umbrella structure, residual denominational entities created various orders for the matching of gifts, callings, interests, and specialties with needs and opportunities, using a network approach.

Some gave themselves exclusively to Minicommission I: contact/encounter missions with nonbelievers out of reach of the gospel. Others engaged in Minicommission II, creating a global approach to interchurch aid, development, and discipling. Research endeavors kept all Great Commission Christians apprised of imbalances between proclamation and discipling.

A broadened understanding and use of Christian laity produced "marketplace martyrs" (living sacrifices). Because of project orientation in short-term endeavors, job security for the "absentee on mission" was provided by churches with trained backup substitutes while the worker was away.

This global mission approach meant endeavors were international in makeup. Citizenship or country of origin was not a factor in the shared commitment. Due to the realities of aging and healthier lifestyles, age considerations of missionaries and their children were not of great consequence. School-age children involved in missions kept up with their own educational needs via satellite classrooms.

The World Council of Churches and old-form national councils had dissolved.

Further developments included new rounds of pentangular dialogue about collaborative missions among Re-formed Orthodox, Re-formed Catholics (including Anglo-Catholics, based on "ground of unity" agreements), United Conciliars, New Evangelicals, and Latfroasia Indigenous.

Charismatics no longer stood as a separately defined group since all of the major ecclesial blocs had more or less effectively assimilated this dimension.

Collaboration among the major church bodies was also encouraged as a means of finding more acceptable ways to relate to the global presence of reformed and missionary non-Christian religions.

Mission was inclusively concerned with personal transformation and systemic application of the gospel to corporate/structural evil that denies justice and opportunity to large segments of the world's population.

*　　*　　*

The scenario just described does not necessarily fall into the category of either probable or preferable in every one of its aspects. It is a *possible* scenario. Why, and what conditions make it so?

During our time of language study in Indonesia in 1963, we made a survey trip from Bandung into central Java, where we would be working. Approaching a bridge spanning one of west Java's rivers, I noticed a large sign that made me very uneasy. It read, "Jembatan ini sangat dikwatirkan," which literally translated meant: "This bridge is in critical condition"! In consternation, we waited until a large truck approached and carefully made its way across. Even then our family was most fearful as we crossed that span.

The Enlightenment Bridge is in critical condition. Whether it can carry us from the past to the future is in serious doubt today. The pilings of Enlightenment presuppositions are stressed and fracturing. In structural engineering, if stress can be contained within the elastic range of a structure there will not be permanent damage. But if the stress is great enough to penetrate into the plastic range, there is always permanent deformity. The mission paradigm of the Enlightenment period has been stressed into the plastic range.

Note that I am speaking of the *paradigm*, not of mission itself. The age of mission is not over, but a certain mission era is coming to an end—a mission model whose rules were shaped by the Enlightenment framework. It would be a deadly risk to trust the old bridge to carry the missionary pilgrimage into the future. Why? Let me simply brush lightly two characteristics of the passing era that would be entropic for third millennium missions, and then flag some key trends that will shape a new paradigm.

A. SECULARIZATION

In a closed universe that denies transcendence, humankind is the be-all and end-all. Progress is measured in terms of growth, scientific and technological progress, and the amassing of means. Neil Postman pokes hard at the impact of all this in *Technopoly: The Surrender of Culture to Technology*. He defines technopoly as "the submission of all forms of cultural life to the sovereignty of technique and technology." He further states that "the milieu in which Technopoly flourishes is one in which the tie between information and human purpose has been severed." Then he levels a blistering charge about its consequences: "Stated in the most dramatic terms, the accusation can be made that the uncontrolled growth of technology destroys the vital sources of our humanity. It creates a culture without a moral foundation. It undermines certain mental processes and social relations that make human life worth living."[1]

The corporate expression of a given group of people—that is, the nation-state—is a late-breaking development in the secularization of society. Islamic scholar Dr. Ibrahim Abu-Rabi' of Hartford Seminary points out in class lectures:

> In the wake of the Renaissance, the West has contracts with the state: constitutions, a contract tradition by which a constitution—not God—guarantees one's freedom. From this perspective, a secular constitution is guaranteed by the state, not God. That is, God is not needed. On these ideas hang all the expansion, aggression, and hegemony of Europe as country after country moved into the Middle East, the Arab world.[2]

Western mission models in particular bear the onus of being a product of an increasingly secularized culture. They reflect its model and the rules of its game more than one would care to admit. Even where mission has been valid and effective, its reporting often carries overtones of triumphalism that make it difficult for the outsider to differentiate it from the action and attitude of a conqueror.

B. ANOMIE

Webster defines "anomie" as "social instability resulting from a breakdown of standards and values; *also:* personal unrest, alienation, and uncertainty that comes from a lack of purpose or ideals." In *Emile Durkheim and His Sociology,* Harry Alpert defines anomie as a "condition in which the social pressures making for self-discipline are rendered impotent."[3]

Maria Mies builds on the concept developed by Emile Durkheim that anomic behavior is deviant behavior due to the disintegration of norm and value systems, and transfers this condition to intercultural situations that arise between a dominant culture and a subordinate one. Thus, Mies's definition:

> Cultural anomie comes into being when two cultural systems collide in international contact. When one system puts forward a claim to dominance and is capable of maintaining it materially and permanently, the people of the subordinate system acknowledge this claim and are enticed into attempting to rise into the dominant system, but are culturally restrained from rising.[4]

This is verified by one who has lived through such a clash of systems. Bassam Tibi, in *The Crisis of Modern Islam,* deals with the impact of Western education on Middle Easterners. He argues that such education produces a normative Westernization conceptually, but without a simultaneous structural Westernization.

Western education and the absence of possibilities for success produce the cultural anomie that Maria Mies speaks of. Tibi says, "Westernization of education produced not modernization but alienation. Sociologists of development coined the term 'cultural anomie' in order to describe the consequences of a merely cultural Westernization. The state of anomie is a deviant state. Thus, the condition of an Islamic society influenced by Western norms is one of anomie."[5]

One of the realities of the modern missions movement of the past two hundred years is that of *ecclesiastical* anomie, in which the dominant church has subordinated the emerging church. Again, a continuation of the models that play by the rules of the dominant paradigm represents a piling that is crumbling. It is too weak to support the bridge for missionary pilgrims traveling from past to future. Since this bridge is in critical condition, we have no option but to take the route of the Valley of Transition. To successfully traverse this valley, one must be able to see differently, to "re-vise." The Latin term *revisere* means to look at or see again. Webster says that "to revise" is "to look over again in order to correct or improve"; or "to make a new, amended, improved, or up-to-date version of." Coupled with a meaning of "vision" that has to do with unusual discernment and foresight, we find a vocabulary of "re-visioning" what we are all about in the church on mission as both sign and agent of the Christly reign. Third-millennium missions will be carried out by pilgriming paradigm pioneers. They will see and learn how to negotiate the patterns emerging in a paradigm so new it doesn't yet have a name.

SIGNS OF CHANGE

The world facing third-millennium missions is being shaped by several key trends:

1. City-state Versus Nation-state

We are experiencing migration on a scale never equaled in history. Much of this is survival migration, refugees fleeing for their lives. The global total of refugees is larger than the population of some countries. But intentional migration related to work and study contributes to a related phenomenon, urbanization. Half of the global population now lives in cities. These cities are increasingly internationalized, creating complex multicultural mosaics. They are really city-states, having their own museums, libraries, cultural/theatrical centers, sports arenas, and commercial and financial nodes that link into the global economic network.

2. Transnational Corporations Versus Local Businesses

These emerging city-states house the commercial nodes of today's global network of about forty thousand transnational corporations acknowledged by the United Nations. Using satellite links, most of the transborder data flow bypasses the old central governments of nation-states. As William A. Henry III commented in the special A.D. 2000 edition of *Time* magazine, "Communications technology is eroding the meaning of nationality, ethnicity and borders."[6] A whole new paradigm has emerged that makes adversarial trade as outmoded as the older competitive trade. We now live in a time when neither protectionism nor free trade can serve the common good, argues Peter Drucker. "One answer is to form economic regions or blocs. . . . Regionalism creates a unit capable of an effective trade policy that transcends both protectionism and free trade. It creates a unit capable of *reciprocity*. . . . Reciprocity is fast emerging as the new integrating principle of the world economy."[7]

Could it be that a coordinated regionalism will in time replace global structures like the United Nations? And could reciprocal regionalism and reciprocity be a model for shared mission involvement as well?

3. People Groups Versus Bounded Countries

There is no single accepted mode for identifying peoples. But on the basis of common language and ethnic roots, about twelve thousand people groups can be identified. As the Enlightenment era loses its grip on universal applications, ethnicity is emerging as one of the key characteristics of this hinge-moment in history. Because so many boundaries were arbitrarily drawn during the nineteenth and twentieth centuries, peoples found themselves "alien" to their own families and ethnic kin. One of the characteristics of the Valley of Transition is the attention given to groups that spill across all kinds of lines, such as the Kurds and the Uzbeks. This new reality will force new configurations, not only socially and culturally within these groups, but also regionally as power-blocs emerge based not only on ethnicity but also on economics and religion.

4. Sustainability Versus Unlimited Growth

The world cannot bear 6 billion people all living "the good life." The concept of progress and growth rooted in the northern technological belt is a victim of today's paradigm shift. Serious thinkers know we cannot continue to ignore the reality of almost half the global population living in poverty, with almost 20 percent existing in abject poverty (below $375 annual per capita income). The growing gap between haves and have-nots is not only intolerable, it is immoral. Our current environmental crises will only multiply unless there is a change of mind, direction, and lifestyle. Where we face the possibility of wars being fought and boundaries redrawn over water rights, or an AIDS epidemic that could take 40 million lives, or food withheld as form of genocide against one's enemies, there must emerge a new commitment to collaborate on humanity-wide issues. And that is a valid interfaith agenda.

5. Pluriformity Versus Pluralism

Pluriformity recognizes diversity among the components while affirming a common core that holds diverse elements together. Pluralism, by contrast, can be described not only as a series of islands that are unconnected by any bridges, but also as a place where no one feels any need to build bridges.

I sense a growing reaction to the idea that all views are equally valid and that everything is relative. The new paradigm rejects the notion that life has no ultimates. In a closed system, values may be relegated to the private domain, where one opinion is as valid as the next. There can be no heresy in the private domain because everything is relative and subjective. In the Enlightenment era, religion and the church willingly bought into this private domain as "a place to stand." Science occupied the public domain and lived by "fact" or observed uniformity. To deviate from that was intellectual heresy.

For decades the battle lines were drawn between the private and public domains. But with the fracturing of the old paradigm, people of all religions and no religion are seeking for a sense of roots, an affirmation that there is something bigger than the existence we know—something of ultimate value. The return to fundamentals in Judaism, Islam, and Christianity is an indicator of this emotional and religious migration from the transitory to the permanent. All monotheistic religions are on a pilgrimage of renewal, re-vision, and re-identification. Professor Abu-Rabi' states the dilemma within Islam: "Muslims know present reality is that society must adjust to modernity, but fundamentalists are determined the adjustment will be with regard for the traditions, the sources of Islamic life. The question is how to adjust?"[8] The dilemma can be paraphrased for those in other traditions, as well.

6. Transdenominational Versus Denominational

Globally, Christ-followers are experiencing a new ecumenicity of spirit. Although nearly thirty-four thousand denominations exist, there is less "brand loyalty" now than at any time during the age of proliferating denominations. The realities of a world in travail seem to put some of these things in a different perspective—a re-visioning, if you please. Replacing the old vertical Catholic/Protestant divide, the axis is now horizontal, cutting through all the various groupings. We are more issue-oriented, seeking common cause rather than common church.

Another trend indicating that the shift has already occurred is reflected in the convergence of eight landmark documents that appeared between 1973 and 1989. Six originated within Protestant, Orthodox, Catholic, or Evangelical circles and two were produced jointly across these lines. These are included in a book published by the Overseas Ministries Study Center that deals with mission in the 1990s.[9] To be sure, the collection is a missiological mosaic deriving from diverse backgrounds and positions. But the amount of agreement on issues that all hold in common— a kind of "missiological transcendence" acknowledging a common Lordship and common task—is striking.

These six signs of change show that a great shift has already occurred. But will the new pilgrims insist on bringing old baggage?

BAGS TOO HEAVY FOR THE JOURNEY

Is the church ready for the new paradigm? Or are we encumbered with too much baggage? Three burdens in particular weigh us down.

1. Lack of Consensus

First there was one, then there were two. Now there are roughly thirty-four thousand churchly expressions. From the early Eastern church to a competing Western Roman expression, evangelization and mission varied between "presence" and "assimilation." Reformation restlessness ultimately led to a proliferation of expressions rather than renewal within. Further complicating the issue, there are currently over thirty thousand parachurch organizations in the world, each verbalizing its understanding of mission differently. The meaning of "evangelization" differs from Orthodox to Catholic to Anglican to Protestant to Pentecostal. And there is great variation within some of these categories. For instance, among conservative evangelicals there is no consensus on the meaning of the word "evangelize." Does it mean to proclaim the good news of Jesus in a clear way so that all peoples can accept it or reject it? Does it mean to complete the Christianization process? Is it synonymous with church growth?

The dilemma is like playing three-dimensional tic-tac-toe. If you can get all the X's lined up on one row, they do not match with the X's on the other levels. This lack of consensus implies a working from multiple knowledge bases, often resulting in strategies that are diametrically opposite to each other. Differing definitions also contribute to a growing insularity of strategies.

2. Lack of Collaboration

In 1989, Singapore was the site of the Global Conference on World Evangelization called by the informal "A.D. 2000 and Beyond" network. It was an *ad hoc* meeting not officially sponsored by any denomination or paradenominational entity. The steering committee was international and interdenominational in makeup. The hoped-for outcome was a common vision for world evangelization. The common problem addressed was the growing number of plans for world evangelization, most being developed without reference to anyone else's plan.

Over three hundred leaders from about fifty countries met to discuss this concern. A kaleidoscopic global action plan was presented as a point of reference for reflection and interaction. It generated heated debate. While definitions provided a surface excuse for disagreements, deeper issues came to the fore, ranging from turfism (accusations of "Western arrogance" in even creating such a document) to authority (who has the right or power to oversee the implementation of a comprehensive plan?). The intention, of course, was to stimulate thinking in order to reach consensus on the priority of world evangelization and how there could be cooperation and collaboration across all sorts of lines.

In the years immediately following that consultation, there seemed to be an increasing go-it-alone mentality in many quarters, although notable exceptions of networking among some affinity ministries could be cited. Meanwhile, the "A.D. 2000 and Beyond" movement has provided both the inspiration and the avenues for much greater cooperation. A clear majority of the participants at the Seoul 1995 gathering sponsored by the movement were from "Two-Thirds World" churches. The potential for collaboration throughout the Body of Christ is greater than ever before. Still evident, however, are the culprits that prevent viable collaboration: mistrust of others' theology, differing ecclesiologies, and the sheer complexity of any collaborative venture.

3. Lack of Comprehensiveness

Although there are more Christians today than ever before, the percentage of Christians compared to world population did not change appreciably during the entire twentieth century. The gap between good news haves and good news have-nots is still alarming (more or less so, depending on one's definitions). But perhaps the most significant gap is that between the application of resources for evangelization and those populations most distant from the gospel. About 24 percent of the world's population has never heard the gospel story for the first time. Despite that, over 90 percent of all missionaries and 99.9 percent of all missions money is appropriated for that part of the world that calls itself "Christian." Every major ecclesial bloc declared the decade of the 1990s the "Decade of Evangelization." Each pursued its own strategy based on its own definitions and tradition. Given this lack of comprehensiveness, the unreached population segments would not have been able to hear the gospel during this period of time. And the next century may come and go with little change. Some mission leaders today may disagree, boasting that the Great Commission could be fulfilled by A.D. 2010. But these are primarily Western voices that have not yet engaged in humble collaboration with non-Western counterparts. Until such cooperation happens, comprehensive missions will remain an illusion.

LEAD ON, O SERVANT LORD

Mission is the DNA of the church. It draws the whole system toward a common future: fulfilling the purpose for which it was created.

"Future Pull" is a phenomenon in which "a blueprint of the future serves as the propelling force of creative change." So say George Land and Beth Jarman in *Breakpoint and Beyond: Mastering the Future— Today.* In an article adapted for *The Futurist,* the authors argue that every single cell in all living things grows, not based on its history, but "by being pulled forward by its internal picture of the possible future. That future is inscribed in the DNA, the genes that reside in the nucleus of every cell. That way, every part of the system can pull together toward the common future. In human terms, this translates into living with a powerful vision of the future."[10]

The Cross-Resurrection-Ascension-Pentecost sequence ushered in a proleptic reality for the church. Our servant Lord not only stands with us but also beyond us, beckoning and pulling us toward that for which the church was created. We must understand the *what, where,* and *how* of that call.

What? Commitment to word and deed missions: combining the proclamation of the gospel in all possible ways with actions of love, compassion, and justice that clarify the Word. These are inseparable dimensions of the one gospel. In the cause of Christ and the kingdom, they must never be divorced and made to stand alone. Bishop Lesslie Newbigin says, "Words without deeds are empty, but deeds without words are dumb."[11] Such a commitment to whole gospel/whole person mission calls for all the spiritual gifts evident within the Body of Christ. But the use of those gifts in specific mission applications should be done within the covenantal context of churchly mission. That applies to the setting apart/sending body as well as to its counterpart elsewhere in the world, if such exists.

Where? The world is the field. The information age is "boundary blind." There are no unique continental or regional areas identified exclusively as "mission fields." If the world is the field, it is the world of peoples. Wherever people are unreached or untouched by the gospel of Jesus Christ, that is the point of entry for the good news in all the ways it can be made known. And entry points imply entry strategies.

How? The commissions of Christ are specific, but built into their specificity are dynamic implications. The imperatives of proclaiming good news and nurturing those who respond to it are not debatable. These clear expectations are contextualized within a *where* and a *how* that must not be ignored. Certainly the *where* is everywhere. Further, the "here-there" question must be simultaneously considered and implemented. Any attitude that succumbs to a "here first and there later" approach reflects a narrow cause-and-effect mind-set that denies God's sovereign power and sovereign ways. The *how* was built into the fabric of the commissions when Jesus said, "As the Father has sent me, so I send you" (John 20:21). The *as* defines the servant heart/servant mode. There is no room for triumphalism, a posture of paternalism, or an air of arrogance in the carrying out of servant duties and opportunities. We do not "minister to" those for whom Christ died. Rather, we minister to Christ as we serve among those for whom he died.

CONCLUSION: QUESTION TIME

How can the *missio Dei* once again capture the heart of the Western church? Is it possible to tailor the missions message at local and regional levels through new emerging networks? How do we bring to some convergent point the data from new research—and new awareness arising from such data—on the one hand, and the various stages of readiness of Christians on the other? How does one infiltrate the grassroots precincts of a church, a denomination, or a parachurch constituency with the seeds of evangelism that will lead those entities to realize their full missions potential? And, are we helping believers understand that their missions potential cannot be uncoupled from what God is doing among other believers and churches throughout the world that look different, worship differently, and bring deeper levels of commitment to Christ than many of their Western counterparts do? Can we be more "missio-preneurial," innovative, and risk-taking, sensitive not only to where the movement of God is, but able to respond to it quickly?

Would that our churches might adopt the basic "I must" chart articulated in 1961 by United Nations diplomat and unashamed Christian, Charles Malik:

1. I must study the facts about the world.
2. I must feel a profound and troubled concern for the state of the world.
3. I must keep in close touch with the world situation.
4. I must pray, daily invoking God's will on earth.
5. I must witness to Jesus Christ in the midst of change.
6. I must work for the unity of the Church.
7. I must remain faithful.[12]

To do these things is to respond to the "Future Pull" built into the church. And that pull is toward all those places where Christ is today. After all, he promised that he would prepare such places, that where he was, there we could be also. A third millennium missionary pilgrimage will carry us through the valley of postmodernity and into all those places where our servant Lord is stooping to conquer.

David Lowes Watson argues that much of the church's evangelism today reflects "the anthropocentrism of North American culture and church life" and needs radical reform. We must "restore the mystery of the gospel to our evangelism" so that the church can be an authentic witness of the good news. "Because Jesus was raised from the dead," Watson says, "we can trust his promises of shalom." With this confidence in God, the evangelistic question becomes not "How many?" but rather "How long?" God's intent is to save "not merely souls, but the whole of planet Earth, that blue and white jewel of the cosmos."

CHAPTER TWO

THE MYSTERY OF EVANGELISM: MISSION IN AN AGE OF COSMIC DISCOVERY
David Lowes Watson

It might seem inappropriate to begin with the words of Isaac Watts, who, along with many Nonconformist clergy of his day, viewed Methodists as doctrinally suspect and emotionally unreliable. At least we might infer this from his warning to Philip Doddridge that association with the likes of Wesley, Whitefield, and Zinzendorf could only lower the character of a Dissenting minister.[1] Yet Wesley was not one to bear a grudge. He recognized Watts as one of the great writers of English Nonconformity, and incorporated many of his verses into the 1780 *Collection of Hymns for the Use of the People Called Methodists.* The following excerpt includes personal pronouns we would no longer use, but which need to be retained to capture the power of the poetry:

> Praise ye the Lord! 'tis good to raise
> Your hearts and voices in his praise;
> His nature and his works invite
> To make this duty our delight.
>
> He formed the stars, those heavenly flames;
> He counts their numbers, calls their names;
> His wisdom's vast, and knows no bound,
> A deep where all our thoughts are drowned!

What is the creature's skill or force,
The sprightly man, or warlike horse?
The piercing wit, the active limb,
All are too mean delights for him.

But saints are lovely in his sight,
He views his children with delight!
He sees their hope, he knows their fear,
And looks, and loves his image there. (1737)[2]

These are important words, combining the grandeur of the God of the cosmos with the parental love of the God who was in Christ. Such perspectives are all the more timely for those of us with leadership responsibilities in the church, because the anthropocentrism of so much contemporary theology gives us little resilience against the hedonism and narcissism of our Western culture.[3] The mystery that tends to absorb us today is that of the human psyche, perhaps the most pointless and fruitless avenue of research ever to preoccupy our intellectual endeavors. Human beings are interesting, but not all that interesting. In point of fact, the great majority of us are quite boring to everyone except our Creator who, providentially, retains a degree of professional satisfaction, and a marked degree of optimism, in how we have turned out.

Most grateful in this regard, perhaps, should be the English, to whose Protestant Reformation those of us in the Methodist traditions owe our pedigree. Anything interesting in British history has usually emanated from Scotland or Ireland or Wales, where social anthropology can prove a marginally worthwhile discipline. However, even in a gloriously diverse nation such as the United States of America, where Methodism first flourished as a church, humanity is by and large fed up with itself. Oprah Winfrey, the self-appointed high priestess of national therapy, is scraping the barrel for subject matter that will sustain her ratings and the millions of dollars she earns each year from these obscene public sessions.

Self-exploration merely leads us into the murk and the mire of what our spiritual forebears long ago recognized as a dead end. They called it sin, and wisely identified it in the Scriptures as something totally beyond our ability to comprehend, still less negotiate. With astounding foolhardiness, however, our secular ideologies and enculturated religiosities attempt to demystify this universal condition as personal or social immaturity and process it through multifarious systems analyses and counseling techniques. Moreover, as it has done so often in the past, the church ham-handedly tags along, twenty years out of date.[4]

Perhaps the weightiest result of this anthropocentrism, even more than the demystification of human sin, is the domestication of God into the self-projections diagnosed by Feuerbach at the genesis of modern Protestant theology.[5] And of all the consequences of this domestication, none is more impoverishing than the loss of our childlike wonder at God's creation. Certainly our astronomers, cosmologists, and mathematicians have not lost their wonder. The more they explore the universe, the more they are awestruck. Far from seeking to understand what they are discovering, they begin with imaginative hypotheses and pursue them by faith until such time as the evidence contradicts them. How ironic that so much of our theological scholarship today does quite the opposite. We question the great mysteries of Christian revelation until such time as human experience or logic suspends our disbelief. As journalist Henry Fairlie has put it, Christians of today are making it awkward to be an atheist.[6]

Ironically, this state of affairs occurs just when human beings, for the first time in history, have seen their planet photographed from outer space, leaving countless church members seriously out of touch, not only with their neighbors, but also with themselves. These first tentative steps into space and the visual images they afford us have occasioned a leap in human consciousness no less profound than the discovery that the earth is round and orbits the sun—a leap which, by and large, the scholars of the contemporary church are taking just as long to assimilate as their medieval predecessors. This is why volumes such as Matthew Fox's *Cosmic Christ* and Leonard Sweet's *Quantum Spirituality* are so important for the work that lies ahead.[7]

OUR COSMIC CONTEXT

To plunge us into a renewed sense of awe, we merely need to note some facts and figures about the universe. One of the most fascinating authors in this field is the Christian futurist David B. Barrett, whose monumental *World Christian Encyclopedia* stands alongside the work of Philip Schaff and Kenneth Latourette as *sine qua non* for the serious student of Christianity and the seriously intentioned Christian disciple. In his monograph *Cosmos, Chaos, and Gospel,* which he describes as a "futurology of evangelization," Barrett interweaves facts and projections from a wide range of scientific fields. While one may question his theological assumptions, even a cursory sampling of his data greatly expands our cosmic vista and exposes the parochialism of our prevailing ecclesial mind-set.

For example, astronomers now estimate that, in our galaxy alone, there are some 300 billion planets suitable for life. Of these, there are probably 100 billion on which astronomers think life has actually evolved, and 600 million planets sufficiently similar to earth for habitation by human beings.[8] Since the universe is estimated to have 100 billion galaxies, the issue we must face is the overwhelming probability that extraterrestrial life exists. As to why we have not been visited by alien life forms, there is not only the problem of time and distance, but also the very real issue of whether we are worth visiting. The perceptive suggestion of C. S. Lewis in his science fiction novels is that we are the planet in quarantine. We have nasty habits, and the rest of the universe has been instructed to give us a wide berth, in case these habits prove catching—though the cosmic grapevine has it that the Creator has dared some strange things, and intervened directly to effect a cure.[9]

As most of us are aware, the universe is not static. What we do not often contemplate, however, is the extent to which it is expanding. New stars are being created at a rate of ten thousand every second, new planetary systems are forming at the rate of ten every second, and one hundred new planets—potentially with life-forms—emerge each day. Clearly, statistics such as these are somewhat artificial, since cosmic dimensions always leave the mind bewildered. How, for example, does one envisage a light year as the distance one travels for twelve months at a speed of 186,000 miles per second? Or how does one process the probability that advanced extraterrestrial civilizations in this vast cosmos conservatively number 10 trillion?[10]

PLANET EARTH

While numbers like these force us to contemplate cosmic laws that Stephen Hawking and others are just beginning to help us understand, our own planet provides us with statistics that are no less staggering. There are some two hundred and fifty countries on earth, with more than two thousand major civil divisions in which approximately twelve thousand distinct ethnolinguistic peoples speak some seven thousand languages. The total population of just over 5 billion people is increasing at a net rate of 1.6 percent every year, destroying nine thousand other life-forms and sixty-two thousand square miles of forest each year in the process. Unregulated burning of fossil fuels continues to produce the well-advertised greenhouse effect, raising the surface temperature of the planet by one degree every eight years. While there is no consensus on this, the majority of scientists warn us that by the year 2045 this warming will have thawed the polar regions of the planet sufficiently to flood much of Europe as well as the gulf states of the U.S.[11]

Meanwhile, technical advances produce endless possibilities to meet these challenges—if, that is, we will avail ourselves of them. Innovating networks already share copious information on health, space, and human potential. Transnational associations of political, cultural, ethnic, and religious groupings rose from 2,600 in 1975 to 4,700 in 1987. In 1988 there were 650 million telephones in the world, 95 percent being on direct-dial from London, and 72 percent dialable from the U.S. In the same year, there were 80 million computers in the world, and 30 million were owned by Christians and churches, of which 98 percent were in Western churches. In the past decade these numbers have increased dramatically.

Yet the very same technical advances raise new demonic possibilities, some of which are already being realized. Political power is seriously challenged by multinational corporations that, by the end of the 1980s, numbered some ten thousand. The international banking community still controls prosperity or recession to a marked degree. Localized conflicts and even full-scale wars continue. Human rights are increasingly violated, the number of governments using torture rising from 98 in 1980 to well over 100 by the end of the decade. Indeed, the number of citizens killed by authoritarian governments since the beginning of the century had reached 130 million by 1990. The Nazi holocaust pales in comparison with the 40 million slaughtered within the USSR between 1918 and 1953 and the 45 million in China since the Maoist revolution. Not coincidentally, worldwide military expenditure rose from $2 billion in 1969 to $4 trillion in 1988,[12] and it continues to soar.

OUR RELIGIOUS CONTEXT

In the midst of such horrors, Elie Wiesel and other holocaust survivors raise the inexorably anguished question, "Where is God?"[13] The question is anguished, not least because the world's religions continue to thrive, the challenge of secular ideologies notwithstanding. According to Barrett, 85 percent of the human race are still religionists—that is, only 15 percent are atheist or agnostic—with religious pluralism increasingly widespread throughout the world. The Christian community alone numbers some 33 percent of the world's population.[14]

Yet most world religions remain intensely self-preoccupied. For example, while Christians during the late 1980s received an aggregate annual income of $8.6 trillion, or 62 percent of the world's total earnings, they spent 97 percent of this money on themselves. Of the remaining 3 percent, they donated 1 percent to secular charities and 2 percent to the work of global Christianity. Even within this global household of faith there are wide disparities: 52 percent of the world's Christians live in affluence, 14 percent in moderate poverty, and 13 percent, or 95 million, in abject poverty. Moreover, Christians spend seven thousand times as much on secular research, including military arms, as they do for research into how they might advance the reign of God in the world. And closer to home, while new construction of religious buildings in the U.S. peaked at $1.2 billion in 1965 and dropped to $0.9 billion in 1970, it burgeoned again to $2.5 billion in 1987. Of all church income, 95 percent, or $152 billion, is spent on home churches and their ministries. Global missions must operate on the remaining 5 percent, or $8 billion.[15]

EVANGELISTIC MYSTERIES AND INVERSIONS

Our initial reaction to these cosmic and global statistics might well be one of amazement or even incredulity. But the task with which they confront us is undeniable. Our North American congregations urgently need an inversion of their religious self-preoccupation and ecclesial self-indulgence. Nowhere is this more needed than in our practice of evangelism, where self-centered attitudes have seriously warped the gospel.

Examples are not difficult to find. First, and most obviously, we find ourselves spending more time talking about evangelism than doing it—a sure sign of self-preoccupation. As a result, when we do engage in evangelism, our differences of opinion often leave us unclear about what we are trying to do. We employ many and varied strategies to reach the "unreached" and church the "unchurched," but seldom do we ask the prior question of what it is we are trying to reach them *with*. And even when we do try to make our message clear, ecclesial polemics can lead us into a partisan view of the gospel, thereby causing us to engage selectively in what ought to be an inclusive ministry of the church.

Confronted as we are by the wonders of cosmic discovery, such parochialisms are increasingly unacceptable. The question is, how do we set about an inversion of our prevailing attitudes so that we might properly present the gospel of Jesus Christ to people whose consciousness is changing more rapidly than we can imagine, and for whom space is indeed becoming "the final frontier"? On the premise that the first step in such an inversion is to recognize and acknowledge our dilemma, we shall proceed to examine five aspects of the church's ministry of evangelism that presently suffer from the anthropocentrism of North

American culture and church life. In each instance, we shall point to the need for restoring the mystery of the gospel to our evangelism, and how such a restoration should—indeed, must—result in the radical inversion of both our evangelistic theology and our practice.

THE COMING REIGN OF GOD

Christians increasingly agree today that the cutting edge of evangelism is the focus on the kingdom of God as announced and embodied by Jesus of Nazareth. A succession of books points us in this direction: *Hope in Action* by Hans Jochen Margull, *Five Lanterns at Sundown* by Alfred C. Krass, *Announcing the Reign of God* by Mortimer Arias, *The Logic of Evangelism* by William J. Abraham, and *Models of the Kingdom* by Howard Snyder.[16]

In considering this kingdom dimension of evangelism, we should keep in mind the distinction made by Mortimer Arias between the gospel *of* Jesus and the gospel *about* Jesus.[17] All too often we focus our evangelism on the priestly work of Jesus, with a view to bringing persons to an awareness of their sin and the concomitant need for repentance and conversion. While this is a vital and necessary dimension of the evangelistic task, it becomes disproportionately anthropocentric if not balanced by the announcement of the coming reign of God. It gives the gospel *about* Jesus an undue predominance over the gospel *of* Jesus, with the result that the obligations of discipleship are given a secondary role at the outset of a person's Christian pilgrimage—a habit-forming mind-set that undercuts the mission and ministry of the church.

Once we do engage in announcing the coming reign of God, we are confronted with a deep, deep mystery. Indeed, were it not so, Christians would be prime candidates for prosecution under the laws of truth in advertising. After all, Jesus' words carried the power, not only of a future promise, but also of a present breaking-in of God's salvation. The good news he brought was that of a new age, a new order, God's revolutionary *oikonomia* or economy that would bring to fulfillment the vision of God's righteousness.[18] In this new age, time and eternity will be fused into a glorious new creation (Rev. 21:1-4). There will be neither Jew nor Greek, neither slave nor free, neither male nor female (Gal. 3:28). The wolf will dwell with the lamb, the leopard will lie down with the kid, and the lion will eat straw like the ox (Isa. 11:6-7). Everyone will know God, from the least to the greatest (Jer. 31:34). Justice will roll down like waters, and righteousness like an everflowing stream (Amos 5:24). There will be no more sound of weeping, nor cries of distress. All children will live beyond infancy, and all old people live out their days. Those who build houses will live in them and not have others possess them, and those who plant vineyards will eat of them and not have others take them away (Isa. 65:19-22).

A cursory glance around the world today must surely raise questions about such pronouncements. Unless, that is, the *evangel* is a deeply mysterious promise: a declaration of what will one day come to pass, accompanied by such a foretaste of sufficient richness that the promise rings true—a vision of such fullness and glory that it plumbs the depths of the human spirit with the Holy Spirit of God. How is this *basileia*, this reign, to come to pass? We do not know. When is this *shalom* to be realized? We do not know that, either. But that it *will* come to pass we are commissioned to announce with certainty and consistency—all worldly indifference, hostility, and charges of irrationality notwithstanding. After all, inebriated behavior was the first characterization of Christianity (Acts 2:13).

When we make the benefits of Christ the focus of our message to the detriment of his teachings, what happens to Jesus' vision of the *basileia*? We internalize it spiritually. There is of course a profound sense in which the kingdom of God must be within us if we are to announce it with integrity. But to internalize it to the point of neglecting its social, global, and cosmic dimensions is the epitome of anthropocentrism. It domesticates the God of the universe into particular human experiences. Most scandalous of all, it cuts the nerve of Jesus' clear commandment to attend to the global inequities that so offend God's justice.

Of course this coming *basileia* makes no sense to the world as it is. It means going out on a limb to announce the impossible and affirm the incredible. But that is precisely what we are called to do. And it is precisely that declaration that will get us a hearing among those with ears to hear.

Just as the promise of this kingdom is deeply mysterious, so is the response it evokes. Yes, there is resistance and vigorous opposition, especially from the powers and principalities of this world. But we also find acceptance when and where we least expect it. Indeed, the ultimate mystery of evangelism is that the world *will* respond to the fullness of a nonsensical gospel far more readily and profoundly than to the truncated messages we attempt to offer in the name of reason and experience.

It is the coming reign of God, with all its love and joy and peace and justice, and therefore its absurdity, that touches humanity at its deepest level. The vision that the earth will be as full of the knowledge of God as the waters cover the sea takes humanity out of itself and into the cosmos of its creator (Isa. 11:9). By the same token, the promise that one day all humanity will know God intimately takes the church out of itself and into the world that God created as part of this glorious cosmos. Frederick Herzog puts it well: "The world is not our parish—our parish is the world."[19]

THE RESURRECTION OF JESUS OF NAZARETH

The second aspect of evangelism to be impacted by our cosmic discoveries is the very content of the gospel. This might seem to be a contradiction, since the originative witness of the gospel tradition is recorded in Scripture, and the task of the evangelists of the church would therefore seem clear. As Paul put it, we have been sent to hand over to the Gentiles what has been handed on to us:

> that Christ died for our sins in accordance with the scriptures, and that he was buried, and that he was raised on the third day in accordance with the scriptures, and that he appeared to Cephas, then to the twelve. Then he appeared to more than five hundred brothers and sisters at one time, most of whom are still alive, though some have died. Then he appeared to James, then to all the apostles. Last of all, as to one untimely born, he appeared also to me. (1 Cor. 15:3-8)

Yet this "traditioning" of the gospel is precisely what we so often fail to do. Our commission as evangelists is to proclaim this good news first and foremost as we have it in Scripture. Then, and only then, can we interpret it contextually. Today, however, we tend to reverse this sequence. So we find ourselves evangelizing with an anthropocentric gospel, the mystery of its scandalous particularities reduced to theological or pastoral expedience.

The most striking example of this is the doctrine that is at the heart of the evangel, the resurrection of Jesus. This is not the place to rehearse the theological and historiographical issues of more than a century.[20] Unfortunately, evangelists have been brought by their academic colleagues to an unhelpful and inappropriate choice. Rather than proclaim the resurrection of Jesus as a spiritual event that is historically mysterious, evangelists must draw on scholarship that either historicizes it as a subjective faith experience of the disciples or spiritualizes it beyond the incarnational significance of the atonement.[21]

The resurrection of Jesus has only marginal relevance to the life cycle of butterflies and the symbolism of rainbows. Still less is it to be equated with the mood swings of fickle Christian disciples. When all of these substitute myths have been explored to their limits—which is to say, their very limited limitations—the deepest questions remain. What happens when I die? What has happened to loved ones who have died? And most important, what is God's last word on the pain, the oppression, and the injustice of this world? While the resurrection of Jesus leaves most of these questions unanswered, it does give us one central assurance: that there is life after death. Because Jesus was raised from the dead, we can trust his promises of *shalom*. Because Jesus was raised from the dead, the children of Auschwitz and Sudan do have an advocate. Because Jesus was raised from the dead, we can trust his word that the God of the cosmos is a parent God who will one day explain all our sufferings.

Until then, however, our message remains a deep, deep mystery. How will the sufferings of human history be explained? We do not know. When will the victims of Auschwitz be lifted up and the children of Sudan be fed? We don't know that, either. But this we do know: Jesus of Nazareth, crucified and buried, was raised on the third day while Pontius Pilate was still governor of Judea. This we must shout from the rooftops and pronounce in places of worldly authority, at the cost of our very lives if need be. What we must not do is to rob the proclamation of its mystery, for in so doing we will rob it of its power. It will be in and through the Holy Spirit, the cosmic presence of the God who was in Christ, that the gospel will be received, not through lofty words or human wisdom (1 Cor. 2:1, 10). To which we might add: nor yet through an anthropocentric evangelism with its sundry strategies and models.

RESPONSE TO THE GOSPEL

This brings us to the third aspect of evangelism that has yet to be much impacted by today's expanding cosmic vista. The issue can be stated very simply: evangelism and church membership recruitment are not the same thing. Yes, both these ministries are vitally important for the mission of the church, which is to say the *missio Dei*. Moreover, there are many missional contexts worldwide in which membership in a faithful Christian community is the necessary and immediate corollary of accepting the gospel, as opposed to the Christianized culture and enculturated Christianity of North America, where television commercials offer Saturday evening worship as a convenience for Sunday morning lie-abeds.[22]

Yet even in those frontline missional contexts, where new converts to Christ find their livelihood and even their lives in danger, evangelism and church membership must be kept distinct. For the one is concerned with the deeply mysterious gospel of God's salvation in Christ, and the other is concerned with human response to the gospel. The one is properly focused on God; the other is properly focused on the human condition. This is not to argue for a separation between the two. They are profoundly inseparable, as are all the ministries of the church. But to identify them as one and the same thing is yet again to render the gospel anthropocentric, not Christocentric, and to reduce the awesome cosmic event of God's incarnation in Christ to little more than the immediate needs of ecclesial institutions and pastoral constituencies.

Most especially is this the case in the North American context, where the cultural accommodations on the part of the church are quite ingenious. The gospel of Jesus Christ, when it is presented with scriptural fullness and contextual integrity, requires no human apology. Evangelistic concerns for more response from gospel hearers, or for more churchly manifestation of gospel fruits, usually emanate from the twin Christian errors of eschatological impatience and soteriological bad manners. But the results of any evangelistic activity will always be as mysterious as the gospel itself.

Some qualification is of course in order here. To emphasize the mystery of human response to the gospel in no way implies that we should not evangelize as often as we can, to as many as we can, in as many ways as we can. On the contrary, the mystery of human response implies the broadening of our evangelistic activities. For when we concentrate our efforts on obtaining a response to the gospel, we will inexorably gravitate toward those persons and those situations where our efforts will produce the most visible signs of success, and thereby afford us the most gratification. By contrast, our commission is to proclaim the gospel of Jesus Christ *irrespective of the response it evokes*. This is so for several reasons. First, any response to the gospel will be a work of the Holy Spirit, as we have already noted. As evangelists, therefore, we never really know what the Holy Spirit is doing with our evangelism. We may be given an occasional hint, or even a glimpse, insofar as God deems it salutary, given our penchant for worldly success. But for us to take any satisfaction from our evangelism, any satisfaction whatsoever, other than having served Jesus Christ faithfully and honorably, is profoundly to misunderstand our task and to usurp the authority of the One who has sent us. Besides, it maligns by default the memory of those who have gone before us, braving danger and risking life and limb, but rarely seeing any results.

For those who have shared in fellowship with the Yellowstone Conference of The United Methodist Church, the following verses will probably be familiar, as will the memory of the fervor with which the pastors of that conference sing them. They tell of the work of William Wesley Van Orsdel, one of the early evangelists on the Montana frontier, who is still affectionately known in those parts as "Brother Van":

> The seed I have scattered in springtime with weeping
> And watered with tears and with dews from on high;
> Another may shout when the harvesters reaping
> Shall gather my grain in the "sweet by and by."
>
> *Chorus*
> Over and over, yes, deeper and deeper,
> My heart is pierced through
> With life's sorrowing cry;
> But the tears of the sower
> And the songs of the reaper
> Shall mingle together in joy by and by.
>
> Another may reap what in springtime I've planted,
> Another rejoice in the fruit of my pain;
> Not knowing my tears when in summer I fainted,
> While toiling sad-hearted in sunshine and rain.
>
> The thorns will have choked and the summer sun blasted
> The most of the seed which in springtime I've sown;
> But the Lord who had watched while my weary toil lasted
> Will give me a harvest for what I have done. (W. A. Spencer)[23]

THE CHURCH INSIDE OUT

To identify the fourth aspect of our evangelistic inversion, the title of J. C. Hoekendijk's groundbreaking book of the 1960s, *The Church Inside Out*, still serves us well. His words are succinct and pertinent, for it is in ecclesiology that our evangelistic inversion has to be most radical, given the "centripetal inertia" that grips most of our North American congregations.[24]

To state the issue directly, eschatologically the church is an anachronism.[25] As Jacques Ellul and Juan Luis Segundo have both argued—and from theological perspectives sufficiently diverse to make the case well-nigh watertight—the church is the sign community of the coming reign of God.[26] Put differently, the *locus* of God's salvation is not the church, but the world. By the same token, the source of God's salvation is not the church, but Jesus Christ—who died for *all* the world. Accordingly, congregations are not safe houses where Christian disciples can hide from the world, but open houses through which the love of God can flow into the world. At their threshold the sin-sick children of God find no preconditions or obstacles, but a gracious welcome home.

Once we accept our true identity as a sign of the coming reign of God, a means of pointing people to God, a symbol of God's salvation in Jesus Christ, and a declaration of God's universal intent through the work of the Holy Spirit, then the anachronistic nature of the community called church becomes very clear indeed. The gospel is the banner of God's truth, and Christians are the standard-bearers. We are to be highly visible in the battle for the salvation of planet Earth; indeed, we are to be in the very thick of the fighting. But our supreme task is to declare the nature and purpose of the battle, and to identify at all times the One who leads us. When the battle is won, however, when we have arrived where the sign has directed us and when the hope that it symbolizes has been fulfilled, then the sign is no longer needed.

How far from these cosmic battle lines are the life and work of so much of our church, and how seriously misguided are so many of our evangelistic strategies! Instead of Jesus Christ at the center of congregational ministry and mission, too often one finds an ecclesial self-preoccupation to match that of the culture. Ironically, those who make the church their consuming priority usually do so with a great deal of self-sacrifice, giving countless hours and much of their substance to continue ministries that have long since ceased to be Christ-centered. The inference is inescapable: any evangelistic strategy or model that makes the church its priority—in whatever shape or form, by design or by default, through deed or word—is seriously mistaken, ecclesiologically, eschatologically, and above all, soteriologically. These faithful servants would be revitalized were they to be reassured that the church is not where people come to be saved, but where they encounter the One who has already saved them—and who badly needs their help in restoring this planet to its rightful place in the cosmos.

THE HOPE OF THE WORLD

This final aspect is the most important implication of our present cosmic discoveries. For salvation is the essence of the gospel, the purpose of God's incarnation in Christ, and the meritorious work of his atonement.[27] It is all the more unfortunate, therefore, if not scandalous, that the scope of this salvation should be foreshortened and even foreclosed by the anthropocentrism of so many of our present evangelistic perspectives.[28] Too often our evangelism is dominated by a soteriology that has become personalized to the point of cosmic affront to the God who was in Christ, and whose love for the whole world saturates the pages of Scripture.

"If you were the only person in the world, Christ would still have died for your sins," the evangelistic dialogue often implies. But that is not so. To begin with, no one has ever been the only human being in the world, and to introduce such an impossibility is to place the gospel on a very slippery slope. Moreover (since we are dealing here with figments of the imagination), if you or I were the only person in the world to be saved, God would find an easier way to do it. The struggle of Christ was not against flesh and blood, but against "the rulers, against the authorities, against the cosmic powers of this present darkness, against the spiritual forces of evil in the heavenly places" (Eph. 6:12).

The cross has dimensions that far exceed anyone's personal salvation. It is a travesty of Christ's passion and death to imply that he went through all of that on account of your sin, or my sin, or any person's sin. For one thing, you and I are not that clever. For another, the great majority of our sins are the social sins, the systemic sins, that escape our consciousness most of the time and that we personally are seldom able to do anything about. A Roman flogging begins to take on significance, however, when we remember the number of governments worldwide that use torture as a routine means of control.[29] A Roman cross becomes contemporary when we remember the millions of human beings in the last one hundred years alone whose lives have been nasty and brutish and short.

To state the matter directly one final time, no one is saved yet. No one is saved as long as one little child is hungry or homeless. No one is saved as long as there is one captive to be set free. No one is saved as long as any of God's little ones suffer. For the salvation brought to us in Christ Jesus is not the aggregate of astute salvific consumers who have made the right choice, but the fullness of *shalom* worldwide. The evangelistic question is not "How many?" but rather "How long?" And God's salvific objective is not merely souls, but the whole of planet Earth, that blue and white jewel of the cosmos.

In other words, God's salvation will be fulfilled only when the sufferings of Christ's little ones are brought to an end. Anything less than this final outcome would make a mockery of the cross. If God so loved the world that he came in person to share its pain and suffering, then we must never forget that Christ suffers with the very least of the world's creatures. The purpose of our evangelism, therefore, is as awesome as the cosmic act of God's incarnation: to bring Christ's sufferings to an end as quickly as we possibly can. For the ultimate mystery of the *evangel* is why God should have thought this planet worth so much trouble in the first place.

We began with the words of Isaac Watts, contemplating the mystery of God's cosmic splendor and parental grace. It is only fitting, therefore, to end with the words of Charles Wesley as he contemplates the same mysteries:

> Let earth and heaven combine,
> Angels and men agree,
> To praise in songs divine
> The incarnate Deity;
> Our God contracted to a span,
> Incomprehensibly made man.
>
> Unsearchable the love
> That hath the Saviour brought;
> The grace is far above
> Or man or angel's thought;
> Suffice for us that God, we know,
> Our God, is manifest below.
>
> He deigns in flesh to appear,
> Widest extremes to join;
> To bring our vileness near,
> And make us all divine:
> And we the life of God shall know;
> For God is manifest below.
>
> Made perfect first in love,
> And sanctified by grace,
> We shall from earth remove,
> And see his glorious face:
> Then shall his love be fully show'd,
> And man shall then be lost in God.

(*Collection of Hymns*, #609)[30]

Some missiologists argue that a theology of religion, and of Christianity in relation to the religions, is the most pressing issue today for global mission. Norman E. Thomas addresses this issue with fresh insight. He argues that "Christ can be presented persuasively both as Savior of all and as God at work among all living faiths." This approach potentially bridges the gulf between exclusivist and inclusivist positions. Such an approach is necessary "if evangelization among persons of other faiths is to be both biblically sound and contextually relevant."

CHAPTER THREE

THE GOSPEL AMONG THE WORLD RELIGIONS
Norman E. Thomas

One hundred years ago "the evangelization of the world in this generation" was the clarion call to Christian missions embraced by most Protestant Christians. This slogan of the Student Volunteer Movement, championed by John R. Mott, expressed the triumphalist spirit of Christians who anticipated the ascendancy not only of Western civilization but also of its dominant faith.

Today we live in a chastened time. Other world religions have not declined in strength. Instead, they are resurgent. Islam is the fastest growing faith in the United States; in Great Britain today there are more Muslims than Methodists in the very cradle of the Wesleyan movement. David Barrett reports that those who claim loyalty to Jesus Christ have remained a constant third of the world's population since 1900, with approximately two-thirds in continuing adherence to other faiths.[1]

Sixty years ago the International Missionary Council (IMC) asked a noted Dutch missiologist then working in Java, Dr. Hendrik Kraemer, to write "a book on evangelism in the modern world, with especial reference to the non-Christian religions." The purpose was "to state the fundamental position of the Christian Church as a witness-bearing body in the modern world, relating this to different conflicting views of the attitude to be taken by Christians towards other faiths."[2] In what became his *magnum opus* and the preparatory volume for the IMC's Tambaram Conference of

1938, Kraemer developed a theology of radical discontinuity between Christianity and other living faiths. He believed that "biblical realism" was the only grounds for normative truth and that evangelization, proselytism, and conversion "belong to the core of the missionary enterprise." The Conference, meeting outside Madras, India, heard other voices from the subcontinent. In response, the delegates confessed their faith that God has not been left without witnesses in any age—that there are "glimpses of God's light in the world of religions," but that each church must be rooted in faith in God as revealed fully in Jesus Christ, his Son and our Lord.[3]

Fifty years later, in 1988, an international team of scholars updated the debate at the same location. Stanley Samartha, former director of the World Council of Churches' (WCC) dialogue program, called for a breakthrough in the present "confusion" over the relation between mission and dialogue. He would have based it upon two premises: the acceptance of the plurality of religions, and the reexamination of all exclusivist claims. But the outcome was thirty-five questions on seven issues for further study, with no suggested answers. They included:

- In what ways is plurality, including religious plurality, within God's purpose?
- What do we say about the saving work of God through other religious traditions?
- How do the confessions in other religions of decisiveness/universality/uniqueness challenge and clarify Christian convictions about the uniqueness of Christ?[4]

That missiologists could agree on questions but not answers is not surprising. Today, Christians vigorously debate a theology of the religions with sharp and seemingly irreconcilable differences in viewpoints.

This essay is a contribution to that debate. It is based on the premise that effective evangelization among persons of other faiths in the twenty-first century will require a clear and relevant theology of the religions. My thesis is that such a theology needs to include faith in the risen Christ at work among all peoples and cultures—the Savior of all.

First, let us consider three common responses to the question "Is Jesus Christ the Savior of all?" These responses are often categorized as *exclusivism, inclusivism,* and *pluralism.* Next, we shall hear from four Asian theologians who bridge the exclusivist/inclusivist divide and believe that the living Christ is both Savior of all and at work among all persons of living faiths. Our conclusion will be that such a theology is needed if evangelization among persons of other faiths is to be both biblically sound and contextually relevant.

IS JESUS CHRIST THE SAVIOR OF ALL? THREE ANSWERS

Is Jesus Christ the Savior of all? No longer is there unanimity among Christians in answering that question. Paul Knitter in *No Other Name?* (1985) clearly outlined the variety of contemporary Christian attitudes toward religious pluralism. Two years later he collaborated with John Hick in presenting essays advocating a pluralist theology in the controversial volume *The Myth of Christian Uniqueness*. Most positions can be grouped under the following threefold typology, although individuals have developed a wide range of creative theologies that deserve a more refined analysis.[5]

Exclusivism

The historic tradition of the Roman Catholic Church prior to Vatican II emphasized exclusivism. Two fundamental beliefs, however, were held in tension: God's universal desire to save and the necessity of the Church for salvation. In 473 the Council of Arles condemned anyone who believed that "Christ, our Lord and Savior, did not undergo death for the salvation of all peoples," yet affirmed that Christ "does not wish anyone to perish." As for the Church, the tradition went back to Origen (d. 254) and was applied by Cyprian (d. 258) that "outside the church, there is no salvation."[6]

Protestants look to the 1910 World Missionary Conference in Edinburgh, Scotland, as the symbol of twentieth-century unity of thought and action in Christian mission. Commission IV focused on "The Missionary Message in Relation to Non-Christian Religions." The two-year study process evoked a full range of responses from hundreds of missionaries, from exclusivism through inclusivism to pluralism. The consensus, however, found clear expression in the final report. While including the "generous recognition of all that is true and good" in the other religious traditions, there was a "universal and emphatic witness to the absoluteness of the Christian faith." There was no sense of Christianity's being one religion among others. Instead, in accord with the prevailing evolutionary thought of the age, there was a strong sense that the other great religious traditions would ultimately be taken up into Christianity.[7]

Evangelical Protestants cite a more recent statement, the *Lausanne Covenant* of 1974, for their consensus on the uniqueness and universality of Jesus Christ. It reads:

> We affirm that there is only one Savior and only one Gospel, although there is a wide diversity of evangelistic approaches. . . . We also reject as deroga-

tory to Christ and the Gospel every kind of syncretism and dialogue which implies that Christ speaks equally through all religions and ideologies. Jesus Christ, being himself the only God-man, who gave himself as the only ransom for sinners, is the only mediator between God and man. There is no other name by which we must be saved.[8]

The eleven scriptural citations given in support of the *Covenant* are those most often cited in support of exclusivism. They include the words of Jesus that "God so loved the world that he gave his only Son, so that everyone who believes in him may not perish but may have eternal life" (John 3:16), the confession of Peter that "there is salvation in no one else, for there is no other name under heaven given among mortals by which we must be saved" (Acts 4:12), and the profession of Paul "that at the name of Jesus every knee should bend . . . and every tongue should confess that Jesus Christ is Lord" (Phil. 2:10-11). Also included from 1 Timothy 2:5 was the affirmation that "there is one God; there is also one mediator between God and humankind, Christ Jesus."

Alan Race commends the exclusivist theology of religions as the most clear-cut of the options for giving a central function to the person of Christ, and as the "position which corresponds most closely to what has generally been held to be orthodox Christianity through the centuries." But the British pluralist then asks: "Is the exclusivist theory an appropriate response to the new knowledge we now have about the world religions?"[9]

Inclusivism

If salvation is through Christ alone, then what about those who have no opportunity to hear the message of the gospel? Karl Rahner broke new ground in 1961 and based his answer on the Church's tradition that God desires to save all humankind. He encouraged his readers not to underestimate God's love and grace, and to "'think optimistically' about the possibilities of salvation outside Christianity." The non-Christian religions contain "supernatural, grace-filled elements," he declared, and can be "a positive means of gaining the right relationship to God . . . a means which is therefore *positively included in God's plan of salvation*" (emphasis added). For Rahner, Christ is the *final* cause of God's universal salvific will. From this theological perspective, those of other faiths could be affirmed not as pagans but as "anonymous Christians." As a consultant and drafter for Vatican II, Rahner was soon to get a wider reception of his more inclusive theology.[10]

"All peoples comprise a single community." With this affirmation the

Catholic bishops opened their Vatican II "Declaration on the Relationship of the Church to Non-Christian Religions" *(Nostra aetate)*. They insisted on the essential unity of the human race, a unity based on the fact that all persons have God both as their creator and as their final goal.[11]

Begun as a limited text concerning Catholic-Jewish relations, *Nostra aetate* was expanded to include relations with Hinduism, Buddhism, and Islam. Concerning other faiths it reads: "The Catholic Church rejects nothing which is true and holy in these religions." This reaffirmed a traditional viewpoint. But it went on to declare that those religions "often reflect a ray of that Truth which enlightens all." Robert Graham, in notes on the official text, comments that this marks an "authoritative change in approach. Now, for the first time, there is recognition of other religions as entities with which the Church can and should enter into dialogue."[12]

Although the Vatican II documents contained no systematically developed theology of religions, concerned theologians welcomed the new openness. Meeting one week after the bishops' adoption of *Nostra aetate*, Hans Küng, Raimundo Panikkar, and others proposed that the old church-centered view of "outside the church, no salvation" be replaced by a theocentric view that the whole of humanity "is embraced by the one salvific plan of God which includes all the world religions." Küng, in the debate, consented to change his assertion that the non-Christian religions were not roads to salvation to the following: "For [the person] who is not confronted in an existential way with the Gospel of Jesus Christ they can be the channel of Christ's saving grace." The Conference Declarations also contained these words: "Christian faith represents radical universalism. Every human being and every world religion is under God's grace. But Christian universalism is grounded and centred in Christ." Concerning the church's missionary task they declared: "The Church will not conquer but serve the world religions . . . rooted in her primary mission, to witness to Christ and his Gospel before the world and its religions." Coming as it did during a large Eucharistic Congress attended by Pope Paul VI, and so soon after *Nostra aetate*, the Küng-Panikkar debate both awakened and polarized Roman Catholics on the issues.[13]

Protestant theologians also pioneered a positive assessment of other faiths in God's plan of salvation. J. N. Farquhar in 1913 proposed Jesus Christ to be "the crown of Hinduism," which was the title of his influential book. This view also dominated the Jerusalem Conference of the IMC in 1928. W. E. Hocking of Harvard University helped draft the "Council's Statement," which affirmed:

> We recognize as part of the one Truth that sense of the Majesty of God and
> the consequent reverence in worship, which are conspicuous in Islam; the
> deep sympathy for the world's sorrow and unselfish search for the way of
> escape, which are at the heart of Buddhism; the desire for contact with
> Ultimate Reality conceived as spiritual, which is prominent in Hinduism;
> the belief in a moral order of the universe and consequent insistence on
> moral conduct, which are inculcated by Confucianism.[14]

The "one Truth" referred to, however, was the *Christian faith*.

Although exclusivism remained the unaltered stance of almost all
Protestant evangelicals, a few began to voice a more inclusivist theology.
J. H. Bavinck, out of his close contacts with Muslims, wrote:

> In the "night of power" of which the ninety-seventh sura of the Koran
> speaks, the night when "the angels descended" and the Koran descended
> from Allah's throne, God dealt with Mohammed and touched him. . . . The
> great moments in the history of religion are the moments when God wres-
> tled with man in a very particular way.[15]

Ralph Covell, reflecting on his own experience in China as well as that
of other evangelical missionaries, writes: "The Christian missionary then
does not bring God or Christ to another culture. God, the Creator, and
Christ, the Logos, who gives light to every person coming into the world,
has been working there long before the missionary arrived."[16]

Covell drew his biblical mandate for inclusivism from John 1:3-5.
Others would appeal to Jesus' teaching that "I have other sheep that do
not belong to this fold. I must bring them also" (John 10:16). They also
point to the final judgment of all the nations (Matt. 25:31-46).

Pluralism

One of the central dilemmas in any Christian theology of religions is
how to relate the universal revelatory activity of God to the particular
proclamation of salvation through Jesus Christ. The *exclusivist* answer
emphasizes God's special revelation in Jesus Christ as normative. The
inclusivist extends the particular to the universal, thereby enlarging the
availability of the work of Christ. The *pluralist*, by contrast, moves away
from "insistence on the superiority or finality of Christ and Christianity
toward a recognition of the independent validity of other ways."[17]

John Hick, the influential British pluralist, calls the shift his
"Copernican revolution" in theology. It demands "a paradigm shift from
a Christianity-centered or Jesus-centered to a God-centered model of the
universe of faiths." As for Jesus Christ, Hick would allow Christians to

continue to adhere to Christ as their unique savior, but would not have them believe that Christ is necessarily unique or normative for others.[18]

Drawing upon redaction criticism, Hick argues that Jesus did not designate himself Messiah or Son of God—his followers evolved the Christ-myth to express what he meant to them. Similarly, Krister Stendahl of Harvard interpreted Peter's assertion in Acts 4:12 that there is "*no other name . . . by which we must be saved*" as "love language," like a husband saying that his wife is the only one for him, rather than an axiom of dogmatic theology.[19]

Stanley Samartha, former director of the WCC's dialogue program, places himself squarely with the pluralists. The exclusive claim, he argues, "is not integral to the gospel or Christian faith in God through Jesus Christ or to the content and practice of mission today." What touches the hearts and minds of India (as evidenced by Mahatma Gandhi) is the life and work and words, the suffering and death and resurrection, of Jesus of Nazareth. He would understand the incarnation not in terms of *deity* but of *divinity*. He presents parallels from Asia of religious leaders who in love sought liberation for themselves and their followers, only to have their followers later believe in them as divine—the Buddha, Rama, and Krishna. "The theory of multiple *avataras* seems to be theologically the most accommodating attitude in a pluralistic setting," he asserts. Samartha calls for openness to "the generosity of God's love and the infiniteness of God's mystery."[20]

Samartha's appeal is that Christians move beyond both exclusiveness and inclusiveness. For him, the distinctiveness of Christ "does not lie in claiming that Jesus Christ is God." To do so relegates Jesus to the position of "the tribal god of Christians as compared to the gods of other peoples." He rejects both the elevation of Jesus to the status of God ("Jesusology") and limiting Christ to Jesus of Nazareth ("Christomonism"). Instead, Samartha advocates a *theocentric Christology*. In it the theological significance of other revelations and other experiences of salvation would be affirmed along with the quest for new understandings of Jesus Christ by neighbors of other faiths.[21]

CUTTING THE GORDIAN KNOT

Must a high Christology be a buttress for exclusivism, as Stanley Samartha fears? Conversely, does openness to divine initiatives among persons of other faiths imply a low Christology, emphasizing Jesus as the man for others while remaining silent or rejecting Christ as the Son of God?

It is my contention that a Gordian knot is restricting effective Christian witness today to persons of other faiths. One strand is the false belief that Christianity is a Western faith and therefore Jesus Christ is a culture-bound Savior. A second strand is the avoidance of the "stumbling block" of Christ's divinity by professing only his humanity.

Just as Alexander the Great cut the Gordian knot to open Asia to Greek civilization, so also must contemporary Christians proclaim the faith with both historical acumen and biblical soundness. Christianity began in Asia, spread first to Africa, and only later went to Europe. Today the majority of Christians, and much of the church's dynamism, are found in Africa, Asia, Latin America, and Oceania.

Confining Christ Jesus, the second person of the Trinity, to the historic Jesus of Nazareth while affirming both the creative activity of God and the indwelling presence of the Holy Spirit would be to wall Christ up in the tomb once again. A biblically sound Christology begins, instead, with the affirmation that Christ, the firstborn of all creation, is the light that enlightens every person (John 1:9). It continues with the conviction that the risen Christ goes before us, just as he went before the disciples on the road to Emmaus (Luke 24: 13-35), when we witness to persons of other faiths.[22]

The thesis of this essay is that Christ can be presented persuasively both as Savior of all and as God at work among all living faiths. Such a theology can bridge the exclusivist/inclusivist divide. It is needed if evangelization among persons of other faiths is to be both biblically sound and contextually relevant.

Four South Asian theologians model in varied ways such a theology of the religions: Paul Devanandan, M. M. Thomas, Raimundo Panikkar, and Michael Amaladoss.

Paul Devanandan (1901–62)

An ordained minister of the Church of South India, Paul Devanandan forged his creative theology of religion as a pioneer in interfaith relations in India. The friendships he formed as literature secretary of the India YMCA, as teacher of theology, philosophy, and religion, and as founding director of the Christian Institute for the Study of Religion and Society provided its experiential base.

"[Christ] is our peace . . . and has broken down the dividing wall, that is, the hostility between us" (Eph. 2:14) was the theme of his Bible studies at the 1957–58 Ghana Assembly of the IMC. The cross of Jesus, by destroying the enmity between Jew and Gentile, created "one new humanity in the place of the two." Therefore, Devanandan suggested, the cross should be preached with the conviction that because Christ rose again, "religion . . . is abolished, creating a new koinonia in Christ transcending the division between Christians and adherents of other religions and no religion."[23]

For Devanandan, faith in Christ transcended Christian religion and traditional Christological creeds. His close friends included leaders of the Hindu renaissance who stayed within the Hindu religious tradition with their faith in Christ. Believing that such faith is a sign of the risen Christ's work, he wrote, "If God's redemptive activity in Jesus Christ is a fact with which we should reckon in every human situation, it is not by total destruction that He manifests his power but by radical renewal. That is why the Gospel we proclaim is the Good News of the Resurrection."[24] Devanandan's evangelical fervor to proclaim the gospel was akin to that of the apostles Peter and John, who could not keep from speaking about what they had seen and heard (Acts 4:20):

> It may not be for us to say that God in His graciousness will not reward the faith of the non-Christian seeker who continues to stay outside the fold, but we press forward with the mission of testimony which has been delivered to us declaring to the end of time that "there is no other Name given under heaven by which men shall be saved except the Name of Jesus Christ." For it remains true for all time that "when Christ succeeds in unveiling for any man the judgement of God on sin, in this very act He cannot help making Himself for that man, the one and only way."[25]

M. M. Thomas

A native of Kerala and lifelong member of the Mar Thoma Syrian Church of Malabar, M. M. Thomas took a career path that paralleled that of his mentor and friend, Paul Devanandan. As youth leaders, both honed their faith in active witness and dialogue with persons of India's living faiths and those attracted by secular ideologies—including both humanism and Marxism. M. M., like Devanandan, became a teacher, but he also became a world ecumenical leader, first as secretary and vice-chairman of the World Student Christian Federation, and later as chairman of the WCC's Department of Church and Society and then of its Central Committee. Upon the death of Devanandan, Thomas took up the mantle as Director of the Christian Institute, which promoted Christian involvement both in social action and interfaith dialogue. In 1990 he was appointed governor of the predominately Christian state of Nagaland.[26]

Surprisingly, Thomas draws the premise for his theology of the religions from Karl Barth's emphasis on the relativity of all religions. He writes that Barth's dialectical theology, in emphasizing the transcendence of the Word and Deed of God in Jesus Christ over all religions and quasi-religions of mankind has provided the basis for a radical relativisation of all religions including Christianity and also of Atheism; and its understanding of Jesus Christ as the humanism of God rejecting and electing all mankind in Jesus Christ points to a transcendent power which can renew them all.

Thomas believes that the cross, or the self-emptying redemptive love of God revealed in Jesus Christ, is the central dynamic of all human history. "It is the Crucified and Risen Jesus," he writes, "who is our evidence that 'we are citizens of a forgiven universe,' and that Being-in-Christ is the 'primary and essential condition of man's existence.'"[27]

In *The Acknowledged Christ of the Indian Renaissance* (1970) Thomas analyzes the impact of Christ upon key nineteenth- and twentieth-century leaders of India, including Roy, Vivekananda, Radhakrishnan, and Gandhi, and draws out implications for the development of a distinctive Indian Christian theology. On the one hand, he asserts that there is no way that humans can "jump out of their religion and culture." But his is not an uncritical inclusivism. Thomas admonishes persons of all faiths to "test the spirits to see whether they are of God" in the light of Jesus Christ. He has faith that this process will exclude all idolatrous and docetic spiritual qualities, including the self-centered spirit of crusade and conquest. This, however, is not a low Christianity that advocates walking "in the steps" of the historical Jesus. Instead, Thomas's vision is of the cosmic Christ who is both active in the present as the *soul* of modern reform movements in the church, other religions, and society, but who is also the One who in the eschaton will disclose "the theological relativisation of all religions."[28]

Raimundo Panikkar

"The mystery of the Trinity is the ultimate foundation for pluralism," declares our third South Asian theologian. The son of a Spanish Roman Catholic mother and an Indian Hindu father, Raimundo Panikkar grew up in his parents' two religious traditions. Both traditions nurtured his life of faith and scholarship. A Roman Catholic priest, Panikkar holds doctorates in science (chemistry), philosophy, and theology. The publication of *The Unknown Christ of Hinduism* in 1964 began his rise to world prominence as a Catholic theologian and scholar of Hinduism and other faiths.[29]

"Does one need to be spiritually a Semite or intellectually a Westerner in order to be a Christian?" With this question Panikkar introduced the dilemma of presenting Christ both as universal redeemer and as incarnate in the historical Jesus. His major contribution is in the articulation of the former.

Panikkar begins with the assumption that God's universal salvific will is present and active in all peoples and cultures and faiths. Further, that activity of God is Christ at work in all authentic religions. He writes:

> Christ is the universal redeemer. There is no redemption apart from him. Where there is no redemption there is no salvation. Therefore, any human person who is saved—and we know by reason and by faith that God provides everybody with the necessary means of salvation—is saved by Christ, the only redeemer. This amounts to saying that Christ is present in one form or another in every human being as he journeys towards God.[30]

The dilemma remains, however. Panikkar wrestles with the dual convictions in Christian theology that "salvation comes exclusively through Christ" and that "God does not condemn anybody." The latter he interprets to mean that "God provides every [person] coming into existence with the *means* of salvation." Since God provides "normal, natural means for leading peoples and individuals to himself," it is within Hindu thought forms and experiences that the saving providence of God will be experienced.[31]

Panikkar believes that Christ "the only Mediator" is present and active in all authentic religions. "There is in Hinduism," he writes, "a living Presence of that Mystery which Christians call Christ." For Panikkar, the Christian religion has no monopoly on Christ. He calls for an "ecumenical ecumenism" in which the dialogue among persons of living faiths becomes a mutual sharing of Christ symbols and of *koinonia*.[32]

Michael Amaladoss

Finally, let us consider a newer voice from South Asia, the Jesuit theologian Michael Amaladoss. Following a year of teaching theology at Vidyajyoti Theological College in Delhi and editing its influential journal *Vidyajyoti*, Fr. Amaladoss was called to Rome to assist the Jesuit superior general in mission concerns.

"In Asia the person and role of Christ is not a problem," Amaladoss contends. "The real problem is the attempt of the church to monopolize Christ." For those of other faiths, he believes, belief in Christ need not be an obstacle to dialogue. It is not Christ's uniqueness, but the uniqueness of Christianity that is in question. Elsewhere he wrote: "We must resist the temptation to reduce the universality of Christ to the universality of the visible, institutional Church."[33]

Amaladoss argues that God's universal salvific will "does not depend on the historic-symbolic mediation of the visible, institutional church alone."[34] Instead of claiming Christ as their exclusive possession, Christians should approach persons of other faiths in a posture of open listening in dialogue.

Undergirding his strategy of mission as dialogue is a clear high Christology. For Amaladoss, "the profound meaning of affirming that the Christ is the universal savior is that God is really the savior of all peoples. He is not the God of a particular people." Our task as Christians, therefore, is "not to carry Christ where he is not present, but rather to discover him where he is, sometimes in mysterious ways unknown to us." As we listen in dialogue, we as Christians may perceive the "salvific dialogue between God and the human person taking place."[35]

"Who is Christ *for us*?" Amaladoss asks. His answer is comprehensive. First, Christ is the Word engaged in creation from the beginning (John 1:3–5:9). Next, Christ is Jesus, the Word incarnate who emptied himself, taking the form of a servant obedient unto death on a cross (Phil. 2:6-11). Third, he is the *risen Christ* who is no longer bound by space and time (Acts 10). He is present "wherever God's saving grace is present." Finally, he is *Christ at the end of time*—the cosmic Christ in whom all fullness will dwell (Eph. 1:23).

"How is salvation in Christ mediated to people through other religions or even no religion at all?" Amaladoss asks. It is by the mystery of divine grace that lives are touched and transformed. This is "*the process of salvation history.*" The church is "the witness and the servant" of that mystery. This mystery is linked to the church in a special but not exclusive way. As the gathered community of faith, the church celebrates the paschal mystery of Christ in the Eucharist. Thus empowered by Christ, the church goes out in *kenosis* and service to others, thereby participating in the process of salvation history through mission and dialogue.[36]

CONCLUSION

Evangelization and interfaith dialogue have often been presented not just as alternative strategies but as opposing models for mission. An underlying reason for that tension is the assumption that dialogue is based on a low Christology that perverts the gospel. Is Jesus to be presented to Jews only as a great teacher and not as the Christ? Are Muslims to hear only about Jesus the prophet with no mention of a trinitarian faith? Echoing these concerns, Lesslie Newbigin asks: "If . . . we are to reject religious pluralism and acknowledge Jesus Christ as the unique and decisive revelation of God for the salvation of the world, what is the proper attitude which believers in that revelation ought to take toward the adherents of the great world religions?"[37]

Newbigin would support the thesis of this essay, that Christ can be presented persuasively both as Savior of all and as God at work among all living faiths. He, too, sought to bridge the exclusivist/inclusivist divide. Newbigin agreed that the effective presentation of the gospel to the world's peoples in the twenty-first century requires evangelization that is both biblically sound and contextually relevant. Such a holistic approach was the crowning achievement of the WCC's 1989 World Conference on Mission and Evangelism in San Antonio, Texas, with Newbigin a catalyst in the creative sharing there.

Most of the work at San Antonio was done in section meetings rather than plenary sessions. Section I, entitled "Turning to the Living God," included leaders and staff representing both the dialogue and evangelism units of the WCC. It was their joint desire to avoid polarization and to achieve a new synthesis between witness, proclamation, and mission concerns on the one hand, and dialogue concerns on the other.

As the participants witnessed to each other about how each had received God's grace through Jesus Christ, a strong consensus emerged that San Antonio must reaffirm the ecumenical movement's evangelistic mandate. They agreed that "the proclamation of the gospel includes an invitation to recognize and accept in a personal decision the saving lordship of Christ." Furthermore, they declared that "Christians owe the message of God's salvation in Jesus Christ to every person and to every people." The statement continued: "We cannot point to any other way of salvation than Jesus Christ."[38]

Next, the section considered the mystery that "the Spirit of God is constantly at work in ways that pass human understanding." They understood that we cannot set limits to the saving power of God. Therefore, "in dialogue we are invited to listen in openness to the possibility that the God we know in Jesus Christ may encounter us also in the lives of our neighbours of other faiths." The mood was one of honest sharing of religious experience, rather than one of Christian triumphalism. "In entering into a relationship of dialogue with others," they declared, "Christians seek to discern the unsearchable riches of God and the way he deals with humanity."

Concerning the relation between witness and dialogue, the delegates concluded that "dialogue has its own place and integrity and is neither opposed to nor incompatible with witness or proclamation." They continued: "We do not water down our own commitment if we engage in dialogue; as a matter of fact, dialogue between people of different faiths is spurious unless it proceeds from the acceptance and expression of faith commitment." With confidence the delegates affirmed that "witness does not preclude dialogue with people of other living faiths, but that dialogue extends and deepens our witness."[39]

In that spirit, the Danish missionary theologian Erik W. Nielsen sometimes shared privately this experience. Once, while visiting India, he agreed to spend a week with a Brahmin friend in his summer home. The two spent the time in meditation, prayer, and conversation, sharing in each other's religious lives. But as the week went by, Erik Nielsen became "increasingly uncomfortable." The "deep devotion, the authenticity, the serenity, and wisdom of his Hindu friend" moved him deeply. In comparison, his own testimony to what Jesus meant to him seemed "groping" and "inarticulate." As he left, he questioned "not his own faith in Christ but the propriety of claiming any sort of uniqueness for the Christian faith in the presence of a man in whom the Spirit of God seemed so obviously to be at work."

Many months passed. Then one day Nielsen received a letter from his friend, who wrote: "Today has been a very special day for me. During the week we were together last summer I saw in you something I had looked for all my life. Today, you will be glad to hear, I was baptized."[40]

In every age, Christians hear and respond to God's call to be faithful witnesses among persons of other faiths. *Confidence* in the gospel, *openness* to the working of the Spirit, and an *urgency* to share the faith— these are the marks of the evangelist in each generation.

This essay has focused on the first of these, the need for a biblically sound and contextually relevant theology for interfaith witness. Those who take up the challenge follow in the footsteps of the apostles after Pentecost. Like the apostles, they often face uncertainties and threats. But confident of the continuing power of the risen Christ and of the indwelling presence of the Holy Spirit, they too will pray, "Lord . . . grant to your servants to speak your word with all boldness" (Acts 4:29).

Five hundred years ago, Christopher Columbus embarked on a sort of global Christian mission. Can looking back over the past five centuries help the church avoid earlier mistakes and be more faithful in the future? Can we speak of "global strategy" without being imperialistic? Mortimer Arias suggests ways toward authentic Christian mission while insisting that "there never was, and there never will be, a culture-less Christianity."

CHAPTER FOUR

GLOBAL AND LOCAL: A CRITICAL VIEW OF MISSION MODELS
Mortimer Arias

"Global" is *in* these days. The United Methodist Church was one of the first to incorporate the word in its all-inclusive missionary Board of Global Ministries. In the last decade some Methodist seminaries started courses on "ministry in the global context" or "global spirituality," or sponsored study trips and exchanges in the search for a global perspective. The American Association of Theological Schools adopted as its priority for a decade the exploration of "Globalization of Theological Education."

Such "global" language has raised some misgivings, especially in the Two-Thirds World. Its origin in the so-called First World—and the adoption of the vision and language of the free market and of the prophets of the transnational corporations who live, move, and have their being in the matrix of "international and global trends"—produces uneasiness. Some Christian leaders suspect that "global" plans and schemes are merely another version of old Western ethnocentrism in theology and missions. We have already had five hundred years of Western globalization of mission, beginning with Columbus.

With these cautions, perhaps our quest for a global understanding of mission today should take a critical look back at the Columbus enterprise and the colonial and neocolonial models of mission that followed it.

The great Mexican writer Carlos Fuentes, in his masterpiece *The Buried Mirror: Reflections on Spain and the New World*, suggests that we can use the history of the Columbus enterprise as a mirror to see

ourselves and as a guide to this "divided night of the soul" that is the
matrix of our present culture.[1]

THE GLOBAL VISION FOR MISSION

All mission, global or local, passes through persons—through their
visions and motivations. Let us start, then, with Columbus's vision and
motivations for mission.

Columbus the Missionary

Christophorus Columbus was a man of vision and mission. He made
this point with his own name and signature: "Christum-pherens," the
bearer of Christ—as in the legend of San Cristobal, who carried the child
Jesus on his shoulders in crossing the river. Though born in Italy,
Columbus belonged to a Spanish-speaking family and wrote his works in
Spanish. He called himself "Cristóbal Colón." "Colón" (Spanish for
"colonizer") was also part of his vocation and destiny: the *colonizer* of
a new world.

Of course, Columbus was also an *ambitious* man. He wanted to be a
pioneer, and was looking for new routes for commerce (like any sailor
worth his salt in the Italian or Catalonian ports). He hoped for gold and
riches, but especially for titles and glory. Though he had nothing in hand
to offer the king and queen, he demanded all the privileges of Admiral of
the Great Sea and Governor of the New Lands for himself and his
descendants, and 10 percent of all the riches and gold he might find.

Columbus was also a *devout Christian*—probably a converted Jew
from a family expelled from Catalonia to Italy in the fourteenth century.
Salvador de Madariaga, one of his Spanish biographers, finds in
Cristóbal Colón several traits of the convert, particularly the eagerness
to make Christians, including converts from the Jews.[2] In his arguments
with King Ferdinand and Queen Isabella, Columbus stressed not only the
importance of the expansion of the Spanish kingdoms—the gold and
pearls and the route to spices—but also the prospect of the conversion to
Christianity of the new peoples to be found. Columbus startled the mon-
archs with his ultimate vision: to earn enough riches to finance the definitive reconquest of Jerusalem from the hands of the Turks!

Columbus was, of course, a man of his time and place. His vision was
a distillation of the ethnocentric European vision in the fifteenth
century; his missionary paradigm was the medieval Roman Catholic
paradigm.[3] His missionary commitment reflected the missional sense of

the Spain of the Reconquista—the bulwark of the last crusade against the Moors, the Jews, and the heretics.

Columbus was in fact the first lay missioner to the Americas.[4] He was the first in a long line of devout missionaries of the main orders committed to the conversion of the "Indians": the Franciscans, the Dominicans, the Augustinians, and later the Jesuits. As Christophorus Columbus's name symbolizes, mission in the final analysis depends on personal Christ-bearers.

Motivations for Global Mission

Pope Alexander VI issued four bulls in the year 1493, immediately after Columbus returned from his first trip. Here the Roman pontifex displays the fundamental vision and motivation of the papacy:

1. The propagation of the Christian religion.
2. The expansion of the Roman Catholic Church.
3. The salvation of souls.
4. The civilization of the Barbarians [sic].[5]

These four motivations would be the rationale for Catholic missions for centuries. Actually, the propagation of Christianity was synonymous with the expansion of the Roman Catholic Church. The newly discovered lands were exclusively reserved for the "Christian princes" loyal to the Pope, and were declared to be the exclusive missionary field of the Roman Catholic Church. For four hundred years, Protestant countries or missions would not be allowed to enter the Iberian dominions, and the Inquisition would not permit "heretics" or "infidels" in this New Christendom. Even today, Pope John Paul II's major concern is the phenomenal growth of Protestantism among the masses of Latin America.

Motivations for Protestant Missions

Let us ask, then: What has been the global vision and the motivation of the Protestant paradigm for missions? They are not very different from the Catholic vision and motivation, except for the name of the church.[6] The propagation of Christianity and *the expansion of the church* appear in the planting of churches in Africa, Asia, and Latin America,[7] reproducing European and American confessions and denominations, especially in the "Great Missionary Century" that transformed Christianity into the first global religion. This model and motivation is prominent in the contemporary school of church growth.[8]

The motivation of saving souls, so strong in the missionary movement in the aftermath of the Evangelical Revival,[9] has been affirmed and reaffirmed time and again by Evangelical conferences to this day (Berlin 1966, Lausanne 1974, Manila 1989) as a non-negotiable "primary" purpose for Evangelicals.[10]

These motivations, church growth and saving souls, do not have the same appeal throughout the world church today, however. Eugene L. Stockwell, speaking for many in the ecumenical stream, proposed a radical revision of some traits of the traditional rationale for missions in his inaugural message at the San Antonio Conference on Mission and Evangelism. After summarizing his trinitarian and Christocentric understanding of Christian faith, Stockwell boldly affirmed the global character of Christian mission. He declared, "We are called to share what we have received from God with all the peoples and nations of the earth, respectfully and with sensitivity to culture and diversity. In a word, the church is called to a mission in Christ's way—no more, no less."

For Stockwell, the salvation-damnation and numerical growth motifs did not seem to pass the test of "mission in Christ's way." Stockwell argued, "Too often the church has threatened hell in the name of heaven, focusing on a future heaven at the expense of an earth God loved so much that to it he gave his only son. . . . Too often the church has stressed numerical growth rather than spiritual depth, power rather than the vulnerability of the cross. . . . We are here at San Antonio," he said, "to say a resounding 'no' to that kind of mission."[11]

These differing perspectives raise a key question: What is the working motivation for global Christian mission today? What is the place of saving souls and church growth in our contemporary global vision and motivation? Can we discern a global trend in this aspect in Christian mission—influenced, perhaps, by the relativism and religious pluralism of our postmodern world?[12]

Protestants have had their own version of the "civilizing the barbarians" motif since the time William Wilberforce and William Carey bracketed together "civilization and the spread of the gospel." The Western missionary enterprise in the nineteenth century proceeded under the assumption of the superiority of Western culture over all other cultures and the divine election of Western nations for their global mission. The "Manifest Destiny" of the new North American nation, shared both by the nation and the churches in mission, was not very different, as a global vision and motivation, from the national sense of mission of Spain three centuries earlier.[13]

What is the "civilization" motif in postmodern global mission? Is it "development," "liberation," "peace," "ecology," or the global vision of "justice, peace, and integrity of creation"?[14]

THE GLOBAL STRATEGY FOR MISSION

The Columbus enterprise involved a lot of global strategizing from the very inception of the Genoan sailor's dreams. Global mission involves global strategizing. It was so with Paul, who strategized with the Roman Christian communities to sponsor his projected mission to Spain to reach the ends of the earth (Rom. 15:24). It was so with the Pope and the Iberian monarchies in the sixteenth century, and it was so with the Protestant powers in the nineteenth century.

What can we learn about global strategy for global mission from the last five hundred years?

The Conquest Paradigm

The first strategy for mission was the sheer *conquest* of peoples and lands and the forcing of conversions. The right of conquest was justified with the "just war" and "crusade" doctrines from the Middle Ages and sanctioned by the Pope, who made the "donation" of these lands to the Iberian kings with the condition that they fulfill the mission of Christianization as the agents of the Pope.

The Indians were told in *The Requirement* (a sort of evangelistic proclamation and ultimatum) that God created the world and sent his Son, Jesus Christ, the Lord of heaven and earth, to save people from hell. Jesus Christ left Peter and his successors, the popes, as his representatives, who in turn had given these lands to the Spanish crown. The Indians were supposed to submit to the authority of the Pope and the king and his governor, and to allow the preaching of the Christian gospel. They would then be baptized and would receive the protection of the Spanish crown. Otherwise, they would be punished—their goods taken and their villages destroyed—and they alone would be to blame for the deaths and losses involved![15]

This was the beginning of the greatest genocide in human history. The native population of the Americas was much more than decimated in the sixteenth century, going from a total of an estimated 80 million (20 percent of the world's population) to 8 million.[16]

Physical violence was followed by cultural violence. The people were treated as inferior; their culture was regarded as nonexistent. The first evangelization in the Americas used the method of *tabula rasa* (the blank blackboard), which started from zero and implanted the invading culture and religion in an abrupt attempt at *Hispanization*. Temples and idols were destroyed; indigenous priests or "witch doctors" were persecuted.

Can we understand, then, why in 1992 the descendants of Indian

Americans and African Americans (brought as slaves to replace the dying Indian population) were not willing to celebrate the Columbus "discovery" or the "encounter of cultures"? For them, it was not a discovery but an invasion. It was not cultural encounter; it was ethnocide of colossal proportions.

The Central Question for Global Mission: The Other

Carlos Fuentes has a touching thought in relation to the "encounter of cultures." He suggests that Spain's uniqueness was its "tricultural reality" of Jews, Moors, and Christians. The conquerors of the New World were "the heirs to a multicultural experience of coexistence, of commingling in tension with Jews and with Moors" that created "a tricultural reality, which stood in stark contrast to the official policy of expulsion and denial of Jews and Moors. . . . The country's cultural singularity was the recognition of the Other: battling him, embracing him, mixing with him."[17]

This was, for Fuentes, "the central question of conquest and colonization in the Americas." Unfortunately, with its adoption of the crusading paradigm, Spain missed the chance of making real that singularity in the New World.

Spain also missed a great opportunity—the chance to incarnate in the Americas the singularity of the gospel, which is not "battling" but "embracing" the other, "mixing" with the other (like the wheat and the tares) until the kingdom of God embraces us all and God will be all in all (Matt. 13:24-30). This is still the *central question for global mission today:* How do we deal with "the other," those we name "non-Christian," "pagan," "unbeliever," "unreached," or "unchurched"? How do we treat them? As object or as subject? As people to battle or to embrace? As folk to be conquered or to be loved and accepted as companions in God's mission?

The Colonization Paradigm

The second strategy for global mission was colonization, the civilization paradigm. The missionaries came to stay and brought with them not only the gospel and the Christian church but also their culture and the instruments and arts of their civilization.

Bartolomé de las Casas, the converted landowner *(encomendero)* who became the defender of the Indians against the *conquistadores* for more than fifty years, was one of the first to try a nonviolent method of evangelization by bringing the dispersed Indians from the jungle to live in community. This model was tried by the Franciscans and later developed by the Jesuits in South America in their famous "reductions" or

Christian villages, which totaled a population of about 150,000 Christian Indians by 1731.[18] The purpose was to concentrate the dispersed or nomadic Indians for evangelization, for protection from landowners and slave hunters, and for the creation of a Christian society.

Admirably intentioned as this experiment was, even those sympathetic to the effort have pointed out that it depended heavily on the authority and direction of the Jesuit missionaries.[19] It was still a transplanting of a foreign culture with paternalistic overtones onto Indian soil. Neither membership in the order nor access to the priesthood were available to the peoples being incorporated into the church until late into the following century. Leonardo Boff, in evaluating Bartolomé de las Casas's noble attempt at a peaceful evangelization through love and persuasion, points out that it was not peaceful or nonviolent enough. True, there was no physical violence, but there was symbolic violence: the destruction of the signs and symbols of the Indian religion. Boff writes, "We know that anthropologically religion constitutes the central nucleus of culture; it is its soul and its most radical meaning." Thus "to destroy this nucleus is equivalent to beheading a community, snatching the skeleton of the social body and decreeing the cultural death of a people."[20]

Protestant Conquering and Civilizing Paradigms

What about the Protestant record on conquest and civilizing strategies of global mission? There are some differences, because the colonialist Protestant countries had a different pattern of church-state relationships and their colonization was mostly a secular enterprise. Still, historians of church and missions are unanimous in recognizing the congruence of colonialism and Protestant missions in the nineteenth century.[21]

The fact that in North America the "Manifest Destiny" ideology has been so pervasive for about two centuries, not only for national mission but for Christian mission, is something to ponder. Being "the chosen nation of the Lord" was used to justify the conquest of the American West, the expulsion and enclosing of Native Americans, and the incorporation of the Southwest into the United States. Meanwhile, missions seeking to reach Mexicans on both sides of the new border followed the "Americanization" model.[22] "Manifest Destiny" assumed new forms in the twentieth century, mixing the kingdom of God with the universalization of American democracy and the crusade against communism all around the world. And what about the new "Manifest Destiny" of the free-marketization of the world, which has been proclaimed as "the end of ideologies" and "the end of history"?

Certainly, Protestants are not innocent of crusading global mission!

Is Global Strategy Feasible?

On the other hand, the international experience of Protestant missions eventually did inspire a global strategy. In this sense it was a noble experiment of incredible fruitfulness, the implementation of John R. Mott's motto, "the evangelization of the world in this generation." We have passed the first centenary of that visionary goal, but we are not closer to reaching it. True, there are more Christians today. But there are more non-Christians, as well. The proportion of Christians is one-third of the total population, but 97 percent of Christians have no contact with non-Christians![23] An estimated twelve thousand peoples are unreached, with no Christian presence.

Global strategy has a long history. Some calculate that there have been nearly one thousand plans for world evangelization since A.D. 30, of which two hundred and fifty are contemporary.[24] Many of these plans are projections of Western technology and methodology of communication throughout today's "global village."

Over the past five hundred years, global missionary strategy has been largely in the hands of Western churches and mission societies. In the last decade, however, a new pattern has emerged: missions from the Two-Thirds World. The figures are certainly impressive: 46,157 missionaries in the first ten years! In 1990 there were 22,497 missionaries from Asia, 19,097 from Africa, 3,874 from Latin America, and 689 from Oceania. And today, approximately one-half of the total Protestant missionary force comes from non-Western countries.

Here is an enormous potential for the true globalization of missionary agents. Yet the question remains: To what degree is this new missionary force a projection of Western theology, ideology, methodology, style, and even control? To what extent does it represent a true renewal of missionary perspective and content, a truly global mission? What kind of gospel are these new missions carrying around the world?

The phenomenal Protestant growth in Latin America over the last half-century is a case in point. The Protestant Evangelical community has been doubling every ten years. It has reached a total of more than 40 million and is still growing. But what kind of gospel is being incarnated in this mass of newly converted Christians? What will be their role in the totality of Latin American and Caribbean society?[25]

A GLOBAL GOSPEL FOR A GLOBAL WORLD

The fundamental question for global mission is not only a geographical matter, encompassing the whole world, but also a matter of content. The issue is a holistic gospel for a holistic mission.

This issue was dramatized by Indian Americans and African Americans in their reaction to the Quincentenary celebrations in 1992. In one of the most dramatic gestures, a group of Peruvian Indians went to the Pope during his visit to Latin America to return the Bible. They asked him to take that Bible back with him, because that book symbolized what had happened to them during the last five hundred years: the loss of their lands, the destruction of their culture, and the loss of their identity and dignity.

What a pathetic symbol! The Bible, with its liberating message of life in its fullness, had become a symbol of impoverishment, domination, and dehumanization.

If we want to be global, we need first of all to *recover the fullness of the biblical message for humanity*. It is time to face the fact that we have been carrying a mutilated Bible and a reductionist gospel. The content and meaning of biblical mission must not be reduced to selective quotations of the Great Commission.

The global potential of the Scriptures for mission is just beginning to be unpacked. We are coming to realize that the future of humanity and God's purpose for this earth are at stake in our ecological crisis, the result of our Western exploitation of nature. The first biblical paradigm for mission is creation, with its global mandate of "toiling and caring for the earth"—a mission of stewardship for all humans, Christians and non-Christians alike.

Equally global and all-encompassing is the prophetic paradigm of justice and peace (*tsedeq* and *shalom*). Even more so is Jesus' universal paradigm of the coming kingdom of God, as well as Paul's sweeping eschatological paradigm of salvation in its three dimensions: past, present, and future. Where did we get our small schemes of global mission? Not from the Scriptures, certainly.

There is great need, secondly, for a global mission that deals with the global realities on which all people depend—that supports justice, peace, and the integrity of creation, as the task has been formulated by the ecumenical movement.

This awareness and demand is not limited to the World Council of Churches. Many Evangelicals are uneasy with the theoretical discussions about the dichotomy between evangelism and social responsibility that have occurred between Lausanne I (1974) and Lausanne II (1989). One of them, Valdir R. Steuernagel, editor of the Latin American Theological Fraternity, concluded his analysis of Lausanne II in Manila as follows: "Lausanne can no longer avoid entering into a study process that would concentrate on justice and would further develop *a theology of the kingdom as the basis for missiology*."[26]

Here is a word of hope for global mission: the increasing realization from all streams of Christianity that a theology of the kingdom is the basis for missiology.

THE CHALLENGE OF INCULTURATION: GLOBAL BUT CONTEXTUAL

We see, then, that mission has to be global in its vision, its strategy, and its content. Finally, I would like to stress what may look like a paradox. In order to be global, mission has to be contextual! Contextualization was the challenge for the Christianization of America five hundred years ago, and it is still the challenge for global mission today.

What precisely is the challenge of *contextualization?* It is much more than *translation,* even what is called "the dynamic equivalent translation." I remember the late Dr. Gonzalo Baez Camargo, when he was dedicating his last years to Bible translation in Mexico, commenting on the perplexity of the translators with "the dynamic equivalent." He asked, "How do you translate for another context the English expression, 'Between the devil and the deep blue sea'?" And he humorously suggested, "I guess we could say in Mexico: 'spending a vacation in Acapulco'!"

D. T. Niles had a parable about the inculturation of the gospel that I have always found suggestive. The gospel is like a seed that you must sow in a particular place and time. When you sow the gospel in Palestine, Palestinian Christianity springs up. In Rome, Roman Christianity. In England, English Christianity. In North America, North American Christianity. This is okay. Christianity takes shape in each context (and I would add in every generation). The problem, said Niles, is that missionaries take to other parts of the world not only the seed of the gospel, but the flowerpot, as well—their own form of Roman, English, or American Christianity. We must break the flowerpot, sow the seed of the gospel in our own cultural soil, and let the plant of Christianity grow.

The Christian church in the sixteenth century missed the possibility of an *autochthonous* or truly indigenous Christian plant in America. And what we have had until recently has been a transplant of European Christianity. The problem, however, is not one of intentions alone, because there is no nude seed of the gospel. There is no such thing as gospel without culture. There never was, and never will be, a cultureless Christianity.

The problem with current and historic ecclesiologies, Gregory Leffel argues, is a question of fundamental models. The church is viewed too much in static or essentialist terms, rather than as movement. Programs of missions are not enough; the church must be fundamentally reconceived as God's missionary movement into the world. "The marks of the world's pain must be stains on the face of the church."

CHAPTER FIVE

CHURCHES IN THE MODE OF MISSION: TOWARD A MISSIONAL MODEL OF THE CHURCH
Gregory Leffel

Susan stands at worship, pressed tightly within the sanctuary crowd. Her visceral awareness of the flood of sound saturating the air she breathes, of the sight of color in motion through frames of moving shoulders and heads—even the smell of perfume and dust, the feel of hugs and warm hands—reinforces her anticipation of meeting God. Joy flows from each movement of the service from celebration to Word, Word to Eucharist.

The entire setting is tuned to transcendence: the place, the format, the performance of church leaders. Indeed, her experience, shared with others, is the very focal point of an organization of special people, housed in a special place, consecrated in entire seriousness by the sanctity of ordained ministry—a complete dedication of time and energy to the glory of God. For her, the experience forms a totalizing image of the church, exhausting (or nearly so) the entire meaning of the concept of the church—a totalizing orientation to the spiritual life shared in Christian community.

For some (perhaps many) Christians, this is the real church—that is, the church as a psychological reality, the church of experience. And the memories of the feelings, both emotional and physical, form a deeply imbedded psychic image defining the identity, purpose, and form of the church. It is a controlling image that motivates and shapes the worshipers' entire involvement and influence within it. Others, of course, have different images. But all who are involved in churches carry some kind of deeply felt sense about what it is.

But is Susan's image of the church, which can be generalized into a fairly standard model of the church as it exists in North America, really what the church ought to be? Perhaps not. Incisive critiques have been raised against this model, calling it into question and raising the larger question, What is the church?

One critique emerges from the experience of planting new churches in other cultures worldwide. In new social settings, many of the organizational and behavioral aspects of North American or European churches made little sense, frequently even retarding the vitality of the Christian communities. These new contexts in very different parts of the world—where Christianity is also much more alive—prompt questions seldom taken seriously before: Why do we do things a certain way? What exactly is the entity we are reproducing?

Further, in reaction to the increasing bureaucratization of Western churches during most of the twentieth century, a corresponding countermovement of rebellion and reform has surfaced. This has introduced a new compulsive of its own, a movement advocating a decentralized, spontaneous, community-oriented church. This may, in fact, be no more than a modern manifestation of an important facet of the very nature of the church in history: the grinding tension hiding below the surface between church as *organization* and church as *spontaneous social movement*. This tension was "discovered" by baby boomer radicals in the Jesus movement, perhaps, but was seen clearly among nineteenth-century primitivist restoration movements, earlier Pietist traditions, the Radical Reformation, and early Anabaptist and lay preacher movements—connecting back even to monasticism and, in all likelihood, to the early church. It is a tension perennially renewing the question, What is the church?

In the West, this is a time of profound unease about what churches ought to be.[1] Growing churches and denominations are abandoning traditional patterns; experimentation, from megachurches to metachurches, is rampant.[2] Are these unique contextualized expressions of church in modern society? Or syncretistic capitulations to inescapable Western market forces?

While such issues get sorted out, the church goes on. Every day, believers continue to form churches, doing what believers do, guided by *images* shaping their behaviors—some formal and incorporated into church rationale, some intuitive, silently shaping expectations and setting agendas. It is important to make these guiding images explicit, both to expose them for examination and critique and to prompt consideration of new ones in an effort to form a (hopefully) coherent theory of the church.

The purpose of this essay is to suggest a new image or "root metaphor" to define and shape churches: *the church as a social movement in the world*. This image emerges from reflection on the historical church, but especially from a shift in vantage point from traditional theories of ecclesiology to a perspective rooted in missiology. It is, therefore, a *missions model* of the church: *"churches in the mode of mission."*

The discussion proceeds in several steps: (1) a review of existing models to provide important concepts and vocabulary; (2) a description of the conceptual shift from ecclesiology to missiology; (3) a description of the primitive churches of the New Testament, in light of both sociological and theological dimensions, to highlight salient themes and criteria constituting any church model; and (4) a development of the central lines of definition of a church self-consciously addressing the world—an image of the *church in mission*.

MODELS FOR UNDERSTANDING THE CHURCH

Contemporary Models

Avery Dulles, in his classic study *Models of the Church* (1987),[3] provides a fine summary of six models for understanding the church, crystallizing the most common forms in which the church has understood itself. Dulles defines models as conceptual frameworks or reductionisms that facilitate the understanding of complex phenomena. They are not absolute reductions or predictors, like scientific laws, but conceptual ways of uniting discrete elements into unified wholes to aid visualizing an entity. Their effectiveness is measured by their fruitfulness in stimulating new insight.

Not only are models useful for reflection *about* something, they also reveal the organizing pattern inherent *in* something. A model of a pattern of human behavior is an "image" of something, a root metaphor operating in the mind that shapes thought and behavior. Accordingly, what models shape our thinking of the church?

The Institutional Model (as Dulles describes it) conceives the church as a structured community, a perfect society preserving apostolic teaching and intentions for the world, perpetuating them through its structure and protecting them through defined orthodoxy and orthopraxy from generation to generation. It is the function of ordained ministry to preserve the structure, which, given its apostolic origin, is authoritative and above challenge from below. Obviously, the strength of this model is in preserving the church and its traditions over time and space. Its weakness is its tendency to coerce behavior, deflate spontaneous community life, and prevent natural ongoing adaptation to changing conditions—to be, in effect, out-of-date and out-of-touch.

A further weakness of this model is a tendency toward anachronistic interpretations of Scripture and history that support current practice by retrojecting its meaning onto historical sources. This model is prominent in Orthodox traditions, and in the Roman Catholic tradition following the Council of Trent—especially as reinforced by Vatican I—although it has been radically confronted by the Church since the Second Vatican Council. All church traditions, however, reflect to varying degrees certain dynamics exposed by the institutional model.

The Community Model takes as its core idea the union of God with believers and the consequent reality that all believers united to God by the Spirit are, as a result, united to each other by the same Spirit in a spiritual or *mystical* community. If the institutional model highlights the visible, structural form of the church, the community model is the opposite. It highlights the invisible experience of shared community with emphasis on its spontaneous expression of love and shared, ecstatic spiritual presence. Its value is in locating the core of the church within the charismatic body of believers rather than in hierarchy. Such an emphasis, though, tends to dissolve strong leadership, with a consequent loss of mission and a sense of the complexity of the church's very diverse and complex role in the world.

This model has been central to spontaneous awakenings and reform movements, from radical Anabaptist communities to the Jesus Movement, and has informed recent Roman Catholic thought and experiments in face-to-face "base" communities. Yet, while powerfully energizing, its dynamic can seldom be sustained over time.

The Sacramental Model. The church, according to this model, exists in the world as a sign of God's activity. And, while encompassing the idea of a sign, it moves beyond a simple sign signifying God's continued presence in the world to the embodiment of that presence, imparting grace to human beings—a sacrament of divine presence. The church as communion with God is the primary sacrament, reflected in specific forms in the Eucharist, baptism, and other recognized sacraments. In this way, the church is a unique manifestation of the divine nature in human society, standing as a mediator that reconciles God and humanity, the nexus of tangible divine contact in the world.

This view of the church fits naturally into Roman Catholic creation and sacramental theology, though the concept of the Body of Christ as ontologically sacred by virtue of the presence of Christ among his gathered people (see Matt. 18:20) is generally shared. The value of this model is in its awareness of the church's innate witness in the world. Its weakness lies in the tendency to totalize sacramental experience and reinforce a preoccupation with self-contemplation, narcissism, and aestheticism. Correspondingly less emphasis is given to verbal witness and mission. These tendencies are clearly recognizable in churches shaped by individualism and privatized religion, whether conservative or liberal, Protestant, Catholic, or Pentecostal.

The Kerygmatic Model. If, in the community and sacramental models, Christ is spiritually present in his "body," in this model he is present in his Word. The purpose of the church is to proclaim (herald) the gospel, calling people throughout the world to faith and emphasizing the power of the Word to effect spiritual change. The church is the repository of the Word on earth; indeed, it is formed by the Word when men and women respond to it in faith. It is responsible for maintaining its witness. Preaching, therefore, is the centerpiece even of worship, and proclamation the focus of ministry.

Being rooted in the Scriptures, this model reinforces doctrinal orthodoxy and defines the major lines of Protestant Evangelical and neo-Orthodox ecclesiology (although through the influence of Karl Rahner's promotion of Karl Barth's theology of revelation, it has been offered as a corrective to an overly mystical view of the Roman Catholic Church). It should be pointed out, however, that Christ is the Word become *flesh*, revelation consisting in his example as well as his teaching. An overemphasis on word is often accompanied by an underemphasis on community, the experiential dimensions of the faith, and ministries of a practical nature. Proclamation and good words are often split into separate versions of the gospel.

The Diaconal Model seeks, therefore, to stress the fact that Christ became incarnate in society as a servant. Thus shall his people be: incarnate in society to participate in its transformation in terms of justice, peace, and freedom—injecting society with the values of the kingdom of God. This model is set within social pluralism, defining the church as one presence among many (including other religions). The church claims to offer a path toward authentic human experience, but eschews a monopoly on truth. Its intention, through dialogue with the world, is to leaven society through the influence of Christian tradition in cooperation with, and respect for, others' points of view. Its tendency in fact, however, is to blur church and society, relativize orthodoxy, and reduce salvation to social transaction, sacrificing the church's unique prophetic voice through which it judges society in the name of Christ.

Each of these models identifies a core of self-perception within concrete church movements and traditions. Yet no church embodies only one model. In fact, each model has some "permanent characteristics" that in one way or another appear in all traditions.[4] For instance, all churches must have structure to ensure permanence, coordination, and discipline. Further, the church in its ontological nature is a spiritual community, and it is for that reason a sacrament in and for the world. The gospel of the kingdom is the defining concept spoken to the world, and revealed to the world through service. The question is one of balance, of nuance or focus, both in what a church claims for itself theologically and what it does practically.

The Community of Disciples. Dulles's preferred model, the community of disciples, balances the central characteristics of the other models. In Dulles's mind, the church is a communion of believers first, but this is expressed not by a primary emphasis on its own nurture and enjoyment, but through service to the world. The church is an "alternative society" standing heroically *vis-à-vis* the world to transform it as Jesus did, keeping a prophetic voice against society.[5] Deep, committed discipleship is set in the frame of the historic church, connected to the apostolic traditions and maintaining the apostolate. In this environment, the community is at home in worship and celebration of its sacramental communion.

Dulles admits the difficulty of formulating a model that integrates so many variables. Does he in fact succeed? Is the community of disciples an effective model or simply a network of balance points that can be shaped one way or another? Is yet another model required?

An Intuitive Model

As defining metaphors, models bring coherence to diverse activities, thematizing them and providing a deep conceptual unity. They provide their greatest value as controlling principles or "big ideas." Still, they are conceptual devices, intellectual tools. What is proposed in theory, however, is often not what is perceived in the mind in actual experience.

The question of models may therefore be turned around to ask, What models are formed in the minds of the community as the result of interaction with the church? What is the psychologically *real* image formed by distilling all of the forms of personal church experience into an inward cognition of the entity "church"? *How do we know if the church as perceived in experience bears any resemblance to the church(es) of ecclesiological theory?* This is an important question. Perhaps behind the rhetoric and behaviors of church members and clergy there lie "hidden" or subliminal images that ultimately, though not intentionally, inform the agenda of community, ministry, and leadership.

It is possible to bring out the contours of cognitive images by using a research methodology refined in cognitive anthropology called *compo-nential analysis*. This method, borrowed from linguistic analysis of the meanings of words, uses interviews to discover the semantic field of ideas (expressed verbally) related to a particular cultural reality (in this case the church). Through comparing and categorizing words and ideas used, descriptive statements can be made that define the inner, cognitive con-cept underlying the expressed words and ideas. The result is not, how-ever, a proposition or concept, but rather a map or a tree of multiple thoughts and powerful associations of remembered sensations, feelings, encounters, attractions/repulsions, and other forms of experiences color-ing one's full inner sense of the reality of a thing.

My own attempt at such an analysis[6] revealed the psychic world of "Susan" (above) as it relates to the church. The study was conducted on a small group of Evangelical Protestant believers who were members of a medium-sized church that was fairly traditional in format and orienta-tion. The study analyzed a semantic field of about two hundred and fifty morphemes (i.e., words) representing a semantic world of cognitive and affective elements. The field was reducible to two central themes, *wor-ship* activity and a specific *place*.

By arranging various elements according to their salience in relation-ship to the central themes, the following description emerged in four lev-els of descending vividness and emotional force:

(1) The experience of standing in a group of worshipers, which was reinforced by high sensory values, including sound, the sight and touch of others, and the smell and taste of the sacraments.

(2) One step removed in intensity was the presence of the physical set-ting that framed the experience, and of the supporting cast of individu-als who provided the aspects of the service, including the sermon.

(3) A further step removed were associations of community support services, including classes, fellowship opportunities, and images of the church as an object in the environment.

(4) The final descriptive layer, nearly inconspicuous, consisted of asso-ciations of the church in relationship to the surrounding community, including a vague sense of service to it.

In order to visualize the findings graphically, they were arrayed in the form of an illustration (see figure 5A). Within the sketch, dominant ele-ments are featured as focal points, with the lesser elements fading into the background, their size and prominence in relationship to their salience. Revealed here is a strong awareness of the worshiper, the *ego*, surrounded by others and aware of the surroundings falling away at the edges of perception, with a lesser awareness of the church as a whole and a very slight sense of its role in the world.

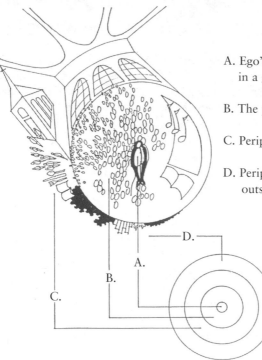

A. Ego's experience of worshiping in a group.

B. The place of ego's worship experience.

C. Peripheral activities supporting the group.

D. Peripheral activity in the community outside the group and meeting point.

Figure 5A. Visual Model of Informants' Semantic Domain

What model of the church is at work here? This inward reality best corresponds to a model of the church emphasizing its *kerygmatic* and *sacramental* modes (Dulles) in a tightly scripted, worship service-oriented format. Presumably the informants chose to attend their church because it largely conformed to their intuitive image; or they had internalized images communicated by this particular church; or personal and institutional images were mutually reinforced. Whether the image formed corresponds to the image desired by the church's leaders is another question, and in this case was not pursued. This image does, however, clearly reveal the church-related values of some of its members—*an image or model falling outside any clear theological categories*, yet directly affecting Christian behavior.

FROM ECCLESIOLOGY TO MISSIOLOGY

Reducing the church to a model(s) in order to express its function and purpose is essential to its self-understanding. Practically speaking, it is important for the sake of keeping the church organized, clarifying its mission and identity, and harmonizing the parts of its "body." The function of *ecclesiology*, both theologically and practically, is to explain the church in its various biblical, theological, historical, and sociological dimensions. Ecclesiology explores the nature of the church in order to bring to light its inner life, strengthen it, and advance its qualities and functions.

Traditionally, ecclesiology is a hub or nexus connecting a variety of related fields and activities—homiletics, pastoral ministries, administration and government, education, missions, and so on. Formally, it considers essential questions related to the church: Who comprises the church community (at any level) and what is the nature of their relationships? What is the function of its ministry, both internally and externally? And what is the nature of the structure holding it all together?

Ecclesiology is also a view from within the church. In fact, this vantage point is tacitly assumed, since those asking about the church—theologians, ministers, other leaders, and Christians generally—are also part of the church and have a vested interest in it. Thomas Oden notes, "The query, What is the church? whether skeptical or plaintive, always silently presupposes the existence of the church that asks the question."[7]

The problem of trying to describe an entity (whether a church, a culture, or one's own personality) from within is an acknowledged epistemological problem. Descriptive statements are subjectivized to the extent one's personal perspective is framed by the entity being described. Thus, describing the church while functioning within it is like moving a box while standing inside it. Objectifying observations remains difficult. Unless the observer achieves marginality from the thing being studied, the study will never escape the compulsives of the thing studied. In other words, the study of the church will always be, for the most part, about the church. This is normally the path pursued in ecclesiological studies: (1) concern for the church's self-performance (i.e., its practical success in the world, and its institutional success as defined by membership, growth rate, income, or other quantifiable measures); (2) and/or theological justification for the church's functions or concerns.

Certainly, this does not preclude serious "objective" studies that consider the church from another point of view. Nor does it exclude a certain objectivity in studying the church in the past or in other cultures. And certainly it does not mean that church-related studies are purposely biased or exaggerated, or that proper moral judgments cannot be formed about the church by those within the church. It simply means that the study of the church tends to be exhausted on the church itself as it exists now or has existed in history.

It is also true that the study of missions can similarly be subsumed under the church's concern for its own well-being. In this case, missiology is limited to enhancing the performance of certain foreign activities.

Mission is visualized as the extension of existing church bodies. Yet missiology in its modern development, accompanying the growth of a truly worldwide church movement, has generally maintained a broader perspective. Well-known voices—from A. B. Simpson, who positioned the church in the mode of heralding the message of the kingdom in all the world as a prerequisite to Christ's return (cf. Matt. 24:14), to Ralph Winter, who defined missions exclusively in terms of the cross-cultural penetration of the world's "unreached" ethnic groups—locate the church as an entity in the wider context of the world. These voices establish the church's *raison d'être* as proclaiming the kingdom and making disciples in all parts of the earth and define its purpose as world proclamation to the Gentiles (cf. Luke 21:24; Matt. 24:14; Eph. 2:11-22).

According to F. J. Verstraelen *et al.*, mission is a global, interethnic, intergenerational vision that forms the "ultimate frame of reference" for the Christian movement. Missions sponsored by the churches are placed within the larger motion of God's activity in the world, *missio Dei*. The church is only a piece of the bigger picture. "'Mission' is . . . the dynamic relationship between God and the world: God *sends* himself, his Son, and his church. . . . We have to speak of—in addition to 'the study of the movement of Christianity'—the exposition of the mission of God."[8] An understanding of missions from this perspective begins in the intersection of "the present evil age" (Gal. 1:4) with the kingdom of God.

From this point of view, missiology takes the church in its concrete form in the world as a datum, treating it as a definable object with a measurable performance relative to the full scope of God's involvement with the world. Thus, the beginning point for understanding the church is, conceptually at least (allowing for the fact that missiologists are also a part of the church), outside of it. Consequently, a different set of questions is asked about the church: What is its relative presence/absence in the world? What is its relative growth/decline? What are its relative strengths/weaknesses? What explains its performance in the world? And how may it be improved?

Such a perspective allows us to see the church from the vantage point of the unevangelized world—an alternative view of the church *as a movement* sweeping outward to include new parts of the world. This view stresses the church's *external* performance over against its inward self-perception and its *internal* performance. The difference is found in the point of integration behind the defining image of the church.

It is possible, then, for the church to define itself in terms of its mission to the world as its primary starting point. This is a missiologically informed "model" that, while not negating other dimensions exposed in other models, roots the church in a new conceptual core: *"church in the mode of mission."* This is a movement of witness in the world, demonstrating the gospel (i.e., the Word incarnate in human flesh) through the actions and words of God's people, unstintingly advancing it to the ends of the earth. It is a model of the church *for others*, not for itself. Just as Christ was incarnate in the world, so also his "body" is in the world, reconciling it to God.

This may seem to be an uncomfortable way to define the church, especially in light of the fact that the church is first and foremost *for Christ*— his bride in a union that will reach full consummation in the *eschaton*. But to say that the church exists for Christ is to say very little about its presence in the world in this age. Perhaps it can be put this way: the second person of the Trinity existed in relationship to the Father and the Spirit without any explicit reference to the world as its redeemer. He became the Christ by offering himself as minister to, and savior of, the world. Similarly, the church captures its true nature in the world as the continued embodiment of the Incarnation, the continued offering of Christ of himself to the world for its redemption. The church cannot find its true identity outside of its relentless mediation for the world.

Such a view sees the church as an event, a motion across geography and generations, a social movement with a specific end, a *telos* that defines its purpose. It is a pulse of divine witness spreading like a wave through human history. The question is, in what sense is this a biblical image? And in what sense was it a part of the psychic reality of the earliest Christians?

THE PRIMITIVE CHURCH AS A MISSIONS MOVEMENT

The most remarkable fact about the early church is that it happened at all. Seldom do world religions erupt, as it were, seemingly from nowhere. Yet the magnitude of the growth of the church, which claimed one-half of the Roman world (not to mention its growth in the East) within three centuries, is a fact of significant proportion, an important focus of study in its own right.

Further, the experience of its unfolding doubtless made a deep impression on the formative identity of the early church. Does the church feel differently about itself in times of rapid expansion versus times of stasis or retreat? How might its awareness of its role in the world be heightened? And how might this be reflected in the records left by the church, particularly the earliest records of its initial mission to the world, the New Testament? The following discussion briefly traces the rough historical dimensions of the Christian movement to about A.D. 350 in order to expose its key dynamics. It suggests that the church perceived itself as a spontaneous movement, and presents this movement in tension with a growing institutional framework. From these historical materials, a missions model of the church can be described.

The Dynamics of a Religious Movement

Sociologist Rodney Stark in *The Rise of Christianity* (1996) describes the early Christian movement in the Greco-Roman world through a quantitative analysis of available statistical data. He compares the rise of Christianity with the dynamics of religious movements in more recent times. Supported by well-substantiated numbers, Stark's reconstruction of Christianity in its formative period challenges long-held understandings of the causes of its growth.

Perhaps most surprising, Stark argues that the growth of Christianity was fairly constant, yet relatively slow. It was a mass movement in terms of its scope, but one that naturally occurred within networks of social relationships, not through widespread public preaching and sudden mass conversions. Positing an initial total of only 1,000 Christians in A.D. 40 (deliberately low in order to demonstrate the nature of steady growth), Stark demonstrates that by growing at a rate of 40 percent per decade (3.42 percent per year), the church, reaching a modest total of 7,500 by A.D. 100, would have grown to 217,000 by A.D. 200; 6 million by A.D. 300; and 33 million by A.D. 350.[9]

Such a growth curve explains why Christianity is comparatively invisible in archaeological and historical records before the late second century, but also why it was inevitable that Rome would eventually fall to the pervasive Christian movement. Surging church growth in the fourth century was a natural extension of the early church continuing to grow at the same rate as before. Thus, Constantine did not create the conditions for Christianity's sudden increase; he simply yielded to its continuing rise.

Stark's analysis does not preclude variations in the rate of growth, such as a rapid increase in the first few years or a decrease at the end of the apostles' lifetimes. Consider, for example, the problems some established churches faced at the end of John's lifetime, as noted in Revelation 2 and 3. There could have also been a modest jump in church membership following the Edict of Milan. Still, the overall dimensions of growth appear to require a constant growth rate of around 40 percent per decade.

Growth of this nature is best explained as influence spreading through preexisting social networks rather than as the fruit of public appeals.

Sociological analysis of religious movements suggests that it is the desire to maintain relationships in good order that makes the conversions of loved ones and colleagues more likely—and ties among religious believers are stronger than with others generally. Doctrine generally serves as a secondary reinforcer of the decision to convert. In other words, the interconnectedness of individuals in relational webs provides a warm environment for conversion that, by contrast, cold public proclamation cannot reproduce or utilize. Stark notes a Mormon claim that cold-call evangelism results in only about one conversion in one thousand contacts, while evangelism through social networks results in conversions about 50 percent of the time.[10]

In fact, Stark cites the Mormon Church—a movement growing at an average rate of 43 percent per decade, from thirty thousand in 1840 (ten years after its founding) to 4.6 million in 1980—to explain early Christian church growth.[11] Specializing in extension through family networks, the Mormons have maintained a stable, steady pattern of growth since their beginning. After their initial period, the Mormons never utilized public mass conversion campaigns.

The obvious question is whether it is anachronistic to project the experience of what Stark believes to be a new world religion (the Mormons) on an ancient movement.[12] However, he argues that such similar phenomena are so widespread in the studies of religious groups that they can be generalized and given broader application. Findings from the study of contemporary religious movements are particularly useful when records of past movements (such as those of early Christianity) allow a fairly thorough reconstruction of events. According to Stark, the early Christian experience fits very tightly with the rate and type of growth to be expected of a new religious movement, based on recent research.

Stark is confident of further correlations between recent religious movements and early Christianity. Most notably, he argues that the mainstream of the Christian movement was oriented toward the middle class: artisans, craftsmen, shopkeepers, merchants, and professionals—people relatively free economically. Some members of the upper class were also attracted. This, he notes, is the consensus of both traditional and the most recent historical scholarship. (The notion of a proletariat church he traces to sociologist Ernst Troeltsch—this theory being popular at midcentury but having less support today.) This also corresponds to the growth pattern of modern cults, which Stark defines as new religions occurring outside of existing religious traditions. Growing principally in the center of the socioeconomic continuum, cults are significantly underrepresented by the poor and the very wealthy. Similar observations have been made in the study of the diffusion of innovations and of church growth itself.[13]

Renewal movements occurring within existing religions, however, are often overrepresented by the poor, leading to the formation of what Stark calls sects. Sects and cults, though, are very different phenomena and must not be confused.[14] As the deviant religion of a small minority, early Christianity falls within the cult category, spreading among the more prosperous, and it is this fact that explains its relatively free access to power (evident despite persecution) and the ready patronage of home-owners and leading citizens. This is not to say that the poor were not represented at all—they certainly were—it is only to locate the strength of the movement in another place.

Stark arrives at another surprising conclusion. Widespread Hellenistic Judaism not only provided the church with its first converts in many cities, but also continued to be a significant source of church growth through the fourth century. It was through the Jewish community that contacts with the Gentile community's "God-fearers" were made, and that Christianity was able to find fresh social networks to support its spread. The Jews provided an audience already equipped to understand the Christian message, facilitating the growth of a core following. For the Jews, Stark notes, Christianity provided—especially after the crushing of Jewish revolts in A.D. 70 and 120—a safe accommodation to Gentile society without the loss of core religious values and traditional morality. The erosion of Jewish identity in the face of pagan culture likely masks the extent to which Jews were swept into the church, while those locked in conflict with the church were reduced to a minority.

Early Christianity grew for other reasons, as well. Women were attracted to the church because of its relative equality, fair treatment, and strong support of marriage. This dynamic was reinforced by the rescue of female infants from euthanasia and by the inclusion of orphans and widows. In fact, Christianity reversed the prevailing numerical proportion of men over women (a male to female ratio of 4:3 in pagan society versus 2.5:3 in the church), creating a situation favorable to women and a fertility rate well above that of society as a whole. The preponderance of women also brought growth through conversion by marriage of pagan men—frequently enough, men of influence or high rank—thus softening the tone of opposition. Women served as "gatekeepers," opening new social networks for evangelism.

Even disaster assisted in the penetration of pagan society. Stark notes that devastating epidemics in A.D. 165 and again in 251 resulted in massive depopulation by a factor of one-fourth to one-third or more. Christian care and concern for the ill, including non-Christians, had a twofold effect. On one hand, their nursing skills substantially reduced their mortality rate relative to their pagan neighbors. On the other, their loving actions attracted non-Christians into their community networks, to which pagans turned for comfort and intimacy after the decimation of their own families and relational networks. As a result, Christianity grew as a percentage of the population even without an increase in absolute numbers. In addition, Christians gained substantial new access to pagan social networks.[15]

Most of this activity was concentrated within the cities of the Roman Empire. Of the twenty-two largest cities, according to Stark, twelve were penetrated by Christianity by A.D. 100 and the others by 200. It was natural for a new religion to grow in the flux of urban settlement, especially in the pluralistic, ethnic confusion of Roman cities. The larger the city, the more freedom from conformity and, consequently, the more open citizens are to new religious beliefs. In the cities, Christianity was free enough to build a critical mass of support. Cities, with their social chaos and physical squalor, provided a unique environment for the gospel. Many major cities, such as Antioch, were administrative centers as well as military outposts. They were constructed within defensive walls and were jammed with soldiers, resettled veterans, and assorted retinues of craftsmen and merchants making a living from the defense spending.

These cities formed an incredible ethnic mix. Antioch alone, with a population of 150,000, housed eighteen separate ethnic quarters. In the face of the collapse of social cohesion, riots and mob violence were constant, and violent crime was a ubiquitous terror. Ethnic conflicts were exacerbated by horrible living conditions. Housing densities well in excess of almost any contemporary example (compare first-century Antioch with 195 people per acre to modern Bombay's 183, Calcutta's 122, Manhattan's 100, and Chicago's 32) jammed human beings together in warrens of shabby wood construction. Streets hardly a meter wide were filled with sewage and smoke—"filth," says Stark, "beyond our imagining."[16] Disease spread without limit; illness was a daily preoccupation. Average life expectancy was less than thirty years.

Those who survived faced catastrophic building collapses, fires, floods, plagues, riots, wars, and earthquakes. Stark calculates that cities were destroyed on average every fifteen years. In this milieu, Christianity made a unique contribution—it

> served as a revitalization movement that arose in response to the misery, chaos, fear, and brutality of life in the urban Greco-Roman world. . . . Christianity revitalized life in Greco-Roman cities by providing new norms and new kinds of social relationships able to cope with many urgent urban

problems. To cities filled with the homeless and impoverished, Christianity offered charity as well as hope. To cities filled with newcomers and strangers, Christianity offered an immediate basis for attachments. To cities filled with orphans and widows, Christianity provided a new and expanded sense of family. To cities torn by violent ethnic strife, Christianity offered a new basis for social solidarity. . . . And to cities faced with epidemics, fires, and earthquakes, Christianity offered effective nursing services. . . .

[I]ts superior capacity for meeting these chronic problems soon became evident and played a major role in its ultimate triumph. . . .

No wonder the early Christian missionaries were so warmly received in this city [i. e., Antioch]. For what they brought was not simply an urban movement, but a new culture capable of making life in Greco-Roman cities more tolerable.[17]

Christianity flourished in the urban religious "free market," outperforming individualistic paganism with a rich, committed community life in which love was demonstrated in intense face-to-face relationships. Christianity outstripped all other religions with its powerful monotheism, ethical values, and inclusive brother/sisterhood.[18] The application of its religious message to the common experiences of life made it a powerful social force in the ancient cities:

It was only as Christian texts and teachings were acted out in daily life that Christianity was able to transform the human experience so as to mitigate misery.

Chief among these miseries was the cultural chaos produced by the crazy quilt of ethnic diversity and the blazing hatreds entailed thereby. In uniting its empire, Rome created economic and political unity at the cost of cultural chaos. . . .

A major way in which Christianity served as a revitalization movement within the empire was in offering a coherent culture that was entirely stripped of ethnicity. . . . Among Christians ethnicity tended to be submerged as new, more universalistic, and indeed cosmopolitan, norms and customs emerged.[19]

Clearly, Christianity resonated with the times. By penetrating webs of personal relationships with a living gospel, by affirming life, by offering hope, and by transforming social networks into communities of equality and acceptance, the Christian faith created a new urban life in the face of persistent pagan failure. Through this natural human contact, Christianity spread rapidly in the plain sight of neighbors close at hand without recourse to mass evangelism campaigns.

Church as Movement, Church as the Ministry

Against this background, it is possible to tease out additional insights into the nature of the early church from the many documents it left behind. Of greatest importance, of course, is the New Testament, a set of documents from the original movement, many of them airing its dirty laundry. From this literature, Edward Schillebeeckx in *The Church with a Human Face* (1985) illuminates both the sociological and theological aspects of the rise of the church and its formal institutional structure, the ministry.[20]

Jesus is the center of the Christian faith. The character of his life, service, and teaching define the nature of the church that bears his name. Schillebeeckx understands Jesus' ministry in terms of apocalyptic messianism looking for the imminent coming king. He also sees Jesus' ministry in light of Pharisaic influence. Pharisaism, despite its negative reaction to Jesus, was a religion of the masses. It expressed political resistance to Roman occupation and to the capitulation of the Sadducees to Roman manipulation of the temple and Jewish religion generally. Jesus echoed this agenda but went further, identifying in the masses a basic equality of persons and the need for freedom from not only political tyranny, but also from the tyranny of excessive religious control. His message was one of freedom in loving, inclusive community, in the strong light of the coming kingdom, and in the power of the coming Spirit.

Jesus' teaching extended into the core of the church's message, refracted in the light of his resurrection, ascension, and Pentecost. It informed the incorporation of diverse people into a united community of the Spirit. Early Christians demonstrated Jesus' loving concern in the sharing of homes and material goods. Yet the church in its cultural expression remained Jewish, virtually indistinguishable from Jews not following Christ and notably skittish about evangelistic contact with Gentiles. The church in Jerusalem came to resemble the synagogue of any community of Jews. It was ruled by a council of elders (presbyters), chief among whom was James, the brother of Christ. The churches connected with Peter appear to have followed this format. Perhaps this was also the case in the East, as it later became in Alexandria.

But the church was not monolithic. The Antioch church, bursting beyond its Jewish core into the Gentile community, moved in a different direction. Schillebeeckx detects in the church and in its spreading influence an intense realized eschatology: the fullness of the kingdom has arrived, and soon the king will, also. In this light, it is understandable that some would refuse to work or marry, or would even abandon their families—problems addressed in the New Testament. At the center, however, was the deep experience of the Holy Spirit, shared equally by all believers, who constituted a community or body shaped and energized by the Spirit's expression through each person. The church was a spontaneous community of the Spirit in which all were in authority to the extent of their contribution of charisma—a body led not only by the contributions of older believers, but by the spontaneous influence of prophetic and teaching gifts. Having its source in the baptism of the Spirit, it was "pneuma-christology," a community of solidarity and equality in which equal partners were free from domination in any relationships.

It is this spontaneous Spirit community (pneuma-christology) that permeates Paul's letters, filling them with a remarkable freedom. The faith, according to Paul, is perfectly egalitarian: "There is no longer Jew or Greek, there is no longer slave or free, there is no longer male and female" (Gal. 3:28). "There is no longer Greek and Jew, circumcised and uncircumcised, barbarian, Scythian . . . but Christ is all and in all!" (Col. 3:11). Freedom from the Law is likewise perfect; no formal structure is to control behavior other than the notion of loving in the power of the Spirit. How else are we to take the words, "But if you are led by the Spirit, you are not subject to the law. . . . The fruit of the Spirit is love"? (Gal. 5:18, 22). The law of conscience is bounded only by loving consideration of others (cf. Rom. 14:21-23). And of course, "To each is given the manifestation of the Spirit" (1 Cor. 12:7).

But Paul also had to wrestle the excesses of pneuma-christology to the ground of real life, tempering hopes of the immediate return of Christ and helping the dynamics of spontaneous community to function within society over time. He tells his followers not to abandon their families or careers, and to marry if they desire. More problematic was fitting egalitarianism into a pagan society that was chauvinistic and oppressive. Options had to be formulated to work out spontaneous brother/sisterhood within the cultural constraints of the empire. In this way, pneuma-christology is tempered by reality, yet does not lose its critical spark. The movement remains spontaneous. Its leadership consists of *ad hoc* arrangements of local leaders overlapping with more-than-local members of the apostolic band, who, moving from place to place, stimulate further outreach to new areas.

In this context, Schillebeeckx defines *ekklesia* not in terms of the formal assembled governing body of the *polis*, but in terms of "free associations," professional guild societies with cultic overtones that were then common throughout the empire.[21] These were communities of identity formed by people of the same trade. Though ethnically diverse, they functioned as personal social networks and, more important, sources of contacts with influence. All freely participated in decision making; however, all depended on patrons to finance them and provide contacts with the elite. L. Michael White describes these complex arrangements, with their extensive, tightly connected systems of influence that were an integral part of society.[22] As late as the fifth century, such networks of pagans worked alongside Christians to influence the selection of community leaders. This, of course, echoes Stark's point about the role of social networks in spreading the faith. Societies of Christians could adapt this social pattern to their particular needs, accepting the offer of patrons to house their assemblies, but determining their own affairs as equals (with some influence from the apostles), free from the domination of patrons or other singular leaders.

Schillebeeckx believes this pattern was distinctly Pauline and did not last much past the end of his life. With time, likely through the influence of more Jewish-oriented churches, a formal pattern of a ruling council of *presbyters* emerged, and later, a president of the council (by temporary, rotating appointment) and eventually a single leader—an *episkopos* or bishop. There was also a conceptual shift from the church as "free association" to the church as "*oikos,*" or household, following the model of the Greek *paterfamilias*. Schillebeeckx sees here a theological realignment from the spontaneous equality of the Pauline churches to the notion of the family head, the leader of an extensive system of family, servant/slave, and business obligations. Culturally this pattern was hierarchical and authoritarian. In it are seeds of later authoritarian development.

In documents as late as the *Didache* (late first century), Schillebeeckx observes a tension between the rule of equals in a college of presbyters (in an ambiguous relationship of influence with the ministry of the prophets) and the rise of a singular leader, or *mono-episkopos*. Beyond this point, the development of church leadership appears to follow the increasingly authoritarian pattern of civil government. By the time of Ignatius, the power of the bishop over the local Christian community was complete, even absorbing the prophetic office. And by the end of the second century, the pattern of episcopal control over a region beyond a single city had been established in Africa.

It is clear on sociological grounds that a spontaneous movement cannot continue without the development of a governing structure to coordinate it, to preserve its distinctive features beyond its original members, and more important, to decide who is empowered to make decisions. As the Christian movement solidified, its government became more structured, formalizing into a three-part ministry of presbyters, deacons, and bishops. This ministry structure was not disconnected from the local community; rather, it grew from it and found its authority as a servant collective expressing the life and vitality of the community. Over time, however, this connection was replaced by a conception of the ministry as an ontologically distinct entity over the community, and later, even free from the community. Along with this, as early as the third century, the church's ministry was increasingly identified with the Old Testament Levitical cultus. With time, this identification funded the notion of the ministry with a sacerdotal character, further removing it from the regular community of Christians.

Schillebeeckx notes that by the fourth century, the church itself was aware of a significant break with the original pneuma-christology of the New Testament, though at the time it saw this as a plus.[23] The ministry came to be expressed as a crystallization of the pneuma *within* the community, taking over its charisma *from* the community. Over time, the community ceased to be the ground of or participant in the ministry. It was reduced to being the mere object of ministry.[24]

Wherever this ministry conception is found in whole or in part in present-day Christian traditions, one also finds an inherent tension between the church of the New Testament and the church of contemporary practice. This tension is located, according to Schillebeeckx, in alternative ministries that seek to recapture the New Testament priority of the community over the hierarchy—the power of the pneuma in the grass roots over against the structure of the official ministry:[25]

> In Paul we can still feel the original power of the whole of the liberating tradition of Antioch and the early church: "Where the Spirit of the Lord is, there is liberty." . . . According to Paul and the whole of the New Testament, at least within Christian communities of believers, relationships involving subjection are no longer to prevail. . . . This early-Christian egalitarian ecclesiology in no way excludes leadership and authority; but in that case authority must be one filled with the Spirit, from which no Christian, man or woman, is excluded in principle on the basis of the baptism of the Spirit.[26]

The church in its concrete existence is not simply spontaneous movement or institutional ministry. It is both. Both concepts are in constant tension, tearing at one another, as it were, to express either pure charisma or pure control.

The "Ideal" Church Within the "Actual" Church

As the discussion above shows, defining the term *ekklesia* in the New Testament is a slippery business. Lothar Coenen provides a definition that roots its meaning in the concrete communities of the early disciples, and shows its usage in multiple levels of reference from the local to the universal.[27] He identifies it as an "event" rather than an institution. But first he provides an interesting contrast with its pre-Christian use in the LXX.

The Hebrew *edah* is used in the Old Testament as a label for the people of Israel, the entire elect community. The Hebrew *qahal* describes the *assembly* of the elect community *(edah)*. In Greek, the term *synagoge* expresses both concepts: the elect community *(edah)* and the assembly of the community *(qahal)*. *Ekklesia*, however, is used to translate *qahal*, assembly, but never *edah*, the elect community.

New Testament use is somewhat different. While *ekklesia* is used in reference to local bodies of Christians, it also refers to Christians universally, the elect community in the sense of *edah*. Moreover, *synagoge* is used only (with one exception in James) in reference to the Jewish community, and here it includes not just the community of the elect, but their assembly in a specific place. Even the buildings in which meetings take place are called *synagoge*.

The question naturally arises, then: Why, given the similarity in the appearance of Christians meeting in homes with Jews meeting in synagogues, does the New Testament avoid the use of *synagoge* as a term for the church, and favor a much more ambiguous term? The reason, it would appear, is to avoid an association of the church with the Jewish community. This is certainly important for strategic purposes. But we have in Paul further cause to distance *church* from *synagogue*: such distancing underscores the immense chasm that has opened in the gospel between Israel and the church, between the Old and New Covenants, between Mt. Sinai and Pentecost, and between law and grace. In Paul, particularly, there is a radical disjuncture between Israel and the Christian movement. For him it is a matter of the freedom of the Spirit against the bondage of the Law—quite literally, a contrast of life and death. Paul views the church as a sign of the breaking-in of a new day, an age of the Spirit penetrating and overturning the present age of darkness from which the Law by itself can offer no escape. This kingdom of God has come suddenly, following the resurrection of Christ; it is the unveiling of a mystery once hidden but now to be announced to the entire world. And slipping out of Jerusalem, it now sweeps through the world, overturning the entire order of things in a divine new economy of life. As the gospel sweeps across individuals, they are transformed ontologically from children of the flesh into children of the Spirit, a change so radical that it is announced as death and resurrection. Sweeping society, the gospel transforms it into a Spirit-community, dissolving ethnic dividing walls into a single, shared body of fraternal love.

It is for this reason—the massive changes taking place in the reception of the gospel—that Coenen refers to the meaning of *ekklesia* first as an *event*, not a thing, and certainly not as an institution. It is only secondly a community modeling the love and justice of the gospel, the appealing fruit of the movement. And third, it is a reference to the Christian community rapidly filling up the world. Often the word *ekklesia* is applied as much to the universal community as to the local. This presents a certain ambiguity that refuses to allow the idea to be tied down to a particular local establishment.

It is possible, perhaps, to draw from Paul an image of the church as the urgent new reality of this age—one that appears in each new time and place as a flash of lightning and a crack of thunder rolling from one place to another. To be caught in its storm is to be absorbed by the wave of God in the world that is reconciling the world to Godself and announcing the reconciliation to the ends of the earth. What appears behind the storm front is, in Schillebeeckx's terms, pneuma-christology: vital, Spirit-filled communities radiating divine charisma. Yet Coenen points out (like Schillebeeckx) that this free expression of the Christian movement must soon meet with James and the Jerusalem church's synagogue image of the church. Freedom is fated to be enshrouded in structure, the "ideal" finding its place inside the "actual" historical development of the church and its formal ministry.

What is it that Paul sees when he reflects deeply on the reality of the church? What quick flashes of insight can we glean from his writings? Is it possible that in them we sense a connection to the tensions of early Israelite society in the pneuma-community of the Judges—a period of anarchy, yes, but a period when God, not a man, was the true king of Israel? The Judges account is preceded in time and followed by the developing monarchy. The monarchy itself was preauthenticated in the Law (Deut. 17:14-20), and very naturally unfolded under Saul and David. God notes its emergence wistfully, with regret: "they have rejected me from being king over them" (1 Sam. 8:7). The period of God's own charismatic leadership has ended. But the point has been made that leadership belongs to God, not to humans. For now, however, it will be traced as a countermovement within a human structure, an institution of the Spirit administered within an institution of royalty.

This profound tension is transferred to the church. Paul the idealist may wonder, *Is it too much to ask that God rule directly through the prophets and the charismatic body?* Certainly, the ecstatic excesses of the Corinthian church point to the impossibility of sustaining a charismatic body for very long without disaster. But the admission of human leadership and institutional structures is nuanced with the power/freedom ideal informing the Christian movement. It is a raw power within a structured frame, a power that must be managed without being crushed, that must be directed toward redemptive ends, and that must be freed from time to time to break out beyond the structure in new surges of growth.

Maybe this pushes the Scriptures too far and presses too hard to find the mind of a great apostle. But can we admit that the picture of the church in Paul's mind captures the reality of the rat-infested, stinking squalor and violence of Roman cities, into which the gospel breaks as a startling force to make things new? Where, in the crush of overpopulation, the church lives right out in the open as a daily witness, forcing open social webs by coercion of love and spreading through relational networks like electricity until the whole world hears about it (see Rom. 1:8)? Is it too much to think that this vital response was, to Paul, an affirmation of his calling to take the gospel to the world, a sign of a radical, Spirit-driven movement that would fill the earth? Perhaps it is in the mode of mission that the energy of the "ideal" church is released, and that we understand Paul's plea and prayer in the name of "every family in heaven and on earth" to "comprehend, with all the saints, what is the breadth and length and height and depth, and to know the love of Christ that surpasses knowledge, so that you may be filled with all the fullness of God" (Eph. 3:15, 18-19).

The act of contemplating the love of God—infinite in power for us, and including all others—leads to the fulfillment of Spirit-people as they behold the *missio Dei* taking the entire world in its grasp. From this summit perspective, Paul can see beyond the church to embrace the world, the focus of his calling; and in the world's redemption, he can see the purpose of the Body of Christ.

TOWARD A MISSIONAL MODEL OF THE CHURCH

One more Old Testament illustration comes to mind, a picture through which to reflect on the church. Following the miracle of the exodus from Egypt, Israel gathered at Mt. Sinai, waiting at the foot of the mountain for Moses to descend with guidance from God. From this time forward, God will dwell among them, leading them by cloud and pillar of fire into the Promised Land of Canaan, which they shall fill with their presence. The ideal picture of Israel—sadly, not actualized—is one of a people in whom God dwells, who, picking up their tents and belongings, are *moving*—moving *en masse* toward a greater world they are to fill. But they move within a larger frame of identity. God said to them through Moses, "You shall be my treasured possession out of all the peoples. Indeed, the whole earth is mine, but you shall be for me a priestly kingdom and a holy nation" (Exod. 19:5-6). Walter Kaiser notes that the object of the priesthood is the world.[28] This is a distinct missionary calling. Filling the land is only a prerequisite for filling the world with the presence of God.

Israel was called, in this sense, to be a movement (though the people abandoned their full calling), not only moving into the land in the conquest, but also in some physical way moving into the world as a whole. This is a suitable image of the church—a called people. Peter later echoes Moses' words, saying to the church, "You are a chosen race, a royal priesthood, a holy nation, God's own people, in order that you may proclaim the mighty acts of him who called you out of darkness into his marvelous light" (1 Pet. 2:9). This is the church: an elect community, commissioned and sent to fill the world with the light of witness to the kingdom of God, the gospel. The image is that of a mass movement entering lands, sweeping through them, occupying them, and moving on. The movement faces outward to the ends of the earth, the endpoint of its calling; it is, freely and energetically, a people on the move. The image has two poles: the ends of the earth, to which the wave rolls on as a spontaneous movement, and Mt. Sinai, caught in a glance over the shoulder as one moves out. Mt. Sinai represents the core of tradition, the central point of identity marking the starting point—it represents enduring structure. Within these poles, the church finds its identity: *a movement in the world*, spontaneous and active, held together by such structure as may be needed to maintain its tradition and keep its wilder impulses in check.

The Character of the Missions Church

This image of church as *a movement in the world* can be described in five dimensions. These are presented as a view from the leading edge of the church as it cuts into the world, but includes a trailing edge that reflects on its traditions and the presence of God within it. The church in the mode of mission is, from this perspective:

Movemental. That is to say, the church defines itself in terms of its end, its growth as a world presence. This end, in the sense of *telos*, is the subject of prophecy; for example, Jesus says that the kingdom of heaven is like leaven in the worldwide lump of dough, or a seed sprouting into a tree of global dimension (Matt. 13:31-33). The parousia waits for the church's world witness (Matt. 24:14). But it would be a mistake to view this passively—an inevitable result of a process of which the church is only vaguely aware. The gospel is to spread as an intentional ministry into all of the nations of the earth prior to the end of the age (Matt. 28:19). And it is to this end that the Spirit is given in order to facilitate world witness (Acts 1:8).

This last scripture brings color to the apostolate, suggesting the various frames in which the church is to live and conduct its mission: Jerusalem, the homefront; Judea, the nation; Samaria, the first movement away from the nation; and the "ends of the earth," a full-blown encounter with the nations of the world. Two dimensions of mission are suggested, a geographical reach from home through progressively more remote regions, and an intercultural reach from indigenous culture to similar culture, on to cultures in various ranges of difference. With time, intergenerational extension also comes into view—the renewing of the faith from generation to generation while the world apostolate continues.

Mission in its fullness takes various shapes in many combinations of physical remoteness, cultural variation, and age. Conceptually, it is a moving forward from any frame of reference, including the local, requiring constant refreshment of its vision to initiate new contact with the world of sin and darkness wherever it is encountered. Thus, mission falls squarely into the domain of every Christian, regardless of location or calling.

Thomas Oden notes that the fullness of the church's identity and purpose is equally the domain of all Christians. He clarifies this unity of self-concept by drawing an analogy to holography. A hologram is a three-dimensional photograph constructed with laser light. A unique feature of a hologram is that the entire image is captured at all points on the film; it is everywhere the same. No matter how many pieces it may be broken into, each piece contains the whole image.[29] The root image of the whole church, then, is likewise the same root image of every church body, every local church community, and every single believer. The calling of all to the world apostolate is, for every Christian, all the same.

From the perspective of the world, then, the church is a fountain pouring out its life into dark recesses yet to receive light, beginning from all points where it is established and proceeding at various levels of locality and extra-locality to complete its calling. It is an event in space and time, and to be a part of it is to be a part of a world movement. Corporate and individual identities are formed *in motion*. To stop is to cease to be, in experience, fully Christian.

The church's literal movement in the world takes many forms, as various studies of mass movements, singular conversions, social webs, suffering witnesses, imperialist expansion, and so on suggest. Relative size, the rate of penetration of the world, and other quantitative measures of change are variables that the church is responsible for accepting in some way as measures of faithfulness. It is an odd situation when Christians cannot have an influence or witness in some definable sphere. The church, though, cannot control the world's response. History shows it often can trace the working of the Spirit only in retrospect. The church is, however, responsible for its intentions and motivations—for a purposeful, concrete engagement with the world. From each church community must arise an agenda for the world that provides a shape for Christian discipleship.

Community-based. Accordingly, the world finds the church where it is, right out in front of it in the community—not in this case in the community of believers alone, but in the wider, public community of which the church is a part. Just as it was in the tightly packed cities of the ancient world—and as it is in the cities of any world—the life of the church, whether it likes it or not, is lived in the full view of the watching world. Despite attempts to withdraw from the world, the church finds itself inextricably in it. The church is based in the community.

This is fully in accordance with its nature. The church is not constituted when it is assembled; it is ontological in its members wherever and whenever they are. This is not to devalue being together, but to note that the church is a living body, alive all the time, functioning as a demonstration community and modeling the kingdom of God in all of its relationships and interactions, including those with the larger, public community. The church may judge itself on criteria related to any number of self-concerns. The world judges it on the basis of its performance in community.

The church's self-awareness, then, must be weighted toward the community life in which it exists *all the time*, rather than on its assembly, which occurs only intermittently. Very little of the New Testament describes either worship services or group meetings of any kind. Most of it, particularly the Epistles, depicts issues of daily living or demonstrates the characteristics of community life, and for good reason: the primary means by which the early movement spread was through personal interaction within social networks. Within plain sight of neighbors from whom they literally could not hide, the first Christians authenticated the words of the gospel by lives of love, gaining influence through good works and making conversions by including outsiders in their own webs of association. The community is the primary venue in which the Christian movement advances.

Mediatorial. The church is called not only to live *in* the world but also to live *for* it. This is implied in the meaning of "royal priesthood," a race of servants proclaiming the "mighty acts" of God before the world.

Christ our high priest stands as intercessor for human beings with the Father. As members of his priesthood, Christians are intercessors for the world, representing God to humankind and humankind to God. The meaning of the priesthood is not exhausted by service to the world— there remain the roles of praising God and ministry within the church. In the light of the church's fundamental role in the world, however, the focus of the priesthood is the cutting edge of its witness to the world.

Christ, our high priest, in fulfilling the type of the Levitical priesthood, offered up a sacrifice—himself—for the good of the world. In similar fashion, royal priests offer themselves. This seems to be the thrust of New Testament passages that bring individual Christians into a deeper identification with their new, regenerate nature: "Present yourselves to God as those who have been brought from death to life, and present your members to God as instruments of righteousness" (Rom. 6:13). "Present your bodies as a living sacrifice, holy and acceptable to God, which is your spiritual worship" (Rom. 12:1). The transition from death to life is to be accompanied by a corresponding offer of the entire self to God for service. It is an acknowledgment of entry into the priesthood of believers.

Mediation requires engagement, a sensitive, compassionate, interpersonal connection to the objects of intercession, and a sharing of affect, of one's subjectivity. It means being close enough to feel and give voice to the feelings of others. We learn this through the example of the Holy Spirit's intercession for us; the Spirit expresses our souls in "sighs too deep for words" (Rom. 8:26). It means, fundamentally, to be for others, to plunge into their passionate world—individually as mediators for the lost and collectively as a body locked in loving embrace with the world in order to save it. It means to identify with it, to be colored by its colors, to sense what it senses, to understand it from the inside in order to intervene in its thought-life and direct it to God. It means that the church must incarnate itself in the world, as Christ did in becoming one of us and offering his life to us as a servant.

The church, secure within itself and preoccupied with its own experience (the common ecclesiological view), has traditionally been terrified by its responsibility to comingle with the world, to be truly *in* it, though not *of* it—a responsibility demanded by the missiological perspective. The result has been a failure of analysis. The church has for much of its history avoided taking the time to understand the world around it. Who knows how many gospel opportunities have been bypassed because the church, like Jonah, failed to notice repentant Nineveh and act on its behalf? The world is a complex reality and the church's performance in it is hinged to its willingness to get its hands dirty and put in the hard work of social analysis required to discover it. But only in this way can it both sharpen its effectiveness and guarantee that it does not unconsciously become absorbed by the surrounding non-Christian culture.

All this is embodied in a church that is for the world. The marks of the world's pain must be stains on the face of the church.

Charismatic. The church is clearly a charismatic community, a pneuma-people. Each Christian possesses the full empowerment of the Holy Spirit for the common good and, through the mission of the believing community, for the good of the world. The pneuma-christology of the primitive church, a vital and sometimes excessive charisma, is reflected in the New Testament somewhat ambiguously as a free movement in tension with a restraining leadership structure. This vital force, however, must not be trapped by structure, for it is the engine driving the Christian movement.

Yet appearances of pneuma-christology in history have been mixed blessings. They have resulted in renewal but been at times a destructive force. Because of occasional excesses, it is tempting for the church as an institution to repress manifestations of the Spirit. What is needed is a disciplining pattern, shaping and coordinating the free, spontaneous energy of the Spirit-community and directing its passionate activity toward a productive focal point. Such a pattern is found in the apostolate: a conceptual management structure coordinating and harmonizing the gifts as a fruitful whole in support of the church's world mission. Spiritual gifts takes on a unique, coherent meaning and structure when viewed from the missions perspective. Instead of finding their meaning in ecstatic experience (often the focal point of charismatic renewal movements within the church), spiritual gifts find their meaning in a harmonious blending that builds up the Christ-revealing Christian community and extends it to the non-Christian community. Thus, the "building up [of] the body of Christ . . . to the measure of the full stature of Christ" (Eph. 4:12-13) is both *intensive* relative to the church, and *extensive* relative to the world.

It is interesting to note the five leadership gifts—apostles, prophets, evangelists, pastors, and teachers—given to the church for the purpose of equipping all the members for the coordinated works of service that build up Christ's ministry in the world (Eph. 4:11-12). Two of these gifts, apostleship and evangelism, are clearly meant to extend outside the community of believers. Note that Paul places prophecy between these two obviously world-oriented ministries, suggesting perhaps that a major role for prophecy lies outside the church, bringing into focus the networks through which the gospel must flow. Connecting prophecy with analysis gives it a role in highlighting obstacles to gospel witness—for example, cold or clogged webs, choked movements, and uneven penetration, as well as hidden opportunities, the wet edges of the flowing movement. This is not a traditional understanding, perhaps, but one coming into view from a missions focus, locating prophecy in a strategic center and reflecting the direction of certain New Testament prophetic activity: the calling and sending of the first Gentile mission; the exposing of Elymas and subsequent conversion of Sergius Paulus; the prohibition of speaking in Asia; and the Macedonian call (Acts 13:2-4, 6-12; 16:6-7, 9-10).

There is no reason to believe that these charismatic gifts are anything other than the normal leadership complement necessary to every church. Yet three-fifths of the gifts point beyond the church: apostleship to new territory beyond the social webs within reach; evangelism to known webs of non-Christian relationships; and prophecy to clarify and direct action on the field. All this is included in the nurture and coordination of the entire body of priest-ministers who are disciplined for engagement with the world.

Alive to God. Jesus said that the world will know his people by their love (John 13:35), which certainly the world does when the church proceeds out into it as a mature body. But God is not content to observe this powerful sign as being outside of it. The church is God's holy temple, God's dwelling place in the Spirit (Eph. 2:21-22), the locus of his direct presence in the world. As with the tent in the wilderness, God is "tabernacling" in the church, transforming it into a true sacrament of his presence. Emmanuel continues to be revealed as "with us." Such revelation is not in a place, but is an essence radiating from the Christian movement. It is an "aroma," a sign to the world that Jesus, who is the "way and the truth," is also the efficacious leader of the church, qualified to bring individuals into the life of God and to introduce them personally to the Father. "For we are the aroma of Christ to God among those who are being saved and among those who are perishing" (2 Cor. 2:15).

The presence of God, tangible to Christians and non-Christians alike, appears when the church, taking hold of its responsibility seriously, builds itself to maturity while in vital engagement with the world. It is the measure of the church's faithfulness, a manifestation of God over which the church has no control other than to work out its life with sincerity and honesty. Its absence is a sure sign that something is wrong and must change. God's presence must be looked for, prepared for, and allowed for, then kept alive and carried into the world as a sign of redemption, the "golden serpent" lifted high for salvation. This is the "product," to use the crude terms of the marketplace, that the church brings into the world.

We are also in this vein closer to "God rule," the spontaneous, Spirit-driven movement of God in the world, and to *missio Dei*, the very heart of God in the world. And after all, it *is* God's mission. We must let God direct it as God chooses.

SUMMARY AND CONCLUSION

Arcane discussions of church theory must not overlook Susan, whose psychic image of the church introduced this study. Hers is the concrete, human experience of the church, not a theological construct. Subliminally it leads to a cognitive construct, or map, of the reality of the church. Her image provides a structure of meaning to interpret her experience, direct her behavior, and most important, define her expectations and frame the extent and nature of her involvement with the church. One can sense in her the power of intuitive models.

Similarly, theological models also have power to shape ideas, both in illuminating new dimensions for reflection and, unfortunately, in conceptually closing off areas of inquiry.

But seeing the power of formal and intuitive models only whets the appetite to grasp the church in its ideal form(s), even as we carefully ask the question, Is there an ideal? It seems clear that perspective is an important determinant in understanding a complex entity like the church. In this sense, ecclesiology and missiology provide contrasting, though related, conceptual fields: the former defining the church primarily in terms of itself, and the latter, from a vantage point marginal to it, placing the church as a discrete item in the broader motion of *missio Dei*.

In order to build a model of the church, it is useful to view the early church through the lens of missiology, describing it in terms of its movement in the world. Sociologically, it is clear that Christianity arose as a social movement, growing steadily through networks of social connections—a pattern apparently consistent with contemporary movements. Theologically, we see that the church grew (in Pauline terms) as a dynamic pneuma-community clearly focused on the unveiling of the mystery of Christ among the nations. The Spirit was given to empower world witness. In many ways the institutional growth of the church has served to retard the dynamism of this movement, trapping the "ideal" church, as it were, within the "actual" historical church.

The question then becomes: What kind of image can set a proper balance between charisma and structure, focusing the energy of the church on its role in the world? The answer is *a model of the church in motion*, a missions model: *churches in the mode of mission*. In this model the church is pictured as a mass movement into and filling the world, finding its identity in its motion. It is, in fact, *movemental*, defining itself relative to its spread in the world; *community-based*, aware of its ontological existence within the world it is called to serve; *mediatorial*, profoundly willing to become marginal to itself in order to live *for* the world; *charismatic*, a focused spiritual body empowered to move the church into the world as a witness; and *alive to God*, spontaneously aware of God's presence filling human beings and directing the church.

Together, these elements represent a compelling, forceful defining metaphor through which to organize and direct the church.

This image is a radical contrast to Susan's worship service-oriented Christianity. Does her model adequately explain the phenomenon of the church? Frankly, no, despite the fact that hers is a popular and widely shared understanding of the church. Collective worship in the Christian community is vitally important. The church, however, must keep its focal purpose straight in order to be fully itself in the world in this age.

Another age is coming in which the church will define itself *in the mode of worship*. That will be a day of great rejoicing. But in this age the church is to be found *in the mode of mission*.

The church often unintentionally alienates people for cultural reasons, George G. Hunter argues. The United States, for instance, includes millions of people who wouldn't fit comfortably in middle-class churches. "Our church subculture has erected dozens of barriers that separate many people from the possibility of becoming disciples. Virtually all of these barriers are essentially cultural barriers" having little or nothing to do with the gospel itself. Hunter shows how to combine gospel faithfulness with cultural relevance.

CHAPTER SIX

THE CASE FOR CULTURALLY RELEVANT CONGREGATIONS
George G. Hunter III

HOW SECULAR PEOPLE EXPERIENCE TRADITIONAL CONGREGATIONS

One Saturday evening, Dave said to his girlfriend Jennifer, "Let's go to church tomorrow morning." Jennifer knew that the tip of an iceberg had just surfaced. Dave had tried football and fraternity life, alcohol and astrology, New Age and nude therapy, and several drugs and several marriages in a driven twelve-year quest to make sense of his life, get his act together, "go for the gusto," experience life to the fullest, and find something worth living for. Until he had an injury, vertical rock climbing had given him an adrenaline rush—this was the closest he had come to really living. Every idol had promised more than it delivered. Somewhere he had heard that "If you have tried everything else, you might try God," and that "the place to try God is at a church on a Sunday morning."

Jennifer agreed to go. A search in the Yellow Pages revealed several churches on the highway Dave and Jennifer both took to work each day—to the regional insurance office where he worked as a claims processor, and to the county courthouse where she worked as a court reporter. Each of a half-dozen churches featured a service at 11:00 A.M.

Dave had no church background; he couldn't even recall the name of the church his parents, who divorced when Dave was fourteen, had stayed away from.

Jennifer had been raised a nominal Methodist and had even "graduated" from a confirmation class, so they decided to visit a United Methodist church. It was a strange experience. The music, the liturgy, the language, and the whole ethos reeked of the 1950s, an era when kids entered yo-yo tournaments, when Milton Berle, Ed Sullivan, and Lucille Ball dominated America's black-and-white television sets, when people drove Studebakers, Kaisers, Frazers, DeSotos, and Hudsons, and when the Volkswagen Beetle was *new* in America. Most of the people were older and upper middle class; Jennifer noticed several mink coats, but no Bibles. The whole service was conducted at a pre-Elvis pace, with massive dead spots when nothing was happening except for long organ interludes. Dave got acutely in touch with something his grapevine occasionally reported: Christianity is "boring." The sermon might have rescued this experience, but the thirty-minute lecture, which advocated saving the peregrine falcon and ordaining homosexuals, did not become a medium of God's revelation to Jennifer or Dave.

They visited an Independent Baptist church the next Sunday and had a very different experience. The people were blue-collar. The church's use of English seemed affected, as the testimonies and sermon referred to "see-in," "Gawd," and "Chriiist." The hymns contained countless allusions to biblical characters, verses, and themes that were not in Dave and Jennifer's memory bank. The sermon, which railed against homosexuality, pornography, high taxes, and Democrats (and against the Methodist church down the street), failed to engage any of Dave and Jennifer's needs and violated the code of "tolerance" so important to their generation.

They tried a holiness church, and could not fathom why the issue of women's makeup was such a big deal; Dave was frightened to think that maybe that is what is important to God! They visited an Episcopal church, but could not relate to the Elizabethan language, the European pipe organ music, or the Latin anthem. They visited an Evangelical Covenant church, but didn't feel as Scandinavian as the members. They visited a Lutheran church and didn't feel that German, either.

Dave and Jennifer visited a half-dozen churches within a two-month period. They were all different, yet Jennifer and (especially) Dave experienced them similarly—as congregations of people they could not identify with, with messages not relevant to their needs and questions, and (especially) as places culturally alien to people like themselves. So they tentatively concluded that God was not for people like them.

Jennifer and Dave experienced the most widespread, entrenched, and formidable barrier that prevents the most people from considering the Christian faith today: the *culture barrier*. Both traditional evangelical churches and traditional liberal churches erect and maintain their own versions of this barrier (however unwittingly), and they thereby block people, including many serious seekers, from faith.

THE CONTEMPORARY RISE OF "APOSTOLIC" CONGREGATIONS

However, the "apostolic" congregations emerging across the land are more different from the traditional churches on this point than on any other. In the same way that the apostle Paul was willing to "become all things to all people" that he "might by all means save some," so we are observing the emergence of entire congregations that are willing to be culturally flexible in order to reach people. These churches are dramatizing a truth that mission scholars and strategists have known for decades: to reach non-Christian populations, it is just as necessary for the church to become culturally indigenous to its "mission field" in Europe or North America as it is anywhere in Asia, Africa, Latin America, or Oceania. When a church employs the language, music, style, architecture, and art forms of the target population, Christianity then has a chance to become contagious within its ranks. But when the church's cultural forms are alien to the host population, it is hard for most people to perceive that Christianity's God is for people like them.

OTHER BARRIERS TO FAITH

The "culture barrier" is not, of course, the only barrier that keeps people from faith. Interviews with secular people reveal other barriers. For example, there is the credibility issue. The church historically has been wrong so many times on issues of science and human freedom that secular people question its intellectual credibility. They also question the credibility of professing Christians. Some secular people think we don't really believe it. Some think we believe it, but we don't live it. Still others think we live it and believe it, but it really doesn't make much difference.

Some secular people are turned off by the church's image. They think the church represents only an inherited folk wisdom on the level of, say,

The Farmer's Almanac. Or they think of the church as being irrelevant, okay for little children and "little old ladies of both sexes," but, they say, "it doesn't scratch where we itch." Or they think of church as "boring," offering dusty old hymns, liturgies that drag, and sermons that offer a plain vanilla, rule-bound, adventureless "Christian life."

Furthermore, some barriers are within the spirit of the secular seeker. Some love their sins more than they love God. Some want their own agenda more than God's agenda. The souls of many people are affixed for now to some idol; their hearts are hardened and not open to the gospel's appeal.

The Culture Barrier

But the largest and most widespread barrier that keeps people from faith is the culture barrier. In my research among secular people in the Western world, I often ask, "What keeps people like you from considering the Christian faith?" At least three out of four unchurched people mention this barrier, among others. In my interviews with Christian converts out of secularity, I often ask, "What almost kept you from becoming involved with the Christian faith?" Over half of our converts mention this barrier. People phrase the barrier in many ways, but we can state its essence in one sentence: they resist becoming Christians because they "don't want to become like church people." They believe that to become a Christian you have to become like church people—that it is a prerequisite! The thought of becoming like church people strikes them as "bad news." Nothing within them wants to meet this perceived requirement.

Why don't they want to be like church people? The answer is found in how they perceive church people. When I ask secular people, "What is it about church people that turns you off?" their responses are revealing. They do *not* talk about Christians who transparently love God and their neighbors, who serve the community and live for others. They never refer to Christians who have discovered the Way to live, or to the kind of persons they would deeply like to be.

What kind of church people do non-Christians refer to? Their main problem with these people is *cultural.* For instance, they are alienated when they overhear church people using an "alien language" or "pious jargon." The jargon problem cuts several ways. It has the same alienating effect if the jargon is the technical jargon of desk theologians, the revival jargon of the late nineteenth century, or the "politically correct" jargon of the late twentieth century. Non-Christians also notice that church people have antiquated, or even foreign, tastes in music, art, and

architecture, that they love their traditions more than they love the surrounding community, and that they dress and act in "abnormal" ways.

So non-Christians typically experience the church as a distinct subculture with its own values, customs, norms, habits, language, music,
aesthetics, and so on. They think they have to dress, talk, and act
"that way" and learn to enjoy, for example, eighteenth-century
German pipe organ music before they can become Christians! They
suspect that the church's agenda is to change other people *culturally*.

Let me quote several such people: "Christians live in their own little
world, in their private pious cliques, with their buzzwords and their pre-
scribed behaviors." "What do church people *mean* when they sing about
being 'washed in the blood,' or 'dwelling in Beulah Land'? What are they
doing when they are 'raising their Ebenezer'?" "What does it look like
when 'angels prostrate fall'?" "Why are Christians always artificially
polite?"

One new Christian reports, "I loathed the possibility of becoming like
nice sociable church people going through the motions. The thought
made me ill." The problem these people experience, and avoid, is that
churches seem to require people to "become like us" before they are
regarded and included as "real" Christians. We have thus rediscovered
Donald McGavran's observation that the barriers that keep most people
from faith and discipleship are more cultural and sociological than theological or religious.

The Culture Barrier in Church History

Let us put this problem in some perspective. The church has seemed
to require people to "become like us" culturally for a very long time. We
find this pattern as early as Acts 15. The early church in Jerusalem was
requiring their Gentile converts to become circumcised, give up pork,
etc., and to become culturally Jewish as a requirement for becoming baptized followers of Jesus the Messiah.[1] Meanwhile, up in Antioch,
Gentiles were becoming disciples in great numbers and were *not* submit-
ting to circumcision and giving up pork. This precipitated a crisis at the
Jerusalem "headquarters" of the young Christian movement and occasioned the meeting of the Jerusalem Council reported in Acts 15. After
the parties of James, Paul, and Simon Peter deliberated the issue, the
Council determined that Gentiles did *not* have to become culturally
Jewish in order to follow Christ and be part of his movement.

The Jerusalem Council's decision was momentous. Without that decision, Christianity might have remained primarily a sect of "fulfilled
Jews" within Judaism. The decision extended the principle of

Incarnation: just as Jesus adapted to Galilean peasant culture, so the church, his Body, could now become "indigenous" to all the cultures of the earth.[2] Now that Gentiles did not have to become Jews to be Christians, the faith was unleashed to spread and adapt beyond itself. Within three centuries it spread to most of the major cultures in the Roman Empire, and later became the world's most universal faith.

The Jerusalem Council settled a very significant matter. Yet the Christian church has still struggled with the problem, in many versions, ever since. In the years following the Jerusalem Council, the party of James (the "Judaizers") apparently reverted back to Plan A and decided that Jewish inculturation was a necessary part of Christian discipleship after all. The Judaizers even grew for a while, and they fanned out across the Mediterranean world, stirring up people in several churches Paul had planted and prompting several letters from Paul, notably his Letter to the Galatians.

In one way, at least, the party of Paul failed to fully implement the Jerusalem Council's decision. The Christian movement became predominantly Gentile, and throughout most of our history Jewish people have not become Christians—in part because they felt required to become culturally Gentile as a prerequisite to becoming Christian! Only in the last quarter-century has it occurred to anyone that there could be a *Jewish* Christian movement, employing the cultural forms of Jews to reach and nurture Jews. Consequently, through Jews for Jesus and the messianic synagogue movement, an unprecedented number of Jews have become fulfilled Jews.

As the Christian faith spread across much of the earth, it was often experienced as requiring some equivalent to circumcision. Indeed, the peoples of Asia, Africa, Latin America, and Oceania were often *expected* to become Westernized as a part of, and often as a prerequisite to, being Christianized. For example, the Roman Catholic Church required that the Mass be held in Latin almost everywhere until Vatican II. Protestant mission has usually been friendlier to vernacular languages, but has often assumed that people could not become "real" Christians without becoming "civilized" first—by a very Western model!

We now know, however, that Western nations have no monopoly on cultural imperialism. For instance, South Korean churches are now sending out thousands of missionaries to other lands and peoples. Seoul Theological Seminary has established a School of World Mission to better prepare missionaries, because they discovered that Korean missionaries were planting culturally Korean churches from Thailand to Zambia!

The indigenizing principle was established in the Council at Jerusalem, but its implementation does not come automatically for any of us. The culture in which we are raised seems natural to us, so we naturally extend "our kind" of Christianity everywhere unless we know how important it is to adapt to other cultures.

The Culture Barrier Today

The culture barrier between the churches and the unchurched people of Europe is the largest single cause of European Christianity's decline in this century. Martin Robinson's book *A World Apart*[3] reports that Great Britain's thousands of Protestant chapels, which once fit British culture and engaged great numbers of people, have not changed as British culture has changed. The result:

> Visitors to such chapels can see all too easily the yawning chasm between what takes place in the culture of chapel life and the culture of those who live in the neighbourhood. It is as if the chapel folk are silently saying to the community: "To become a Christian, you not only have to believe that Jesus Christ was the Son of God, that he died on a cross and was raised from the dead on the third day; you also have to find a way of living in a culture that no longer exists in everyday life."[4]

Robinson also observes that the church's "cultural blindness" prevents it from even perceiving "the distinction between the gospel and the cultural forms in which we express it," and that fact "is responsible for a great deal of the failure of the church to make a significant impact on the society of which we are a part."[5]

The culture barrier is an even bigger problem for mainline American Christianity. We bought almost totally into the early-twentieth-century myth of the American melting pot. That myth taught that people come from other nations and enter a "melting pot" experience in which everyone comes out as assimilated mainline Americans. But the myth really assumed a more imperialistic process—that people who came from Earth's nations would become like those of us whose ancestors came from Great Britain! So we have added to the usual expectations that the people who join our churches will become "like us." But with the rise of what Michael Novak called "the unmeltable ethnics," we observe people of many cultures and subcultures whose culture seems as natural to them as ours does to us, who like their art, music, style, and language (or dialect) about as much as we like ours, and who are not motivated to "become circumcised" and become like us.

My suggestion that cultural imperialism afflicts the churches of America may, of course, be met with denial, because this is virtually no one's conscious intent. Are America's church people the North American "Judaizers"? Do we really expect people to become like us? Do outsiders really perceive us as requiring that?

Let's ask our own youth, who, since the 1950s, have developed their own subculture, with its own distinct and changing norms for clothing and hair styles, its own jargon, and its own dance and music. In this same forty-year period, youth ministry has declined as a priority within most mainline denominations, and the numbers of youth in our churches today are far less than half of what they were. Bishop Richard Wilke suggests a causal connection in these questions:

> When did we get turned off, we church people, to kids? When did we begin to ignore them, isolate them, even despise them? Once in the late '40s and '50s, we had deputation teams, college age Christians, pouring each summer into the churches to witness, lead Vacation Bible Schools, develop youth programs.
>
> Once in the '50s, every preacher worth his or her salt worked in a youth camp, offering life to kids who would give their hearts to Jesus, challenging young Christians to become missionaries, deaconesses, nurses, doctors, preachers and Christian educators in full-time Christian service.
>
> Lay people taught kids in Sunday school, took them on hotdog fries and scouting weekends, helped them go to college. An official officer of the Women's Society for Christian Service wrote them personal letters when they were in the service or away at school.
>
> When did we turn them off—these kids of our towns and cities? Was it in 1965 when they grew their hair long? Was it in '66 when they strummed guitars? Was it in '67 when they marched for integration? Was it in '69 when they protested Vietnam? Was it in '70 when they smoked marijuana and began to sleep together in a single sleeping bag? Was it their music—first rock and roll, then rock, then hard rock, metal rock, acid rock?
>
> When did we cut back our scouting, disassemble our church camps, destroy our national leadership for youth teams, forget to offer them Christ and let our local youth programs dwindle? . . . When did we declare kids off limits for the gospel?[6]

Do we Christians seem to require people to become like us? Let's ask the American peoples of non-Anglo races and cultures. For years we heard that the most segregated hour of the week was 11:00 to 12:00 on Sunday morning. We repented and made the achievement of integrated congregations the *de facto* priority in my denomination and many others. We were unable to achieve it. Why? The way the objective was often phrased gives a clue: we wanted African Americans and others to "join *our* churches." Ethnic minority people *visited* "our churches" in those years, but they seldom came back and almost never joined. Why? We seemed to be requiring them to become culturally Anglo, "like us." They resisted their "ethnocide"—the elimination of their culture by absorption into ours.

If you still harbor doubts about this reading of our history, I invite contrary evidence. When did any Anglo congregations say to African American visitors, "We will change to an African American style of music"? When did any Anglo congregations say to Hispanic visitors, "We will conduct the worship service in Spanish"? When did the denominations say to ordination candidates from Korea or the Caribbean, "We will ordain you on the basis of your denomination's ordination standards in the land you came from"? Peter Wagner's tough phrase is all too accurate: mainline American Christianity has followed, usually unconsciously, a policy of "assimilationist racism."[7]

Or let's ask ourselves some questions like the following: How open are we to people who drink or smoke? How open are we to people with addictions? How open are we to young men who ride motorcycles, who wear jeans, long hair, earrings, and leather jackets with the words "Life Sucks"? How open are we, really, to illiterate people, homeless people, and people with AIDS? How open are we to people with dirt under their fingernails or unshined shoes, or people with bad breath or body odor who might belch or split an infinitive in the church building?

Such questions are important because the U.S.A. has tens of millions of people who have some rough edges, who lack middle-class social graces, who can't read music and wouldn't know how to second a motion, who aren't quite "refined," and who lack many of the "civilized" standards of church people. Our church subculture has erected dozens of barriers that separate many people from the possibility of becoming disciples. Virtually all of these barriers are essentially cultural barriers, and have little or nothing to do with "the faith that was once for all entrusted to the saints."

REMOVING THE CULTURE BARRIER

There is a solution to the culture barrier. The church can choose to cooperate with the Acts 15 decision and develop what missiologists call "culturally indigenous churches" in the American mission field, just as we do in other fields. We can start Sunday school classes, house groups, worship services, and new congregations that fit the cultures of the various unchurched populations in North America. We can choose to use language and music they understand and can relate to. We can encourage clothing and styles they are comfortable with. We can minister to their felt needs. The U.S.A. is a vast secular mission field with many cultures and subcultures. Are we imaginative enough and compassionate enough to sponsor and unleash many forms of indigenous Christianity in this land?

One powerful theological affirmation can point the way: To reach an undiscipled population, our outreach, ministry, and worship must be indigenous to their culture, because each people's culture is the natural medium of God's revelation to them.

This primary guideline contains one indispensable qualifier. In effective mission, Christians adopt and employ the outer forms of the target culture, its language, music, styles, and so forth. However, Christians in mission must understand, but must not adopt, the inner "worldview" of the culture, because much of that changes profoundly in Christian conversion. A new relationship to God, a transformed self, and life in the messianic community provide new lenses through which one sees life and the world and a new set of core beliefs and values that drive one's life.[8]

Several additional theological insights can ground and guide a more indigenous strategy:

1. Just as Jesus came and adapted to a particular culture, so his church is called to extend his Incarnation into every culture on earth—so that every people will perceive that the triune God of Christian faith is for people like them.
2. A saving revelation of God is possible in any culture. Every culture has enough to work with and the Holy Spirit makes up the difference, so the meaning of the Christian gospel can be communicated in any culture. (If you doubt this claim, please recall that God's original revelation did not come to Anglo people in the U.S.A. What we have in Anglo-American Christianity is a cultural adaptation of original biblical Christianity; if we got the meaning, then presumably any other society can get it, as well.)
3. We have received the gospel treasure in "earthen vessels," but we often mistake the vessel for the treasure—then we confuse faithfulness to the gospel with perpetuating and extending the cultural forms in which we received it! Instead, we are called to unwrap the gospel's meaning from the cultural forms in which we received it and rewrap it in the cultural forms of the target population.
4. We believe that just as Jesus came not to destroy Jewish law, tradition, and culture but to fulfill them, so he came not to destroy but to fulfill all of the earth's cultures.
5. This principle calls the indigenous Christians in each society to function in their society as "salt" by preserving everything in their

culture that is possible within God's will, and as "light" by changing what is necessary.

6. This strategy would align the Christian movement with the basic
   apostolic principles modeled by Paul, who communicated everywhere the one gospel of "Jesus Christ and him crucified," but communicated this gospel by being "all things to all people, that I might
   by all means save some."

Reflecting this kind of apostolic perspective, the Lausanne movement's
Willowbank Report declares that "No Christian witness can hope to
communicate the gospel if he or she ignores the cultural factor."[9] A faithful strategy calls "us" to adapt to "their" culture and not require them
to "become circumcised" and adopt our culture. Fortunately, we do not
need to consider this principle merely as an abstraction.

Martin Luther pioneered the principle in earliest Protestant
Christianity by abandoning the Latin Bible and mass. Luther translated
the Scriptures into the vernacular German language of the people he
served, and Lutheran churches worshiped in German and developed a
German hymnody around the music the people already knew and loved.

The Methodist heritage extended the indigenizing principle. John and
Charles Wesley led their apostolic movement by adapting to eighteenth-
century British culture. They "agreed to become more vile" and preached
in the fields and town squares, on the unchurched people's turf. They
wrote Christian poetry to be sung to the tunes the people knew and loved
to sing in the public houses. They built chapels in which common people
would feel comfortable. They coached Methodists to speak in "the most
obvious, easy, common words wherein our meaning can be conveyed"
and to "never . . . deviate from the most usual way of speaking."[10] A century later, General William Booth asked, "Why should the Devil have all
the good tunes?" and introduced urban streets to Christian band music
in the popular genre of nineteenth-century Britain.

OPTIONS FOR CHURCH LEADERS

Over time, the tastes and styles of cultures change. Words, music, and
attire that once fit the culture are now experienced as old-fashioned or
even alien. Most unchurched people today are no longer culturally
shaped to understand the hymns of Martin Luther or Charles Wesley or
Fanny Crosby or traditional Salvation Army band music.

What are the church's options as it reflects upon its mission in a
changed culture? Church leaders, typically, have responded in one of
three ways:

1. Often, leaders have unnecessarily bonded the gospel treasure to the cultural forms that were employed in the past when the movement was most successful. They assume that the mission must perpetuate those forms. If the target population does not respond to our cultural forms, they are rejecting the gospel.

2. Often, some elitists (usually "high church" musicians) impose foreign forms upon the church to "raise" the cultural aesthetics of Christians and non-Christians. The elitists really do believe that everyone would be "better" if they were force-fed eighteenth-century pipe organ music! When people, both Christians and non-Christians, are exposed to that type of cultural imperialism, they usually vote with their feet—in other words, by absentee ballot!

3. The most faithful and effective option, I suggest, is to recover the vision and imagination of our founding geniuses—to "exegete" the culture God entrusts to us, as they did theirs, and to indigenize the faith's language, music, and style once again. We do not honor our founders by blindly perpetuating in a changing world what they once did, or by hijacking their tradition and imposing something culturally alien. We honor them by doing for our time and culture what they did for theirs.

Fortunately, the Christian movement in our time gives us a wealth of cases and examples. For example, the pre-Christian shamanist religion of Korea had a tradition of prayer mountains. Korean Christians discovered that this institution could be retained and filled with Christian content, permitting their people to experience retreats at Christian prayer mountains.

E. Stanley Jones observed that Hinduism in India featured a kind of retreat called an "ashram." Jones developed Christian ashrams that were similar in outward form to Hindu ashrams, but at the meaning level were planned experiences in Christian community. In contrast to Hindu customs, no one attending a Christian ashram was addressed by any title except "Brother" or "Sister." Contrary to Hindu caste patterns, everyone did manual labor, such as sweeping floors or cleaning toilets. A Christian ashram began with a "service of the open heart" and closed with a "service of the overflowing heart," and filled the middle with days of Christian teaching and nights of silence.

The contrasting philosophies and styles of the two Methodist conferences in Mexico provide an interesting case study. The conference to the south employs more Western music, themes, liturgies, and theologies, is more dominated by the clergy, and its membership strength is stagnant. The conference to the north is experiencing contagious growth, largely through "lay" ministry and more indigenous *Mexican* worship with guitar, folk hymns, hand clapping, and unrestrained celebration.

Saddleback Valley Community Church serves laid-back Orange County, California. The church has no organ ("and never will"), but does have a band. They have no choir robes, because they have no choirs! But they feature many singing ensembles. They generally use no music written before 1980. The pastor usually preaches in shirtsleeves, often with no necktie. They fill three Sunday morning services, and for years met in a high school gymnasium.

One well-known story from Bishop Gerald Kennedy's legacy illustrates the kind of sensitivity, empathy, and flexibility that a culturally appropriate strategy requires. Years ago, Wisconsin Methodist churches targeted a given Sunday to invite unchurched people to attend church. A Methodist woman invited an unchurched dairy farmer's wife and her family to "be our guests at church this Sunday." The wife replied, "We would love to; I will wear my best apron." The Methodist woman knew, of course, that women do not wear aprons to church, but she prevented a social crisis for the farmer's wife by calling every woman in the church and announcing, "This is apron Sunday. Wear your best apron to church." When the farmer's wife later pieced together what had been done for her, she was moved by such caring and was baptized into the faith.

More recently, in a United Methodist church in Moore, Oklahoma (part of metropolitan Oklahoma City), a young man in his late twenties named Bill experienced a deeper gift of faith and began serving as a counselor in the youth ministry. He launched efforts to revitalize the Men's Fellowship, and he began reaching out to undiscipled young men. He has had two experiences that illustrate, negatively and positively, Christianity's options on the culture challenge.

First, Bill observed that most of Moore, Oklahoma's young men liked to gather together in the fall to watch Monday night football on television, and that the only places providing that option were bars. He wondered if the Men's Fellowship could bring a large-screen television into the church's fellowship hall on Monday nights and host unchurched men. He asked an acquaintance with long hair, an earring, and a motorcycle if guys would be interested in watching Monday night football at the United Methodist church. The fellow replied, "I would like to, and I could bring other guys." When Bill proposed this Monday evening agenda to the Men's Fellowship president, he heard this reply: "Sure, we could meet on Monday nights, but we like dominos more than football; invite them to come and play *our* game."

Even with this revised agenda, Bill's friend visited the Men's Fellowship. His friend liked the men, most of whom were older, and was attracted by what he understood of Christianity's message. But he felt uncomfortable, saying to Bill, "Look, with my long hair and earring, I'm out of place here. Christianity is not for people like me. After tonight, I'm out of here." Bill found himself saying, "If I get my ear pierced, will you come back?" His friend was moved and said, "If you care enough about me to do that, sure, I will come back, and I will bring my friends!"

Some new congregations—and even movements—are now being started that target people who aren't like most church people culturally. Recent years saw the launch in the Los Angeles area of "Sanctuary," a network of churches now found in many West Coast cities. These churches reach out to rebellious, drug abusing, "baby buster" teenagers and young adults—some of them suicidal, most of them loving heavy metal music. Sanctuary's services have featured Christian heavy metal bands. Their ministries included a toll-free phone line, "Boot Camp" Bible studies for new believers, and especially "RAD Studies" (RAD standing for Radical Active Discipleship). By communicating to baby busters through their culture, Sanctuary churches have reached, in each city where they have a ministry, hundreds of people whom no other churches would be reaching.[11]

A growing number of pioneering Christians and churches are demonstrating the Christian movement's way forward in our secular mission field by *extending* the decision of the Jerusalem Council. They have discovered that we do not usually reach people by requiring them to become like us culturally, though a few will become "circumcised" church people in order to become Christians. We will reach many more people when some of us are willing to "become circumcised" and adopt enough of their culture to identify with them and communicate through their culture's forms, creating whatever new units and ministries are necessary and thereby helping them discover the gospel as good news for people like them.

A CHALLENGE TO THE CHURCH FROM HOLLYWOOD

Even Hollywood seems to be challenging the church to forsake its cultural captivity, to identify with unchurched people and their struggles and their communities, and to offer culturally indigenous worship that will actually *attract* unchurched secular people.

Perhaps you saw the movie *Sister Act*, starring Whoopi Goldberg and Maggie Smith. As the movie opens, Whoopi Goldberg is a nightclub performer in Las Vegas who witnesses a murder. The police hide her in a Roman Catholic convent where she is to live, for the time being, as a nun. She and the other nuns attend the local parish church adjacent to the convent. After the nuns' choir sings badly before an almost empty church, the priest announces, "We are a *small* congregation this morning. Too many mornings. Something has gone terribly wrong. Where is faith? Where is celebration? Where is everyone?"

Whoopi Goldberg accepts the challenge to lead the choir and reform the music. The choir of nuns sings the same hymn the next week, "Hail, Holy Queen," but the harmony, the style, the energy, and the spontaneous life in their music are so different that people in the street hear the music and are attracted into the church. Though Maggie Smith, the convent's Mother Superior, resists the new style, the priest and Whoopi Goldberg gain the freedom for the nuns not only to continue the new music, but also to leave the convent daily in conversation and service with the people of a rather dangerous community outside. They develop a day care center and a food kitchen for homeless people, and they converse, laugh, and pray with the people in the community. The word spreads and the church grows. In the movie's final scene, the Pope comes to the church that is now full to observe this wonder.

The movie's most important moment occurs after the first service in which Whoopi Goldberg leads the choir. The exchange between Whoopi, Maggie, and the priest in the choir room after the service shows Maggie Smith beginning to get in touch with the discovery that could transform thousands of congregations.

Maggie Smith: "Boogie-woogie on the piano? What were you thinking?"

Whoopi Goldberg: "I was thinking more like Vegas—you know, get some butts in the seats."

Maggie Smith: "And what next? Popcorn? Curtain calls? This is not a theater or a casino!"

Whoopi Goldberg: "Yeah, but that's the problem, see. People *like* going to theaters, and they like going to casinos. But they *don't* like coming to church. Why? Because it's a *drag*. But we could change all that, see. We could pack this joint."

Maggie Smith: "Through blasphemy? You have corrupted the entire choir!"

The priest overhears the conversation as Maggie Smith announces that Whoopi can lead the choir no longer. He enters the choir room and engages in a redemptive bluff worthy of any Las Vegas poker dealer, saying to Maggie Smith: "Reverend Mother, I just wanted to congratulate you. I haven't enjoyed Mass this much in years. What a marvelous program—innovative, inspiring. You are to be commended. I can't wait until next Sunday when the choir performs again. Did you see the people walk right in from the street? That music, that heavenly music! Reverend Mother, it called to them."

She replies: "It . . . it did?"

SHARING GOOD NEWS

Look at theology through the lens of mission, Andrew Kirk says, and you will see that the church's whole theological enterprise needs rethinking today. Genuine theology is necessarily personal and present-oriented because of the personal nature of God. Sound theology therefore requires commitment, and in fact all theology should acknowledge the particular commitments from which it begins. Concerned with an authentic missionary encounter with today's global culture, including Western postmodernity, and with theology's role in that task, Kirk writes: "It is urgent that theology recover a self-conscious mission to contemporary culture to help arrest its further slide into the abyss of nihilism."

CHAPTER SEVEN

THE MISSION OF THEOLOGY AND THEOLOGY AS MISSION

J. Andrew Kirk

INTRODUCTION

The main headings of this essay were inspired by a visit to the stadium on the top of the San Juif hill in Barcelona, before it was completed for the 1992 Olympic Games. The work of transforming an old sports arena into one fit for a major sporting and telecommunications event had only recently begun. The whole interior of the old building was being torn out. Only the external shell would be left.

My thesis is that, in a sense, the same has to happen with the enterprise of theology and theological education in the new millennium. On the one hand, theology in the Western world has been constructed on intellectual assumptions that are no longer believable; on the other hand, it is palpably inadequate to the task that now faces the Christian community worldwide. Like the stadium, the old internal structures must be cleared away before a more serviceable model can operate. It is even questionable whether the external structure itself should survive.

CLEARING THE GROUND

The set of perspectives that I develop in this study constitutes an ambitious and risky undertaking. I am investigating an operation on which hangs in large part the healthy life of the whole Christian community, for if we do not get the theological task right, every other task is likely to be out of kilter. It is a topic that lies at the heart of the whole educational and training enterprise of the Christian church—one which, among other considerations, absorbs an immense amount of human and financial resources.

Assuming that the church can only exist as truly itself when dedicated to the mission of God, a burning question ensues: How should one reinvent[1] theology and theological education so that they flow naturally from an integral perspective on God's constant will and activity in the world? I do not myself stand outside this concern, having been intimately involved, both in Latin America and Britain, for more than thirty years in many different kinds of theological education. For many reasons, I believe the time has decidedly come for a "sea-change" or, in the current jargon, a "paradigm shift" in the way we view the whole theological enterprise.

The title of the essay points to an overwhelmingly influential heritage that has shaped theology universally: the conjunction of the Latin *(missio)* and Greek *(theos* and *logos)* languages and cultures. Now, however, the influence of the Roman and Hellenistic worlds on the subsequent development of Christian thought and practice is being challenged in many ways by Christians from the "South"[2] eager to see the gospel closely related to their history and traditions.

Some may question the association of mission with theology. They may argue that theology has various tasks, even an overall purpose, but to talk about it having a *mission* is dubious. Mission, it will be said, connotes undisguised commitment to a particular cause, while theology, traditionally understood as an academic discipline alongside its peers in other university faculties,[3] is surely a detached, careful, and tentative process of reflection.[4] I intend in this study to show that this standard response is based on inadequate assumptions. I will then go on to show that theology and mission are inextricably linked both in theory and practice.

Theology is a vast subject. It is still a major area of human endeavor, in spite of the battering that it has received from secular culture. For example, the number of books published each year in this field is still very substantial, and the number of theological institutions in existence across the globe is immense.

Theology used to be called the "Queen of Sciences." It gave the adequate reason for the whole scientific enterprise. Though now its status in academia has been demoted and in many institutions of higher education it has been transmuted into religious studies, it is not ignored. Over the last two hundred years its rationale and methods have changed very substantially; nevertheless, the distinct methods, motives, and content of its two-thousand-year history should be recalled at this time of reevaluation.

I do not want to limit the understanding of what constitutes theology. There are a number of different species; all, in their separate ways, have a right to be called theology. None of them can make a substantiated *a priori* claim to take precedence or to be wholly normative for the rest. The following headings give a rough indication of the taxonomy, or classification, of the main kinds.

Academic Study

This is the model we first naturally think of, if we live in the Western world with its strong tradition of university departments, faculties, and schools of theology. It is epitomized by the methods required to obtain a doctoral degree, by the various professional associations of scholars that in some sense regulate, by generally accepted convention, what are the acceptable methods of investigation in each discipline, and by the professional journals of theology's various disciplines. Its main symbol is probably the library.

Church-Related Theology

This type might also be called "confessional theology." We have in mind the work that goes into papal encyclicals, reports of the World Council of Churches (particularly those of the Faith and Order Commission like *Baptism, Eucharist, and Ministry* or *Confessing the Apostolic Faith Today*),[5] bilateral and multilateral statements coming from commissions set up by world communions of churches (for example, the report that came from the Anglican Consultative Council and the World Alliance of Reformed Churches, *God's Reign and Our Unity,* 1983), and substantial affirmations of faith that emerge from world gatherings of Christians like the *Lausanne Covenant* (1974). Its symbols today are probably the conference center and the computer: the first is used to provide accommodation in the right environment for carefully selected commissions, and the second is used to facilitate the process of working through endless draft statements to a final agreed-upon document.

Alternative Theology

These are ways of reflecting on the meaning of the Christian faith that are either outside or critical of mainstream church theology. Examples include the oral theology of the African Independent churches, the environmental spirituality of Matthew Fox, the ecclesiological thinking of liberation theology, the advocacy of "pluralism" as the only authentic approach to interreligious dialogue, and the promotion of the so-called "prosperity gospel," which emphasizes the twin blessings of health and wealth to all who claim them in faith. Though these examples differ vastly in conception and content, they are often characterized by taking one element of the Christian tradition and pushing it to an extreme.

Grassroots Theology

The best-known example of this way of doing theology would be the biblical/hermeneutical reflection going on in the base ecclesial communities.[6] However, it also takes place wherever and whenever ordinary Christians examine the relevance of their faith to the world around them, particularly in the exploration of ethical issues related to the various professions and to political and economic policies.[7] Some of the most exciting theological discoveries today are happening as people struggle to put the story of the gospel together with their story. For a number of years in London, I had the privilege of accompanying many people from various parts of the world in this kind of theological pilgrimage.[8]

Local Theology

This kind of process has been mapped out most thoroughly by Robert Schreiter.[9] It is characterized particularly by prior concern with the cultural context, rather than with the received faith, as data for the theological task. Its emphasis is on the contextualization, indigenization, and inculturation of the Christian faith. Schreiter's book has a long section on the relation of the gospel to "popular religion" in its many manifestations. The significance of this lies in the fact that religion in this form, whatever the "purists" might desire, is the most widely practiced variety throughout the world. It must therefore be taken into account in any theological reflection on the beliefs and customs of the people.

There is not always a rigorous separation between these species. We recognize a certain degree of overlap. Nevertheless, one can detect substantially different emphases, according to the *aims* set out, the *methods* used, the *assumptions* made, the *degrees of personal commitment* expected, and the *situations* in which they are done. These different factors have not always been given their due weight in discussions about the nature and task of theology.

UNDERSTANDING THE NATURE AND TASK OF THEOLOGY

There are probably almost as many definitions of the essence and intention of theology as there are people engaged in doing it.[10] Theology may be understood as scientific *(wissenschaftlich)* investigation into the texts and historical engagement of the Christian community over the centuries. The ambition of this method is to pursue detached, critical research according to the best criteria of professional scholarship.[11] Theology may be understood as the process which provides systematic training for church-related accredited ministries, in which the traditional requirements of the different churches shape the curriculum. Charles Wood defines theology as "critical inquiry into the validity of Christian witness,"[12] in which the contemporary practice of Christian communities is an essential element in theological reflection. Orlando Costas believed that theology has the task of producing a faithful, obedient missionary community that always strives to understand its vocation more adequately. Theology, he said, is "the reflective activity of the Christian Church that tries to understand the mystery of faith, describe its implications for life, and make visible its mission in the world."[13]

Though I would not necessarily dissent from these explanations, my own understanding of theology takes a different focus. It can be outlined as follows. Theology is a reflective, intellectual process that is carried out by a community of faith whose concern is with God and his relationship to the entire universe, and that gives a privileged place to certain sources of knowledge, namely the Bible, the ecumenical creeds, and other historical confessions. It has two fundamental tasks: to make sense of the whole of life by reference to God, and to be an agent of the transformation of the whole of life, so that it may reflect God's intentions.[14]

Later in this study I will elaborate on these two main tasks (or overall mission) of theology. First, however, for reasons that have to do with its potential for standing in the way of a fresh calling for theology, we must look critically at the academic model of theology.

The academic model has had a dominating, almost exclusive, influence for about two hundred years. During this time it has assumed the right to be the arbiter of good and bad theology, valuing more highly its own methods of rigorous criticism over all other types of theological work. Moreover, academic theology *per se* might well reject both of the tasks outlined above as being necessary definitions of theology's aims and objectives.

Theology done within the confines of the academy has appeared to operate according to different criteria from those presupposed in the definition I have suggested above. It has tended to concentrate on an analytical, interpretive, and reconstructive process concerned mainly with the linguistic forms of original texts, their genre, their original historical context, and the mode of their transmission through various stages of mutation till they came to rest in their final historical setting. Basic to this mode of investigation are these questions: What did the text mean? In what context was it written? What parallels with other texts can be suggested? What effect did it have? These are all questions about the past.

The fruit of academic study suggests that the scholarly ideal is to leave the present behind. Through imagination and the creative use of data, theologians should immerse themselves in past realities. It is not surprising, then, that theology has relied so heavily on the renowned "historical-critical" method. Even where new approaches have arisen that concentrate on the finished text or on transpositional, hermeneutical considerations, the method remains pervasive.

Now, I believe that a good deal (though by no means all) of this work is a basic *resource* for theology, *but it is not theology itself*. Nor is what often happens as a next stage, namely the comparative process of bringing the ideas and beliefs of others (secondary sources) into parallel lines, as it were, in order to discuss different interpretive theories.[15]

Theology, to be theology, must have a personal dimension oriented to the present—to personal, openly declared preferences involving engagement and commitment (including a solid identification with the Christian community). One overriding reason for this, often spelled out but not yet sufficiently heeded, is that the major *object* of the reflective task—God, or the Word of God, in relation to the universe—is also the *subject* who calls, makes demands, and sets tasks. In the course of study it is therefore impossible to remain detached from the evident fact that the text presents us with a living God who calls us to be part of his righteous rule *on God's terms*.

The interpreter cannot remain detached from the message of the text, in a kind of cocoon of suspended judgment. The attempt to remain free from any interaction with the text as communication is already a judgment about one's method and one's relation to the particular configuration of words. For this reason I have never understood how it is possible to study the text of the Bible as if it were any piece of literature from the ancient Near East. On the grounds of both its content (the prophetic demand for repentance, conversion, and change) and the impact of its message (turning around the lives of individuals, communities, and whole cultures), it manifestly is not.[16]

Perhaps the unquestioned object-subject distinction is what distinguishes religious studies as a phenomenological pursuit from theology proper. The study of religion as a discipline has its own rationale and method. However, even here both the nature of religious communities and what they claim about their religious beliefs make this far from being a purely dispassionate study undertaken by an isolated thinking subject. There is also the relevant question of the motivation that leads the individual to undertake study in this particular field. To pretend that rigorous research can take place in any subject (even the exact sciences) independently of assumed human preferences and ideals is now an old-fashioned and quite illusory myth.[17] Only an ingenuous dreamer could imagine that the pursuit of intellectual knowledge as a disinterested operation, having purely theoretical goals, is possible.

For a number of reasons, however, it seems to be hard for the academic community to recognize the dimension of "subject" in its work of investigation—in other words, the idea that we do not confront the text so much as the text confronts us. First, the methods of study used have traditionally been aligned with the natural sciences, reflecting a desire to be counted a legitimate part of the universal rational program of the academy, whose characteristic method has been that of observation by the seeing eye from outside (through the microscope or the telescope). In the case of theology the eye looks not at cells and galaxies, but at texts from the past.

Second, it has been widely assumed that research could be done by neutral individuals on an unbiased basis. Theological knowledge is believed to be "publicly accessible to any interested person who has the necessary competencies. Indeed, as the result of disciplined and orderly critical inquiry, it is supposed to be accessible independent of any prejudices or special interests of either the researcher or the competent observer."[18]

Third, though perhaps unconsciously, Cartesian dualism, which postulates an imagined isolated thinking subject able to explore the world as if emerging from a cave for the first time, has been treated as a true account of all rational endeavor.

In contrast to these presuppositions, I believe that theology has to begin from a fundamentally different location. Although the following claims may seem somewhat scandalous in the context of the pursuit of academic excellence, I am convinced they are more easily defensible, partly because of their theological integrity and partly because they are truer to what happens in practice than those which underlie the hitherto generally accepted academic model.

In the first place, *belief is prior to understanding (credo et intelligans)*. The first act of theology is to believe and trust that the core of what the Christian community has always held to be the case is valid. In a sense, theology is a sacramental act in which one's own baptismal vows are being constantly reaffirmed. Or, to argue from a secular perspective, our very experience of being human obliges us to acknowledge that a faith-stance prior to and pervading all intellectual work (for example, in deducing criteria to test truth-claims) is inevitable.

In the second place, *grace is prior to works.* Understanding (which is distinct from both information and knowledge) is first and foremost a gift from above, not primarily the result of heroic human exertion (see Matt. 11:25-27).[19] Hence the oft-repeated phrase "the pursuit of truth," as a human task or achievement, is unreal and illogical. Unless truth is already given or assumed, there is no means of knowing when it has been discovered! Truth is received, not hunted in order to be preserved as if it were an endangered species!

In the third place (and this will be even more controversial), *submission to God's Word is prior to intellectual freedom.* Whatever might be argued theoretically, in practice the choice is stark, though real: either one submits to the external authority of God's Word written or one submits to another authority. This latter may be one's own or someone else's reason (as in the whole project of modernity) or the authority of feelings and experience (as in postmodern belief). In the last two cases there can be no doubt that the same processes are at work as in the first: the selection by faith of an external authority and an implicit submission to its criteria.

The idea of freedom as a state or stance without boundaries and wholly impervious to the (often hidden) coercion of cultural expectations, which confine choice, is another modern illusion. It is fascinating to note how the word of Jesus Christ has been totally reversed by the expectations of modern epistemology. He claimed that "if you continue in my word . . . you will know the truth, and the truth will make you free." Modern human reason says, "If you reject all authoritative assertions, you will indeed be free, and the freedom will lead you to truth."

THE ILLUSORY CLAIMS OF TRADITIONAL ACADEMIC THEOLOGY

In the light of these introductory remarks, I would like to survey a number of inherent methodological deficiencies in the academic model of theology. This will be prior to setting theology in a much wider context and coming to ways of working that do justice to the integrity of theology when it is allowed to be true to its own rationale rather than being confined within a logic that alienates it from its proper foundation.

The Invalid Claim to Be a Scientific Method

It is hard to know what is the status of this oft-repeated claim, but as an analogy to the disciplines of the natural sciences it does not fit. Yet it does not, as a result, have any less intellectual honor than subjects that are studied according to other criteria. It is simply the case that different methods are appropriate to different subjects.

The scientific method begins with the universally accepted assumption (or, in current terminology, faith-commitment) that the processes of the natural world function in a regular or uniform way—for example, that our blood will be pumped round our body in the same direction tomorrow as it is today.

It proceeds then by imagination as the scientist proposes certain hypotheses ("What if . . ."). The central work, following from this, is that of testing the *hypotheses* by carefully *regulated experiments* according to universally accepted *criteria*. The final phase is that of the *verification* of hypotheses (for example, that smoking leads to a deterioration of health, that obesity is caused by eating fatty foods, or that increased emissions of carbon dioxide in the atmosphere produce the phenomenon called "global warming") to establish whether they should be accepted, modified, or abandoned.[20]

Science deals with the kind of data that is, in principle, susceptible to direct investigation. Theology cannot apply the same methodology because the nature of the data is fundamentally different and because there are no universally accepted criteria for testing. In one sense, the only thing it has in common with science is the use of hypotheses. The ascription of "scientific" to the methods of theology ought to be dropped because they thereby receive, within a particular cultural framework, an undeserved aura and sense of invincibility.

In practice, in much theological scholarship, particularly in the field of biblical studies, the necessary relationship between theory, substantive evidence, rigorous testing, and conclusion is tenuous. Much too much is built on unproven (and probably unprovable) conjecture. Perhaps this is one reason why fashions in theology can appear and disappear on a seasonal basis. Like trends in clothes, they originate in the creative imagination of the fashion designer, only to be replaced the following year by something even more wondrous than the style that went before.

Pretensions to Being a Genuinely Critical Method

In traditional academic theology, the historical-critical method has been the bedrock of any work able to claim intellectual rigor and credibility. In accordance with certain Enlightenment emphases out of which it grew, the method begins with a first principle of doubt (or suspicion). Thus, the historical accounts of the biblical narrative are assumed to be guilty of exaggeration or of reconstructing stories to fit a predetermined theological stance, until proved innocent. The principle of "Occam's razor" is used against the *prima facie* account of the text.

In my estimation, this whole procedure disastrously confuses skepticism with criticism. For two hundred years theological faculties and departments have gone about their work under the illusion that the critical method is an impregnable fortress from which we sally forth to do battle with theological naïveté, fundamentalism, and other forms of strong Christian belief in the accessibility of final truth. The assumption is made that there is a clear divide between a critical and a confessional approach to theology. As David Kelsey says, "Only after critical testing do we have true 'knowledge.' 'Intellectual intuition' and 'reason' are strictly separated, and only human capacities for critical, disciplined, orderly problem solving in the framework of research agendas, or other situations approximating such research agendas, count as 'rationality.'"[21]

This confusion has led to a certain schizophrenia between academic pursuits on the one hand, and spirituality, mission, and pastoral concerns on the other. In many cases the divide is imagined, for critical method has to presuppose a particular vantage point that is itself not exempt from criticism from other vantage points. In fact, none of them can claim *a priori* a superior rational standing. It is for this reason also that convinced belief cannot necessarily be equated with naïveté.

One of the aims of the critical method has been the partly justifiable goal of wanting to distinguish between unassailable historical fact and ideologically convenient interpretations of history.[22] It has sought to fulfill this objective by the onionskin process of stripping away alleged layers of bias in the belief that it must be possible to lay bare a core of unprejudiced facts. That is why so much theological investigation proceeds by conjecture and reconstruction.

In more skeptical hands, however, doubt is erected into an article of faith (beyond mere method)—a negative belief, starting from a series of propositions that "cannot any longer be believed by modern, rational people." What specifically cannot be believed are "miracles," because presumably the absolute uniformity of nature is more believable than God's special action to achieve specific ends.[23]

The method, therefore, often assumes the doctrine (or dogma) of "naturalism"[24] as a necessary starting point for a truly critical process. The problem, however, is obvious to all who have not succumbed to the theory: the assumption on which it is built has to be accepted as incontrovertibly self-evident and, therefore, made immune from doubt and criticism.

Of course, there is a proper historical approach (often more clearly spelled out by professional historians than by theologians) whose proper task is to illuminate the meaning of texts by reference to historical location. As Professor Eric Ives says, "The analogy closest to the activity of the historian is the detection and trial of a crime. What matters is the evidence, and what that is worth. . . . The role of the historian is to achieve the highest level of probability congruent with the state of the evidence."[25]

Another analogy would be the instruction given to juries that they bring in a verdict only when the evidence convinces them of the guilt or innocence of the defendant "beyond all reasonable doubt." According to the widely accepted principle of fairness, in the absence of such evidence the accused remains innocent and the prosecution's case is declared unproved.

The Growing Tendency to Use Theology as a Transmitter of Symbolic Significancies

Inevitably, the doubt-inspired method of historical criticism led to a culture of skepticism. But, as it is impossible to doubt all propositions simultaneously, a new search for meaning through the use of texts is going on. No longer are some theologians concerned with original significance, which is generally considered to be archaic and anachronistic, but with "significance-for-me" or "significance-for-us." The two levels of meaning—the original and the contemporary—do not need to have any continuity at all.

This process adopts, consciously or unconsciously, the deconstructionist dogma that texts have to be read in the understanding that there is no meta-narrative (either the historical-Christian or the universal-rational) that has any basis for indicating, or even illuminating, what it means to be human. The poet Micheal O'Siadhail uses the phrase "never again one voice" to capture the mood of revolt against the kind of all-embracing theories that have led in the twentieth century to the "utopias" of communism, national socialism, and autonomous-market capitalism or to the comprehensive certainties of religious fundamentalisms.[26] The Christian and the liberal-humanist worldviews are both deemed irrecoverable. We, as autonomous subjects, now have to give ourselves the freedom to decide which meaning from the text we will accept or to create our own individual meaning.[27]

The method perfectly fits the mood of the times. It is a "consumer" approach to theology:[28] I construct out of my experience whatever I choose. The text becomes a tool for shaping the history of the individual, the group, or the whole species in ways that seem personally liberating, contextually significant, and culturally self-evident. The clear assumption is that one can live with integrity in the modern world only by accepting the equal validity of a multiplicity of different religious views. The "one voice" is identified negatively with the struggle of certain communities to secure for themselves a dominating or controlling place within society:

> It is very difficult to give material content to the idea of an "essence" that unifies schooling without its becoming dangerously open to ideological distortion. The danger of proceeding in this way is that one may unify theological schooling but in doing so may hide larger inequities in the arrangement of social power and may validate particular oppressive arrangements of power.[29]

Of course, this method reverses the age-long tradition that human beings find perfect meaning and freedom in listening obediently to God's Word written (*the* "one voice"). Now the text is to be conquered and shaped so that it provides "mythological" support for beliefs and actions deemed right on quite other grounds (life is to be a celebration of the many voices that contribute to the universal storehouse of meaning and value). Theo Sundermeier, in his response to the missiological thinking of David Bosch, illustrates this process very well: "Texts are 'open' in the sense that they constantly invite renewed and deepened interpretation. They are like works of art in that they only acquire meaning in the process of reception. In passing through the understanding of the recipient they are changed. . . . In this process of understanding the message changes."[30]

Because of the strong drift of contemporary Western culture toward anarchy of belief-systems, it may take a long time before the manifold problems of this method are recognized. The consequences, as is already evident, will be a steady slide into irrationality, isolation, and meaninglessness, what fits comfortably into a cultural consensus among certain groups in society. This is not easily dislodged by argument. Orlando Costas argued that a pluralist approach to theology undermines its missiological possibilities because it sanctions theological provincialism.[31] If *situation* is the supreme criterion for the utmost integrity in theological construction, there are no grounds for distinguishing between opinions that emerge out of particular, isolated, individual, and subjective judgments about the rightness of beliefs and actions. "Academia needs to take seriously the problem of how to relinquish a claim on a set body of knowledge as somehow containing the 'truth,' without succumbing in the process to every current and tide of new expression."[32]

One is inclined to say: Exactly so! The pluralist thesis about diversity and the contingency of all beliefs on the ground that they are historically conditioned makes an interesting theory, but it cannot work in practice. Action springs from commitment to particular beliefs and objectives. If people held, at all moments, that these were entirely provisional, their decisions would become totally paralyzed by an all-encompassing uncertainty and apprehension. More important, consistent pluralism renders all resistance to manifest evil innocuous.[33] Neither textual interpretation nor the general task of theological reflection can possibly sidestep the always prior question of truth.

A General Confusion About Aims and Objectives

Academic theology has thrived on the false distinction between "doing" theology, with its implied perspective and committed interaction with living reality, and teaching and studying theology, with its implied disinterested, impartial presentation of a variety of viewpoints.

This dichotomy can best be summed up, perhaps, by considering what is required to achieve the higher academic degrees. The test of excellence and competence lies in what is known, who is quoted, and how one argues, not on what one believes (which may be highly suspect and therefore should be bracketed out) or what kind of action is required.

An illustration of this would be the experience of a friend in defending his doctoral thesis on the phenomenon of the "Messianic Jews."[34] Neither his research nor the conclusions he drew were put in question, only his own conviction, which informed his work throughout, that the existence of "Messianic Jews" was a legitimate result of a justifiable evangelistic approach to Jewish people. The expectation of the examiners was that a critical approach to the study should end up in a noncommitted stance. A little reflection, however, shows that in a case like this, belief of one kind or another is inescapable. One has to accept that, according to prior convictions, evangelism and conversion are either legitimate or not. Even a person who might maintain a stance of indifference to the question does so on the basis of other beliefs.

Of course, anyone engaged in serious theological reflection has to acknowledge, analyze, and face objections to their own views and, if persuaded by the weight of evidence or the arguments put forward, change or modify those views. Such a procedure, however, is a long way from admitting that there is any difference in kind between theological work done in a strictly "nonconfessional" academic environment and that done in the confessionally committed locale of a seminary or college whose purpose is to train leaders for Christian communities.

This brings us back to Kelsey's disjunction between "Athens" and "Berlin." The distinction between a method that strives to inculcate the tools necessary to pursue theological inquiry as a disinterested intellectual exercise and one that seeks to form people theologically, pastorally, ethically, and spiritually within a particular tradition cannot be sustained. The simple and obvious reality is that the mind cannot be separated from the person and his or her history and context. It is much better, therefore, for all approaches to theology to admit the particular commitment from which they begin.

BUILDING THE STADIUM

Starting with a brief summary of the discussion so far, I will list some of the main factors that are pushing the whole enterprise of theology in new directions.

Inadequacy of the Existing Paradigm

The combined weight of Michael Polyani's thesis of "tacit knowing"[35] in his work on the methodology of science and the insights coming from the sociology of knowledge (that knowing is socially constructed) has led to the recognition that no one engaged in a discipline like theology can stand outside it in a zone protected from the subtle influence of personal beliefs and interests. They cannot act like umpires arbitrating a tennis match, elevated above the arena of play, final judges of the way the rules of the game are to be interpreted. It is impossible, therefore, to move from some kind of sanitized, unideological "pure thought" to its application to events in the everyday world.

The theologian is already committed in all sorts of ways both before and during the pursuit of his or her craft. It is liberating to recognize this, since everyone is in the same situation. No one is more or less biased than anyone else. Each has particular preferences that show in different ways.

One cannot, for example, rule out the way that the benefits of the academic teaching of theology influence the results of one's study. The pressure on those whose livelihood is bound up with their tenure in a university to conform to particular intellectual conventions is great. The maverick who consistently steps out of line with the established norms of academically approved performance is unlikely to go far. However, only those with a simple and naive faith in academic neutrality could imagine that such norms are unquestionably valid or that it is possible to suspend belief (usually someone else's belief—rarely their own) while engaged in the pursuit of knowledge and understanding.

It follows from this, I believe, that all theology should begin with a "prototheological" phase in which the theologian reveals and discusses all hidden assumptions and a general kind of health warning is given against all pretensions of the academy to a universally valid vantage point.

One example of the way unexamined assumptions come to supplant open processes of reasoning is the dispute about the plenary inspiration of Scripture. In the nature of the case, there are no facts, historical or otherwise, or any universally accepted, rational norms that oblige all intelligent beings to accept one position over another. We may weigh the evidence and accept for ourselves the probability of one position, but the factors that influence us are often cultural in the wide sense, and may be unconscious. (Indeed, the less we are aware of the conditioning force of extraneous factors, the more likely we are to be influenced by them.)

Thus, not believing in the plenary inspiration of Scripture is just as much a matter of disposition or inclination as is believing. Each carries all the weight of an *a priori* faith-commitment. Ridiculing another's belief is no substitute for substantive argument. And yet, what chance would an otherwise highly qualified person who admitted to believing in the full inspiration of the text of Scripture have to secure an academic post in a university? Why should only certain kinds of belief be deemed acceptable or unacceptable? Would there not be a terrible outcry among "advanced" thinkers if a person who denied the plenary inspiration of Scripture were to be rejected on this ground alone from being a candidate for a teaching post in a "conservative" college? Would this not be condemned by more "enlightened" people as unacceptable discrimination, even as having contravened equal opportunity principles?

To take seriously and to be rigorously honest about every kind of bias is the first step toward helping theology in general to be more widely self-critical than it is at present.

A Recognition of the Need to Rethink Educational Practices

Possibly because of a tendency in recent years for more mature students to study theology, there is gradually emerging a greater willingness to involve them in the whole process of their own education than has been the case formerly. It is now more widely recognized that programs that serve first the needs of the educator, and into which the learners must fit, are pedagogically and ethically inadmissible. In the place where I am involved in mission education, we try not to use the term "student" of those coming to learn, but rather the term "participant." The idea is to use language to signify the ideal that education is about processes of learning in which all (the tutor and the tutee) participate.

At the same time, the educational method highlighted by liberation theology of "see," "judge," "act" is also gaining currency. In engaging the participant much more in a whole process of observation, discernment, decision making, and action, the balance between the input of the "expert," previous experience, and practice will be changed, lessening the control of the first. In this way we move from a teacher-centered model to a learner-centered one. The teacher's task is to be a facilitator, a resource, and a stimulus, helping participants to relate gospel, church, and world in critical, creative ways.

The advent of the Internet has given rise to new concepts of the resources that educational establishments need in order to maximize the potential of participants to be involved as subjects in their own learning. Access to computer technology should mean that much less attention is given to the classical lecture, even perhaps to classroom activity that involves the use of multimedia presentations and discussion. The future of adult education is likely to be conducted in between the three points of the "learning resource center," exposure/placements, and the tutorial group.

Theological Incursion from the South

Whatever we may think of liberation theology, there is a sense in which we now live in a post-liberation theology age.[36] I will list some of the major concerns that have begun to transform the whole enterprise of theology from the perspective of the South.

Owing to a growing awareness in the postcolonial era of the perennial identification of the church and its theological underpinning with politically conservative and oppressive regimes, theologians have applied Marx's famous dictum about philosophy to theology thus: "The [theologians] have only *interpreted* the world in various ways; the point, however, is to *change* it."[37]

The impossibility of separating intellectual work from life commitments, either by commission or omission, leads inevitably to a critique of Western intellectual assumptions. Western theology is interpreted as one part (even though this has been obscured by its claims to universality) of Western colonial expansion. The present world order, characterized by the North-South divide and the fragmentation of peoples in many parts of Africa, Asia, and Latin America (and not forgetting post–Cold War Europe) into artificially constructed nation-states, belongs to a history imposed from outside. This is why people from the South speak of living on the "underside" (in Spanish the word means literally "the reverse" side) of history.

Dominant industrialized societies are almost incapable of forgoing a certain "messianic" pretentiousness about being able to solve all problems everywhere. Peoples of the South, quite rightly, are mightily unimpressed by the state of Western societies. They say, "Physician, heal yourself!" Yet the deeply felt superiority of Western culture and civilization (the norm of being a "civilized" society) dies hard. One can see in this an absurd, even manic, obsession with the benefits of one particular economic system, and how consumer choice has become the chief criterion for defining human identity.[38]

Christian theology, unfortunately, has participated in this sense of superiority—in spite of the fact, seen clearly from the South, that Western theology has hardly begun seriously to challenge Western culture. One of the interesting aspects of the proposals put forward by Lesslie Newbigin is the sharp, even angry reactions that his writings quite often receive. Newbigin proposes to test the thesis that, because "the gospel is public truth," one of the major missionary tasks of the church in the West is to call the culture to conversion to the gospel.[39] Yet some overly defensive Christians hold that modern Western culture, as the result of a certain unquestioned way of thinking and being, is sacrosanct. It may be questioned at the margins, but not at the center of its core assumptions, for then the "emperor" (the new imperium) would lose his clothes and his ugly nakedness would be exposed. Newbigin, quite unjustifiably in my opinion, is then accused of wanting to turn the culture-clock back to an imagined era when culture was friendly toward and supportive of Christian beliefs and values,[40] trying to reclaim the public square in the name of the gospel.

The doyens of the interreligious theological scene, people like John Hick and Wilfred Cantwell-Smith, openly acknowledge their indebtedness to the dualism of Greek thought and the rational dichotomy of Kant's philosophical scheme—in other words, to powerful strands of Western cultural history. Challenge this influence in the name of an alternative intellectual heritage and their rational structure collapses. Surely, at the heart of its view of the world, Christian faith challenges two cardinal assumptions of Greek philosophy and its subsequent intellectual tradition: the distinction between sacred and profane and the separation of reality into phenomenologically contingent and noumenally absolute worlds. In other words, Christianity can be true to itself only when it is prepared to disengage itself from some of the central thought-forms of Hellenistic culture.

To the question, wherein lies the validation of the plausibility of the gospel message, Western theology is likely to say: with the criteria of the modern (or now for some the postmodern) mind. In other words, does the gospel conform to accepted standard norms? Theological thinkers from the South answer quite differently, putting the emphasis on its missionary effectiveness, its ability to inspire people to be agents and embodiments of the life of God's new creation in Jesus Christ. If they are correct, then theology's main purpose is to elucidate in different situations the imperatives of the *missio Dei* and the *missio ecclesiae*.

The Western World Poses the Greatest Contemporary Missionary Challenge to the Church

This dawning of consciousness has been extremely slow in coming because of countervailing tendencies like the sheer inertia of ecclesiastical structures (which, like the great oil tankers, need much time and space to turn around) and the deeply powerful pastoral model of ministry inherited from the past. The Church of England, for example, with which I am particularly familiar, behaves like an institution dominated by a rural mentality, though ostensibly engaged in urban ministry.

Mission historian Andrew Walls says that up to the present "the missionary movement has always been considered as an extension of the Church at the margins."[41] In other words, mission always occurs in places where the church is not already established. This view is part of the long and deep legacy of the 1910 Edinburgh Missionary Conference, with its strong distinction between the Christian and the non-Christian worlds. At the same time, in the West the more vigorous evangelistic work of the church in the United States of America, in comparison to that going on in Europe, may be due to the tenacity with which

European Christians have bought into, and often still defend, the "territorial principle" of established churches. In this model, mission work is still based on the assumption that the European peoples are implicitly Christian, not overtly pagan.[42]

The response to the "Decade of Evangelism" shows that there is great confusion in Europe about the missionary task and how to implement it. Ordinary Christians point to a need to regain confidence in the truth and power of the Christian message, while many of their leaders confess to knowing more about what the gospel is not than what it is.

Andrew Walls has also put forward a theory of church history as consisting of great missionary ebbs and flows. The ebb in Europe is patently obvious, particularly among the young (a fact constantly remarked on by Christians visiting from Africa, Asia, and Latin America). Perhaps there must yet be further decline before the church can countenance any radically new responses, not least in the area of theological education. For example, the challenge to communicate the gospel to a "non-literate" or "semi-literate" culture is a matter that requires deeply serious theological exploration.

THE TWO TASKS OF THEOLOGY

Finally, I would like to elaborate further the two major tasks (or mission) of theology that I stated programmatically at the beginning of this essay, and test their validity.

To Make Sense of the Whole of Life by Reference to God

I agree with the pivotal emphasis of liberation theology that concepts of God are absolutely central to all theological work.[43] At its heart, biblical faith is prophetic. Of the three mediators of God's word highlighted in the Old Testament—priest, prophet, and sage—the prophet speaks with greatest clarity and forcefulness about the nature and intentions of God. Moreover, the word of the true prophet is least able to be manipulated by religious or political elites in the interests of maintaining their privileges over against the clamor of the disinherited.

Theology, if it is going to be anything other than the esoteric pastime of a small professional coterie, must recapture the centrality of the prophetic word. Here, however, it may find itself in a dilemma on two scores. On the one hand, emphasis on the Word has been associated for most of the past century with the dialectical theology of Karl Barth. Though Barth was a master theological craftsman, no contemporary reconstruction of theology should, by an association of language, be aligned immediately with that of someone else, however brilliant.

Barth has a reputation for having developed a theology in which the transcendent communication of God is in sharp discontinuity with human-constructed cultural effects. This emphasis tends to negate the impact of the prophetic message, because its forcefulness is its ability to penetrate to the heart of a culture, deliver its message there, and be heard as judgment, warning, and promise. Too sharp a separation of the Word from the world may imply that the former becomes incomprehensible to the latter. The prophet, then, would not be so much "crying in the wilderness" as "proclaiming into a void." The messages of Jeremiah, Jonah, and Jesus were clearly understood, even when they were morally unacceptable to the hearers. Barth's dialectical theology is less than helpful when one reflects on the pressing necessity to communicate the meaning of God to a generation that has lost touch.

A theology of the Word has also been part of the evangelical tradition of the church. Unlike Barth, many evangelicals have deeply imbibed the Reformation belief that God's special revelation is transparent to anyone who is open to hear its message. The gap between the mind of God and the minds of men and women is not as great as Barth seems to suggest. Nevertheless, modern culture finds it difficult to take the evangelical witness seriously. Many commentators identify certain characteristics, such as the supposed need to possess spiritual certainty, the appeal to moral absolutes, the rejection of certain scientific theories (like evolution), and the bizarre, literalistic interpretations of the Bible made by some, as evidence of a precritical, premodern mentality.

A rediscovery of the centrality of the Word of God in its faithful communication through prophet and apostle has to be freed from association either with dialectical theology or with the triumphalistic gospel and simplistic exegetical methods adopted by some conservative groups of Christians. Liberation theology may provide another perspective. It is not tainted by the kind of negative views of theologies of the Word noted above, and yet, because it insists that God is knowable through his Word, it too is decidedly a theology of the Word.[44]

On the other hand, certain strands of modern thinking are deeply suspicious of "the Word" and words. Postmodern literary theory assumes that words, particularly when allied to truth-claims, have the totalizing effect of imposing an absolute prohibition on all forms of difference. Thus theology, which insists on the givenness of the word of God and the non-negotiability of the narrative of the Word, is dismissed as a dissimulated will-to-power: "never again one voice!"

A theology of the Word thus has a difficult task, both in relation to the past "dialectical" emphasis on the profound break between the Word and culture and to the present deconstructionist insistence on the break between culture and all universal words.

Nevertheless, it is urgent that theology recover a self-conscious mission to contemporary culture to help arrest its further slide into the abyss of nihilism. John Milbank says that all modern critical thought is itself under suspicion of being a "will-to-power." Postmodern suspicion leaves "no possible residue of secure, humanist meaning."[45]

It is not surprising that this generation has seen a resurgence of interest in Nietzsche. As Allan Bloom says in his trenchant critique of the mindless contemporary cult of open-mindedness and tolerance above all things, "Nietzsche with the utmost gravity told modern man that he was free-falling in the abyss of nihilism. . . . Nobody really believes in anything anymore, and everyone spends his life in frenzied work and frenzied play so as not to face the fact, not to look into the abyss."[46]

Anyone aware of the gravity of the present crisis of culture and concerned about its destructive human consequences[47] should welcome the call of Newbigin and others to a missionary encounter with contemporary culture. Two major areas have to be tackled, both of which profoundly affect this generation's sense of meaninglessness and the possibility of recovering again an adequate basis for meaning. First, there is the inability of a world dominated by scientific culture to comprehend human life in any other way than by reference to biological origins and the final physiological destiny of deterioration, death, and disintegration. The insistence on referring everything to "nature" (quite deliberately chosen as a word in contrast to "creation") has led to the deep oppression of experiencing life as imprisonment in a mechanistic universe.[48] The loss of an overarching teleology that would restore purpose to human existence is an exorbitant price to pay for banishing God to the realm of personal and private opinion and experience.

Second, there is the present intoxication with pluralism. The hermeneutic of suspicion finds an ontological imperialism in every claim to universal validity. This finds expression in the apparently self-evident cultural relativity of all our views. This leads further to a kind of cultural positivism, which affirms that every culture is right simply because it is. Such a view is held to be particularly true in respect of minority cultures because, without doubt, they have often been brutally suppressed by other conquering cultures.[49]

Our age wants to celebrate the relativism of all perspectives. We live now "beyond good and evil," even though, as Bloom points out, that gives us severe difficulties in making sense of human rights. The current emphasis on cultural diversity as an end in itself may be one way of trying to escape from the impasse of "scientism" and get a toe back into teleology, on the basis that cultures, by their very nature, cohere through commonly shared ends.

The globalization of theological education, which has become something of a fashion within progressive theological circles, seems to draw much of its inspiration from the imperative to recognize the benefits that accrue from celebrating a pluralism of cultures.[50] What appears to be self-evidently true—namely, that Western cultural/theological hegemony must be destroyed by demonstrating its imperialistic and humiliating effects—in the hands of some theologians actually reinforces the status quo.

The convictions and commitments of Christians living in other parts of the world can be accepted as a witness to the truth of the gospel. This implies that we in the West should repent of our blindness, hypocrisy, and unfaithfulness and change our views and our missionary and pastoral practice. It is certainly the intent of some who have embarked on a process of globalization that the possibility of such an outcome be squarely faced. On the other hand, globalization can be construed as the celebration of an incommensurable variety of different stances, which forces Western theology to recognize its parochialism and obliges it to desist from criticizing other theological positions. Otherwise, however, it leaves it basically unchallenged, secure in its culturally relative cocoon. Schreiter delineates the problem that multiplicity continually poses:

> One way of answering the multiplicity question owes a great deal to the dominant culture in North America where an ideology of plurality (as opposed to pluralism) is cultivated. In this ideology, no unity or universality is sought, since that might be construed as the triumph of one view over the others. Rather, a plurality is maintained, wherein all are allowed to coexist, *provided that none threatens the existence or well-being of the other* [my emphasis]. . . . In theological education, in an interest to help students and faculty see the diversity of culture and of God's world, we can sometimes fudge a bit the questions of universality, dismissing them as signs of anxiety or intransigence.[51]

Thus, the acknowledgment of a polycentric world can either enable the prophetic word of the gospel to penetrate more deeply through the shell of resistance to its life-changing message or it can hold it off at a safe distance, out of range of our secure, culturally autonomous bunker.

I believe that, in the same way that some handle the question of cultural multiplicity, the present fascination with the pluriformity of religious convictions and practices among some theologians and the attempt to construct a viable theology of pluralism are related to the refusal to countenance one universally valid prophetic word that comprehensively tells us who we are and what we are to become. Robert Zaehner, former professor of Eastern Religions and Ethics in the University of Oxford, began his tenure in the chair as a convinced believer in the uniqueness and finality of Christ among the religions, but finished by laying the blame for the ills of Western society (and the rest) at the feet of the prophetic faith of the Judeo-Christian tradition and advocating in its place the stance of Zen Buddhism and other examples of philosophical mysticism, beyond reason, revelation, and ethical norms.[52] His own intellectual trajectory mirrors that of the society to which he belonged. Like so many others, he was apparently unable to withstand the relentless *Zeitgeist* of his day.

The mission of both Old Testament prophet and New Testament apostle was carried on in a social milieu not dissimilar to our own. A substantial period of political stability in the eighth-century kingdoms of Israel and Judah and in the first-century Roman Empire led to economic prosperity and, in turn, religious pluralism. Idolatry, to use the prophets' characterization of the religion of their time, was both commercially profitable and religiously necessary. The false prophets and soothsayers were paid handsomely for encouraging the neglect of the terms of the covenant and for despising the warnings of impending doom. In the New Testament we have the example of the silversmiths of Ephesus!

Demetrius "saw clearly, as did the practitioners of magic, that a choice had to be made between Jesus and the new order of things which he represented and the common religious beliefs that the ordinary people had hitherto practised. Unlike some modern global religious ecumenists, they did not envisage any way of bringing the faith of Jesus and the faith of Artemis into some kind of creative harmony."[53]

In both cases religion is the occasion for and the legitimating power of corrupt business practices. On a pluralist view, however, the religions should not be questioned at their very core.

Our pluralist world, then, oscillates dangerously between what would be, if believed and acted on, the prophetic word that destroys idols and brings life from the dead, and the immensely confusing babble of words. Because there is no basis for discernment, an insidious, creeping mood of cultural doubt and paralysis is gripping all Western societies. It is a significant task of theology to persuade (not to try to coerce) our generation to listen again to the Word in order to be able to make sense of the contemporary confusion of words.

To Be an Agent of Transformation, So That the Whole of Life May Reflect God's Intent

Solid, disciplined, and prolonged intellectual work in the context of a missionary encounter between the gospel and contemporary cultures is an essential part of the mission of theology. To fulfill such a task, theology has to be much more self-critical of its tendency to acquiesce in whatever happens to be the currently ascendant worldview. It has, from its own "autonomous" roots (in the sense of being independent of the traditional Western metaphysical dichotomy between reason and revelation), to develop its own integral hermeneutic of suspicion.

Though admittedly not a straightforward assignment, the apostolic message of Jesus has within itself the implements necessary for distinguishing between corrupt and corrupting ideologies and beliefs and actions that genuinely free people to be and do as God intends. It is able to act in this way because it challenges the assumption that listening to the cacophony of many voices is the most certain way to discover truth and goodness, as well as the assumption that the single, direct voice is automatically imperialist and oppressive. Within the word of Jesus there is a perfect combination of truth and freedom.[54]

However, it is crucial to the integrity of theology never to isolate its intellectual work from the call to be a force for the transformation of human life, so that it might be remade in the image of Christ, "the image of the invisible God" (Col. 1:15). This is the message of theology from the South, from the "margins of humanity," from the "underside of history." In the North it would seem that often we may find comprehensive intellectual theological systems looking for a praxis. But in the South there is plenty of praxis, striving perhaps to find an adequate theological underpinning.

At the risk of using overworked jargon, I would argue that theology has a crucial part to play in the missionary task of leading human beings from alienation to wholeness. Theology works from within the framework, given to us by God's revelation, of the reality of creation, the fall, redemption, and consummation. Human beings have been created to enjoy fellowship with God, with one another, and with creation, but they do not. Rather, they have constructed an order of violence—anger against and rejection of God's just claim on their lives, brutality and disorder within human communities, and the violation of the environment—in which they are always on the edge of self-destruction.

Theology begins not just with the prophetic word but with the incarnate Word. When it is true to itself, it follows the movement of the Word from the heart of God (John 1:18) to the depths of the world (Eph. 4:9) and back again. As well as a prophetic role on behalf of God, it has a priestly and servant role to fulfill on behalf of wounded humanity.

The true theologian, then, cannot avoid the challenge of knowing personally life in its most traumatic forms. Again, this is a fundamental aspect of the globalization program of theological education: "crossing . . . boundaries and discovering the realities that lie on the other side."[55]

Moreover, in order to understand better the way social life develops historically, the faithful theologian will have to learn to use wisely the tools of sociopolitical and cultural analysis, though without ever making a fetish of pure methodology. Here the warning of Douglas Meeks is timely, though dire: "It is true that both criticism and innovation stem from what we may call the power of suffering. But seminaries [theology] will not be changed by the mere experience of the poor and poverty. Modernity's pervasive liberalism can absorb and co-opt any experience of the negative."[56]

Together with experience and analysis must go the tough, universally valid, hope-inspiring project of the redemptive reign of God. Thus, theology can only help the missionary church to move from observation, feeling, and intellectual appraisal to a project of transformation by setting out a model of what transformed human beings and communities would look like. Changed conditions of living and changed people are mutually reinforcing.

Transformation means leaving behind one form of living and working out of another. In biblical terms it is the renunciation of the pattern of this age (under judgment and passing away, 1 Cor. 2:6-8) and an entering into the pattern of the age to come, which is the eschatological fulfillment of God's righteous rule in the joy and power of the Spirit of Christ.

Theology, in all its disciplines, is to be done unapologetically as a conscious handmaid to this process of renunciation, conversion, and entering into the birth pangs of a new world. It does not need, any longer, to bow to the alien criteria of the academy (it never did), for its real identity and purpose are fulfilled by being a resource in the service of God's mission to bring all things into subjection to Christ.

A key question for any theology of mission is: What is the nature of this material world in which we live, move, and have our being? If the gospel is good news for human beings, is it also good news for the world in which they live? Luís Wesley de Souza shows that there are rich resources in John Wesley's theology for an affirmative answer, exploring the ways in which "the wisdom of God in creation" is relevant today. In the process, he provides an insightful critique of the so-called Wesleyan Quadrilateral of Scripture, reason, tradition, and experience, showing that Wesley also drew significantly on creation as a theological resource. This fuller understanding of Wesley's theology, then, is fruitful for a contemporary theology of mission.

CHAPTER EIGHT

"THE WISDOM OF GOD IN CREATION": MISSION AND THE WESLEYAN PENTALATERAL

Luís Wesley de Souza

INTRODUCTION

Protestantism, it is sometimes said, has an underdeveloped theology of creation. We have been strong in developing a theology of redemption, while Roman Catholic and Orthodox theologians have been masters in developing a theology of creation.

From my point of view as a Brazilian Methodist, John Wesley is one of the most promising historical sources from whom we can gain insights for a renewed and contemporary theology of creation. Looking at *The Works of John Wesley*, one sees that the theme of creation (including variant words and possible correlated concepts, such as "creature" and "Creator") is almost everywhere. Wesley's interest in the natural creation and its significance to Christian theology and mission are evident, though often overlooked.

The theme of creation occurs throughout Wesley's writings, from the earliest to the last period of his theological production. Creation is, at the very least, a major point of constant and insistent use that seems to be intentional. Even a comment such as the following suggests Wesley's sensitivity to creation: "We opened the Scriptures, and considered the account which is given therein of the whole economy of God with man, from the creation to the consummation of all things."[1] For Wesley, creation is a frame of reference always present as an *underlying assumption* that can be identified from the beginning to the end of his theological development.

My own reading of Wesley suggests that *God's purpose in creation* is a basic assumption that defines much of the silhouette of his theology. The issue is not simply whether there is a theology of creation in Wesley, but whether God's creation is a methodological point of reference. As will be noted later, some Latin American theologians consider creation to be part of Wesley's theological method, along with Scripture, tradition, reason, and experience (the so-called Wesleyan Quadrilateral). Creation in Wesley seems to be more than one theme among others. It is in fact a key element of theological method. This raises then the question: Is there in fact a *Wesleyan Pentalateral*?

WESLEY'S THEOLOGICAL METHOD

John Wesley used some key principles in doing theology that in effect constitute his theological methodology. Wesleyan scholars have highlighted four methodological marks in Wesley's theologizing. These elements have often been called the *Wesleyan Quadrilateral*, as illustrated in figure 8A.

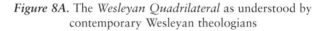

Figure 8A. The *Wesleyan Quadrilateral* as understood by contemporary Wesleyan theologians

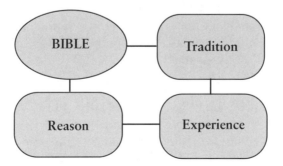

Discussion about the adequacy of the Wesleyan Quadrilateral and whether it is even genuinely Wesleyan notwithstanding, Wesley does give us a helpful example of how to *do* theology. He recognized the interdependence between Christian piety and reason. And his journal, books, sermons, and letters testify to the integration of Scripture, tradition, reason, and the experience of God, which are so often fragmented today.

Each theologian has a particular way of formulating his or her theology. In this sense Wesley is no different from others. Yet Wesley's way of doing theology can surprise us. According to Donald Thorsen, "Wesley did not articulate an explicit theological method. He was concerned more for the practical relevance and applicability of theology than for its theory."[2] Wesley never intended to write a textbook of systematic theology or develop a new theological system. Yet he did have a distinct theological method. He had principles of interpretation—a hermeneutic—of Scripture and of the Christian faith that made him stand "majestically alone, towering head and shoulders above his contemporaries,"[3] as Hugh T. Kerr put it. Thorsen suggests, in fact, that this is his most important contribution theologically: "Wesley's distinctiveness rests not in a systematic theology, but in a theological method—that is, the framework in which theological questions are handled."[4]

Theology is the science of God and divine things, based upon the revelation made to humankind in Jesus Christ, organized and kept by the church under the guidance and supervision of the Holy Spirit.[5] It is "the study of God, his attributes, and his relationship with [human beings] and the universe."[6] Here, the idea of "[human beings] and the universe" encapsulates the whole dimension of God's creation.

Albert Outler described Wesley's theology as "the interpretation of spiritual and moral insights sparked by the prevenient action of the Holy Spirit, deposited in Holy Scripture, interpreted by the Christian tradition, reviewed by reason, and appropriated by personal experience."[7] One can also define theology in Wesley as the work of elucidating the things of God toward society and its individuals. And it is true that in Wesley's theological methodology, he does use the four sources of Scripture, tradition, reason, and experience. But does he not also, and importantly, draw on a fifth source—namely, *creation*?

THE WESLEYAN QUADRILATERAL

Influenced and inspired by his Anglican formation and heritage, John Wesley developed a theological methodology that today is commonly called the Wesleyan Quadrilateral. His method combined the four basic sources of religious knowledge and authority: the Scriptures, the Christian tradition, reason, and experience. According to Thorsen, "Wesley appealed to tradition, reason, and experience as complementary sources of religious authority. These sources, together with the primary religious authority of Scripture, contributed to an approach to theology that continues to provide insight for Christians today."[8]

Scripture

In Wesley's theological methodology, Scripture is "the primary religious authority,"[9] as Thorsen notes. The Bible is nothing less than a revelation of God's acts throughout history and eternity. Yet it was ordinary people, motivated and inspired by God, who wrote it. In other words, the Bible is a result of a partnership between God and human beings created and inspired by God. It is this that makes the Bible both fully human and fully divine. In one of his sermons published in 1746, "The Witness of Our Own Spirit," Wesley says, "The Christian rule of right and wrong is the Word of God, the writings of the Old and New Testament."[10] Although he affirms that God's Word cannot fail because "God speaks not as man, but as God," he also recognizes that the human contribution in recording and transmitting the Bible makes textual mistakes a possibility. God's Word permeates all of Scripture. The Bible alone is sufficient for men and women to know what is right and wrong and to discern what is really good or evil. Thus, Scripture is the lamp that illuminates and clarifies the path of those who seek to interpret and understand God's designs. "My ground is the Bible. Yea, I am a Bible-bigot. I follow it in all things, both great and small," Wesley declares.[11]

Tradition

In Wesley's understanding, the wisdom of the church fathers is an important confirming source of the truth contained in Scripture. In addition to the early fathers, Wesley appealed to the first four general councils of the church. As John Deschner says, "When [Wesley's] systematic statements are examined, they are seen to follow classical models: the Anglican Thirty-nine Articles, the ecumenical creeds, or the doctrinal formulas of Protestant orthodoxy."[12] Thorsen adds, "The theological gestalt [Wesley] developed drew from the theological method that he inherited from the Reformed and Anglican traditions, along with a catholic spirit that sought to incorporate a wealth of insights regarding true Christian tradition."[13] Although Wesley's theology does not simply repeat the historical tradition, Wesley does consider history (with its theology) as a legitimated and authorized source of doctrine. Working with the historical sources, he brings new light and fresh understanding to Christian theology.

Reason

Though salvation is by faith, one cannot find God's truth without the use of reason. Reason is a gift from God. If God gave us the capacity to think, we should use it to understand and explain his Word. "Wesley's appeal to reason often followed appeals to Scripture," notes Thorsen.[14] Yet reason is not a law unto itself. "True reason knows its limits. By recognizing the limitations of reason we learn humility, resignation, and faith (or trust) in God. . . . To Wesley, faith still represented the 'grand desideratum'—the grand *fact* of knowledge concerning God and all things pertaining to our salvation."[15]

Experience

The experience of God is another of Wesley's sources to elucidate biblical truth. "Because of his dual stress on divine sovereignty and human freedom, Wesley focused on Christian experience. . . . Wesley stressed both doctrine and experience, . . . 'faith working by love.' If faith didn't produce moral change, including good works, it wasn't true faith."[16] According to Wesley, the real change comes when we experience "not . . . a cold, lifeless assent, a train of ideas in the head; but also a disposition of the heart. . . . So that he who is thus justified or saved by faith is indeed 'born again.'"[17] This had proved true in his own experience.

Thorsen notes that "Many consider Wesley's insights into experience as a source of religious authority one of his greatest contributions to the development of Christian theology. . . . [Wesley] was the first to incorporate explicitly into his theological worldview the experiential dimension of the Christian faith along with the conceptual."[18]

CREATION IN WESLEY'S THEOLOGY

Useful as the Wesleyan Quadrilateral may be, it has a serious drawback. It fails to make clear the important role of *creation* for John Wesley and for his theology.

Identifying creation as part of Wesley's theological method is not entirely new. A few authors have proposed that creation be seen as a key methodological aspect for Wesley's theology. Some South American Wesleyan theologians, especially the Brazilians Ruy Josgrilberg, Tércio Machado Siqueira, and José Carlos de Souza, have argued this. Another strong supporter of creation as a key aspect of Wesley's method is Duncan Alexander Reilly, an American missionary who has lived and worked in Brazil for more than forty years. These scholars argue that creation itself should be seen as a fifth dimension of Wesley's theological method, thus forming a Wesleyan Pentalateral: Scripture, tradition, reason, experience, and creation (or God's purpose in the creation). In fact, since the 1960s the Methodist Church in Brazil has incorporated in all its doctrinal literature the concept of a Wesleyan Pentalateral, as illustrated in figure 8B below.

Figure 8B. The Wesleyan Pentalateral as understood by Robert W. Burtner and Robert Chiles, along with some Brazilian Wesleyan theologians

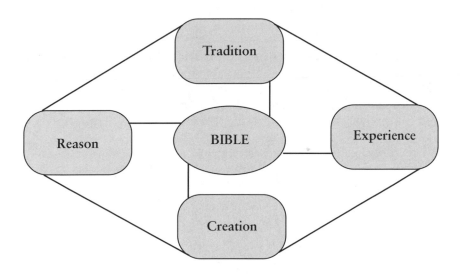

In what sense is creation a matter of theological method? Siqueira begins with the creation of human beings. "If humans are beings created *of* the dust of the ground, according to Genesis 1:7, then they are part of created nature, and thus identified with the reality of the world." But since they are created "in the *image and likeness* of God, man and woman confirm and reveal God's power, wisdom, and majesty."[19] Siqueira notes:

> God did not create humankind as a *spirit* only. He created humans with a *spirit* and a *body*. This perception leads us to the conclusion that the Christian life is not enjoyed only at the spiritual level. When God created man and woman, he intended them to live together in society. Also, [creation] "in his image, and according to his likeness" (Genesis 1:26) [means that] his *image and likeness* is the foundation for communication between God and human beings.[20]

While few have seen creation as a basic element of Wesley's theological method, some well-known American and Continental authors have emphasized its importance. For example, Robert W. Burtner and Robert Chiles in *John Wesley's Theology: A Collection from His Works* explicitly include "The Natural Creation" as a part of Wesley's theological method, considering it to be one of Wesley's sources of religious knowledge and authority. After noting the important roles of Scripture, reason, and experience for Wesley, Burtner and Chiles note: "Two further sources of religious knowledge and authority [for Wesley are] Christian tradition, which reflects Wesley's background in the Church of England . . . and *the natural creation*, which suggests his deep interest in the physical world."[21]

Thus Burtner and Chiles elaborate what is in effect a Pentalateral: the Bible, reason, religious experience, Christian tradition, and the natural creation.[22] They base this on Wesley's sermons, letters, hymns, and especially his book *A Survey of the Wisdom of God in the Creation: or A Compendium of Natural Philosophy*.[23] Burtner and Chiles cite a letter sent from Wesley to Dr. Conyers Middleton in which he writes:

> In contemplating even the things that surround him, that thought strikes warmly upon [one's] heart—"These are Thy glorious works, Parent of good"; while he takes knowledge of the invisible things of God, even His eternal power and wisdom in the things that are seen—the heavens, the earth, the fowls of the air, the lilies of the field. How much more while, rejoicing in the constant care which He still takes of the work of His own hand, he breaks out in a transport of love and praise, "O Lord our Governor, how excellent are Thy ways in all the earth! Thou that hast set Thy glory above the heavens!" While he, as it were, sees the Lord sitting upon His throne, and ruling all things well; while he observes the general providence of God co-extended with His whole creation, and surveys all the effects of it in the heavens and earth, as a well-pleased spectator; while he sees the wisdom and goodness of His general government descending to every particular, so presiding over the whole universe as over a single person, so watching over every single person as if he were the whole universe;—how does he exult when he reviews the various traces of the Almighty goodness, in what has befallen himself in the several circumstances and changes of his own life! all which he now sees have been allotted to him, and dealt out in number, weight, and measure. With what triumph of soul, in surveying either the general or particular providence of God, does he observe every line pointing out an hereafter, every scene opening into eternity![24]

This may seem mere poetic expression, but it is much more. The creation here seems to be a theological referent for Wesley. Similarly, in his letter to Miss March, Wesley writes, "It does not require a large share of natural wisdom to see God in all things—in all His works of creation as well as of providence. This is rather a branch of spiritual wisdom, and is given to believers more and more as they advance in purity of heart."[25] In "A Farther Appeal to Men of Reason and Religion: II," Wesley writes: "I grant, the existence of the creatures demonstratively shows the existence of their Creator. The whole creation speaks that there is a God."[26] Burtner and Chiles also cite this quotation from Wesley's *Compendium of Natural Philosophy:*

> The world around us is the mighty volume wherein God hath declared himself. Human languages and characters are different in different nations. . . . But the book of nature is written in an universal character, which every man may read in his own language. It consists not of words, but things which picture out the Divine perfections. The firmament every where expanded, with all its starry host, declares the immensity and magnificence, the power and wisdom of its Creator. Thunder, lightning, storms, earthquakes and volcanos, shew the terror of his wrath. Seasonable rains, sunshine and harvest, denote his bounty and goodness, and demonstrate how he opens his hand, and fills all living things with plenteousness. The constantly succeeding generations of plants and animals, imply the eternity of their first cause. Life subsisting in millions of different forms, shews the vast diffusion of this animating power, and death the infinite disproportion between him and every living thing.
>
> Even the actions of animals are an eloquent and a pathetic language. Those that want the help of man, have a thousand engaging ways, which, like the voice of God speaking to his heart, command him to preserve and cherish them. In the mean time, the motions or looks of those which might do him harm, strike him with terror, and warn him, either to fly from or arm himself against them. Thus it is, that every part of nature directs us to nature's God.[27]

It appears that the Brazilian theologians who support the idea of creation as part of Wesley's method in doing theology take Burtner and Chiles's argument as the foundation for their argument. This was confirmed to me by José Carlos de Souza in an interview. Wesley's own writings, of course, are the chief support for creation as a key component of the Wesleyan Pentalateral. Primary examples are the sermons "God's Approbation of His Works" and "The Wisdom of God's Counsels" and of course his *Survey of the Wisdom of God in the Creation: or A Compendium of Natural Philosophy.*

THE IMPORTANCE OF THE CREATION EMPHASIS

I agree with those Latin American Wesleyan theologians who identify God's purpose in the creation as a key aspect of Wesley's theological method, along with reason, experience, and tradition. Scripture is the central and normative source in this method, around which all other key aspects are formed and shaped. This can be visualized as indicated in figure 8C.

Figure 8C. Reconceiving the Wesleyan Pentalateral

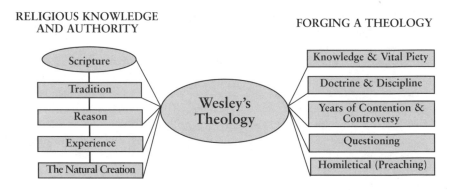

Clearly, the natural creation should not be seen as having equal authority with Scripture. Yet creation is one of the basic theological orientations used by Wesley, and it plays a large part in determining the way he does theology.[28]

An examination of *The Works of John Wesley* reveals that he uses the word "creation" 223 times in his writings, including sermons, letters, and journal. The word "Creator," referring to God, appears 248 times, and the words "creature" and "creatures" are used 695 times. Speaking of the world and human beings, Wesley uses the word "created" 291 times. Along with other cognate words, this makes a total of 1,462 instances (based on an electronic search in *The Works of John Wesley* on compact disk).

We may compare these instances with Wesley's use of other terms related to the Quadrilateral. Thus we find that the word "reason" appears 1,352 times; "experience," 532 times; and "tradition," 28 times (though no doubt including synonyms would increase the numbers significantly). The words "Scriptura," "Scripture," "Scriptures," "scriptural," and "scripturally" occur some 1,370 times.

Obviously, one's theological method is not discerned simply by counting the frequency of key terms. Still, the terms used to elaborate one's thought provide some footprints, some indications of a theologian's epistemology. Knowing the terminology thus helps us trace the process of constructing a theology.

Wesley's repeated use of terms relating to creation suggests that for him, the created order was a source for knowing what is true. This is a key Wesleyan epistemological approach—*the hermeneutics of the creation*. We may see the original creation as the point of departure and *the new creation* as the point of arrival. Thus, theology becomes an expression of how we experience, affirm, and elaborate the gospel. In this sense, creation is indeed a cornerstone in Wesley's theological methodology. In the same way that some "Third World" theologians view solidarity with the poor as "the hermeneutical locus of theology," Wesley sees God's purpose in creation as one of the most significant epistemological keys. Thus, drawing on what may be learned from creation is part of Wesley's theological method.

In practice, Wesley's theology has its own "integrative motif." Stanley Grenz and Roger Olson define an "integrative motif" as "the central idea that provides the thematic perspective in light of which the theologian understands all other theological concepts and gives them their relative meaning."[29] Generally, a theological system is ordered around one specific concept through which a theologian seeks to present the Christian faith, and around which all other concepts are formulated. "This concept acts as the central organizational feature of the systematic theology. It is the theme around which the various doctrines are structured."[30]

Could one say that Wesley's integrative motif is creation, or perhaps "the wisdom of God in creation"? Wesley worked out his mature theology as a sort of history of redemption. In this sense creation is the starting point (creation and fall), a continuing theme, and the ending point (the new creation) of his theology. Yet properly speaking, it is not the doctrine of creation that is Wesley's integrative motif. As Howard Snyder writes, "While creation is important for Wesley, it is not precisely his integrating motif. Rather it is more of an underlying presupposition."[31] Mildred Wynkoop and others have argued that the integrating center of Wesley's theology is the love of God.[32] Others, especially in the holiness movement, have contended that Christian perfection (which of course Wesley defined in terms of love) is Wesley's integrating theme. Snyder believes that Wesley's own writings show that "the redemptive, healing love of God is Wesley's integrating motif." Yet the theology of creation is important "because it reveals God's original intent and therefore the final scope of God's healing, redeeming love."[33] If, however, creation is a key "underlying presupposition" in Wesley's theology, it is important to reflect upon it. In fact, creation is a pulsating assumption throughout Wesley's writings, a sensitivity that permeates all his thought.

Wesley's mature theology can be seen in his eleven sermons numbered 54 to 64, beginning with "On Eternity" and ending with "The New Creation." In this sermon series Wesley shows that "God has a general plan of redemption that is being worked out on the plane of history. . . . History is moving toward the 'redemption of all things,' a general consummation and restoration that will bring about not only human redemption (holiness) but the redemption, healing, and reordering of the entire created order."[34] Theodore Runyon argues that

> the original creation, as it is portrayed in the biblical account, is not a matter of reason or experience, Wesley recognizes, but of divine disclosure. There is no way to reason back from what humanity is now to what we were originally created to be. The Fall stands between us and our original condition. Yet, from two sources—from the biblical accounts of creation and from the biblical prophecy of the fulfillment yet to come—Wesley is convinced we can arrive at an understanding of the divine purpose in the original creation.[35]

As noted above, in Wesley's theology creation is the starting point and the new creation is the ending or arrival point. This framework permeates all his theology, and thus underscores the fact that creation is an essential part of Wesley's theological framework.[36] Indeed, as Runyon points out, "The cosmic drama of the renewing of creation begins . . . with the renewal of the *imago Dei* in humankind. This is the indispensable key to Wesley's whole soteriology. . . . Wesley distanced himself from [Lutheran/Moravian] identification of salvation with justification alone, insisting that the 'great salvation' cannot stop short of a renewal of that original vocation for which humanity was created, to live as the image of God in the world."[37]

We can go further than this, however. Since creation is a basic theological orientation for Wesley, we can affirm that his theology is done from a fundamentally "creation-centered" perspective, as Stephen Bevans would phrase it. Bevans suggests:

> A creation-centered orientation to theology is characterized by the conviction that culture and human experience are generally good. Its perspective is that grace builds on nature, but only because nature is capable of being built on, of being perfected in a supernatural relationship with God.

> A creation-centered orientation sees the world as sacramental: The world is the place where God reveals Godself. Revelation does not happen in set-apart, particularly holy places, in strange unworldly circumstances, or in words that are spoken in a stilted voice. It comes in daily life, in ordinary words, through ordinary people. . . . Creation-centered theology approaches life with an analogical, not a dialectical, spirit or imagination, and sees a continuity between human existence and divine reality.
>
> It is not that the world is perfect and sinless. Creation-centered theology certainly acknowledges the reality and ugliness if sin. But sin is sin precisely because it is an aberration in such a beautiful world, an attempt to "get out of life what God has not put into it," and the only way that sin can adequately be exterminated is by confrontation with the power of good.[38]

This sentiment is in fact very Wesleyan. It characterizes Wesley's own theology well.

The way Wesley understood creation in relation to God's redemptive purposes is clarified by noting some of the ways he speaks about the world God made. Through the beauty of the natural creation, God communicates his own nature, goodness, and perfection to all created things. "The world around us is the mighty volume wherein God hath declared himself," Wesley writes. "It consists not of words, but things which picture out the Divine perfections. . . . Thus it is, that every part of nature directs us to nature's God."[39] As William Ragsdale Cannon notes, "In the Wesleyan conception, creation as the sovereign act of God has prior claim to providence, or the process of divine government. A thing is what it is: that is to say, it possesses the nature that it has, because of the creative act of God. And God remains always faithful to that which he has created. Thus in his government of the universe he is free to use inanimate objects as he pleases simply because inanimate creation is by nature passive in his hands."[40]

Wesley taught that "God has limited himself in the very act of creation. . . . Once God performed the creative act and called things into existence, he obligated himself to respect the creation which he had made and to remain faithful to the works of his own hand."[41] In fact, "the brute creation differed from man himself in only one instance. Whereas man was created for communion and fellowship with God, the brute creation was not."[42] Wesley believed, however, that human beings can actually "oppose God's will and so create numberless irregularities in God's government," as Cannon points out.[43]

For Wesley, "The space from the creation of man upon the earth to the end of all things is *the day of the sons of men.* The time that is now passing over us is properly *our* day. When this is ended, the day of the Lord will begin."[44] God created human beings as "the channel of conveyance between the Creator and the whole brute creation."[45] It is the duty of each person therefore "to 'glorify God, who hath bought him with' so high 'a price, in his body and in his spirit, which now are God's' by redemption, as well as by creation."[46] Note that in his theology of redemption Wesley ties his argument back to the fact of creation.

CREATION AND THE DYNAMIC OF LOVE

Wesley's theology is much more than simply the application of a particular method. In fact, its center, motivation, and deepest conviction is not a method, or any one element of the Quadrilateral or Pentalateral, but *love*. As noted earlier, Mildred Wynkoop stresses this in her book *A Theology of Love*, and in fact relates this to the question of method. Wynkoop writes:

> John Wesley has contributed a sound and usable approach to theology which is worthy of consideration in the solution of the problems relating to the theology/life syndrome. His "hermeneutic" was "love to God and man." This theme runs throughout his works. At least, when each doctrine of the Christian faith is identified and defined by him, the basic meaning invariably comes out "love." Wesley's thought is like a great rotunda with archway entrances all around it. No matter which one is entered, it always leads to the central Hall of Love, where, looking upward toward the dome one gazes into the endless, inviting sky. There is no ceiling to love. The return flow of love back through each doctrine in preaching and life serves to link every doctrine together into one dynamic architectonic and to show the theological stature and integrity of John Wesley.

This "rotunda theology," circular in form rather than being a "stairstep" approach, creates a problem for the theological analysis of Wesley. Theology, many believe, should have a systematic form. Each element should be clearly distinguished from every other element or doctrine. Each should follow logically from the one before it and lead comfortably into the one ahead. But in Wesley such neatness is impossible to capture because it is not there. Wesleyan doctrines cannot be so sharply separated from each other and from the whole idea of love. They are not "abstract."[47]

Wesley himself wrote that "Love existed from eternity, in God, the great ocean of love. Love had a place in all the children of God, from the moment of their creation. They received at once from their gracious

Creator to exist, and to love."[48] Here again one sees Wesley relating his most basic theology to the fact of creation. From Wesley's perspective, God's fundamental purposes in the creation of human beings cannot be useless or meaningless, for they are what God himself has wanted throughout eternity. In fact, this is one of the reasons why redemption and restoration are needed. To love and glorify God is the purpose of the creation of humanity. Thus Wesley says, "Since the enjoyment of these [powers to love and glorify God] was the one end of our creation, the recovering of them is the one thing now needful."[49] Only humans are able to understand, desire, and serve God. Wesley affirms that the human person "alone of all inhabitants of this world can acknowledge and praise him that made it."[50] The ultimate end of God's creation of man and woman is happiness in God, which due to the Fall is possible only by their restoration. "It is wisdom to aim at the best end by the best means," Wesley writes. "Now the best end which any creature can pursue is happiness in God. And the best end a fallen creature can pursue is the recovery of the favour and image of God."[51]

Wesley elaborates this in a passage that neatly combines his teaching about creation and redemption:

> And, first, why must we be born again? What is the foundation of this doctrine? The foundation of it lies near as deep as the creation of the world, in the scriptural account whereof we read, "And God," the three-one God, "said, Let us make man in our image, after our likeness. So God created man in his own image, in the image of God created he him." Not barely in his natural image, a picture of his own immortality, a spiritual being endued with understanding, freedom of will, and various affections; nor merely in his political image, the governor of this lower world, having "dominion over the fishes of the sea, and over the fowl of the air, and over the cattle, and over all the earth"; but chiefly in his moral image, which, according to the Apostle, is "righteousness and true holiness." In this image of God was man made. "God is love": accordingly man at his creation was full of love, which was the sole principle of all his tempers, thoughts, words, and actions. God is full of justice, mercy, and truth: so was man as he came from the hands of his Creator. God is spotless purity: and so man was in the beginning pure from every sinful blot. Otherwise God could not have pronounced him as well as all the other work of his hands, "very good." This he could not have been had he not been pure from sin, and filled with righteousness and true holiness. For there is no medium.s If we suppose an intelligent creature not to love God, not to be righteous and holy, we necessarily suppose him not to be good at all; much less to be "very good."[52]

CONCLUSION

What does Wesley's focus on creation as a key element of theological sensitivity and methodology suggest for the church's global mission today? The interweaving of creation throughout Wesley's writings provides some important clues. Six points seem especially relevant in an emerging global society. They are profound precisely because they are so simple and basic:

1. God is love, and his purposes for creation are good and redemptive.

2. Every person in the world is created in God's image and is "capable of God"—may know, trust, enjoy, and serve him, and even "partner" with him in the healing of creation.

3. All creation, and most basically the human heart, is damaged and diseased by sin and thus needs the redemption God provides through Jesus Christ by the Holy Spirit.

4. God's grace is always active in the world, drawing people to himself and seeking to restore all creation to God's purposes.

5. All people are stewards of God's creation, and Christians bear a special responsibility to model this—particularly in their concern for the spiritual and material needs of the poor.

6. God is progressively working out his purposes in history, despite Satanic opposition, and will eventually bring about the judgment of evil and the "restoration of all things."[53]

The gospel is global good news because there is no better news than the facts that God created all things good; loves all people on earth and the whole universe he has made; and is working to restore the dynamic of love to the whole warp and woof of his creation. The mission of the church is to announce this public truth, to invite people of all races and clans to participate in God's mission through faith in Jesus, and to form Jesus communities that live out the good news in all dimensions of the created order.

Finding effective models for mission in a postmodern world requires learning from the way nationals in "mission" lands have in fact experienced mission, argues Seth Asare. Drawing on mission history in Ghana, West Africa, Asare explores the ways that response to the Christian message can take quite different forms. Sometimes it is a response of mere convenience. At other times the response is based on some perceived relevance. But the deeper and more authentic response is characterized by genuine transformation consistent with the biblical vision of the kingdom of God.

CHAPTER NINE

CONVENIENCE, RELEVANCE, AND TRANSFORMATION: AN AFRICAN RESPONSE TO CHRISTIAN MISSION
Seth O. Asare

INTRODUCTION AND BACKGROUND

In his chapter in this book, Mortimer Arias makes a number of observations on the theology and history of Christian mission.[1] These relate especially to: (1) the bearers of the message of Christ, (2) the motivations for mission, (3) the global strategy for mission, and (4) the challenge of inculturation. Arias cautions that inculturation has contextual and global dimensions and that charges of syncretism should not deter the incarnation paradigm in global missions.

David Bosch has suggested several paradigms for Christian mission during the modern period.[2] These paradigms reflect theological shifts in Western culture. The challenges to mission in the postmodern era include how to shape a mission strategy that is informed by a mosaic of theologies. The situation is further complicated by the way in which the fact of pluralism in society is being confused with the ideology of pluralism.[3]

Statistics of global trends (summarized in table 1) reflect what is happening in the growth of Christianity worldwide. The figures in the table were computed from the annual Statistical Table on Global Mission 1992.[4] The data show that increase in world Christianity is lagging behind world population growth. Yet there is a phenomenal increase in

Table 1. Statistics of Global Trends (1900–2000)

Global Christian population as a percentage of the current world population: 33.0%

	Percentage Increase	
	1900–2000	1970–2000
Overall World Population	274%	64%
World Christian Population	240%	62%
Pentecostal/Charismatic Population	53,291%	625%
Christian Population in Asia	1,381%	216%
Christian Population in Africa	3,727%	186%
Christian Population in Latin America	693%	80%
Christian Population in North America	256%	26%

These figures were computed from David Barrett, "Status of Global Mission, 2001," *International Bulletin of Missionary Research* 25:1 (January 2001), p. 25.

Pentecostal/Charismatic Christianity. Also, the data indicate a rapid growth in Christianity in Third World countries compared to the Western world. These trends point to the continuing shift in the center of Christianity.

This shift in global Christianity necessitates a closer look at the theology and the mission history in so-called Third World countries.

The theology of a "mission-sending unit" has a considerable impact on the strategies and even the results of missions. This is why some of the assertions made by Maxie Dunnam with respect to evangelism can be modified and applied to missions. Dunnam says, "What you think about Christ determines what you do about evangelism," and "What we do about evangelism is shaped by what we think about grace."[5]

Thus, one's understanding of Christ will affect one's praxis in Christian mission. History seems to confirm that people's understandings of God and other cultures have certainly influenced mission methods. Also, there is another factor that is often neglected, and that is the self-understanding and the response of the recipients. The response of "mission recipients" shapes the short- and long-term results of all endeavors in mission.

In the history of mission, the responses of receiving cultures to the mission enterprise have sometimes been puzzling to mission-sending groups, to say the least. For example, for three centuries early Christian missions that went to West Africa struggled unsuccessfully to make any headway.[6]

This apparent failure of early Christian missions is not unique to West Africa. In Japan, two centuries of repudiation and persecution of the Christian faith preceded the establishment of the gospel.[7]

It is also important to add that after centuries of Christianity in Western culture, the dichotomy between profession and praxis of the faith still persists. Moreover, the rejection of Christianity by various groups in modern Western culture continues to be a major challenge. Thus, the hypothesis being explored here is not something that is limited to developing countries; and neither is it confined to premodernity. The initial negative responses to mission in Africa and Japan find parallels in all societies today. These dynamics suggest the need for continual reflection on the responses not only to Christian mission, but more basically to the gospel itself.

THE AIM AND HYPOTHESIS

In this chapter, therefore, I wish to formulate a theoretical hypothesis concerning the response to Christian mission based on the experience of the local people in West Africa. I will use a few incidents in the mission history of Ghana to illustrate the hypothesis. Lamin Sanneh's book *West African Christianity* will be the major source for the historical material.

I propose the terms "convenience," "relevance," and "transformation" as models of response in this theoretical hypothesis. These will serve as three models of responses by nationals to the missionary outreach. (I have chosen not to consider "indifference" or "rejection" in the hypothetical models presented. This is because the number of locals rejecting a religion has not often been factored into the evaluation of mission history. I have also decided not to consider issues dealing with "continuity," "discontinuity," and "adaptation" of Christianity into African traditional religions. This decision is partly due to the gradual but radical nature of the transformation I am proposing. Also, a proper understanding of transformation in the realm of God may mute some of the debate surrounding the subject.)

Convenience is used in this context to designate a situation in which a group welcomes the Christian faith because they do not have much choice. The close relationship between colonial power and mission activity often warrants this type of response to the Christian message. Under circumstances in which there are only a few alternatives to development and survival, it becomes convenient for the nationals to profess the faith of the one with the gun. Yet in many cases the nationals tried to manipulate the situation to their advantage.

Relevance in this context means some portions of the Christian message are deemed by the nationals to be relevant to their lives. They attempt, therefore, to conform. This conformity is partial, however, because it is based on whatever is not in conflict with the tradition or worldview of the people involved. This is a "pick and choose" attitude. What is lacking in this model is conviction that leads to commitment.

Transformation, on the other hand, refers to the situation in which nationals own the faith and their lives are changed by the gospel. Transformation is a continuous work of the Holy Spirit. The process of transformation is possible because of a response that has led to deep commitment. Under this category the bearers of the message become the nationals who are testifying to what has happened in their lives. The missionary is relegated to the periphery with regard to witnessing to the content and power of the message.

These models of response are not mutually exclusive. Neither should they be seen as progressive stages. As used here, these are simply models of observed response to Christianity from nationals in West Africa. They may also be models of response to Christianity even in Western culture.

THE HYPOTHESIS IN THE CONTEXT
OF MISSION HISTORY

A few cases in the mission history of Ghana will illustrate and expand upon the hypothetical models suggested above.

In 1503, the King of Efutu (a town eight miles from Elmina, on the coast of Ghana) decided to become a Christian. His six elders and a number of palace officials followed the noble example of the king. A church building was erected in the town by the Roman Catholic mission at the king's request. This was hailed initially as a breakthrough for the Roman Catholic mission in Ghana. However, later events revealed that the king was only interested in the Portuguese trade and the political protection that he believed this conversion would afford.

Again in 1513, the next King of Efutu similarly requested baptism. The local Roman Catholic mission did not greet this request with any enthusiasm because of their experience ten years earlier.

Four Augustinians arrived in Elmina in 1572. They began a serious attempt to bring the gospel to the local people. Residential segregation was introduced in the town. Local people who became Christians were settled near the castle, thus separating them from their cultural and family ties in the township. These new Christians were shielded from the traditional or cultural laws of their people. There is no doubt that the local people joined this commune for more than one reason. For some, it was a convenient way of escaping cultural demands or retribution within their society.

In 1577, the increasing presence of the Europeans precipitated a conflict between the traditional religion and the Christian faith. People reacted violently, resulting in a tragedy for the missionaries. The whole project was abandoned. The Augustinian mission suffered this fate partly because it was challenging the local people to critically examine their traditional religion in the light of the Christian faith. This was exactly what the local people did not want to do because they had always assumed that it was possible to get the benefits of Christianity without any commitment or any abandoning of their traditional worship.

These incidents in the mission history of Ghana show that the nationals, in many cases, found it *convenient* to respond positively to early Christian mission. Sometimes the responses reflected a different understanding of what was being presented in the light of their traditional religion. Other times the responses were seen as subordination to a superior colonial/religious power. These convenient responses, however, could not be the basis for establishing a lasting mission.

As an example of *relevance* I offer another story from Ghana. Wilhelm Johann Mueller, who served as chaplain in Fort Frederiksborg (1662–70), requested that the Bible be translated into the local languages. He made his contribution by compiling about eight hundred practical words and phrases. Other chaplains encouraged the African children to enroll in the castle schools. Thomas Thompson, one of the missionaries sent out by the Society for the Propagation of the Gospel (SPG) in Britain, helped in the development of the Fanti language and encouraged education.

There is no doubt that these efforts in the area of translation, the development of the local language, and education helped to make the missionary enterprise relevant to the local people. Sanneh, in his book *Translating the Message,* has documented what happens when nationals hear and read the gospel in their languages. The mission schools were a major factor in the education of nationals, and the graduates of these schools became the pioneers of liberation. Sanneh notes, "In their vernacular work, Christian missions helped nurse the sentiments for the national cause, which mother tongues crystallized and incited. The dramatic effects of vernacular translation thus prejudiced the colonial cause as much by historical coincidence as by ideological justification."[8]

It would be a mistake to consider all the graduates of the mission schools as Christians, of course. The nationals of Ghana saw aspects of Christian education as relevant to their development and to the new way of life that was emerging. The relevant portions of the missionary's message were, therefore, embraced by the nationals. Church membership and formal Christian practices (such as church weddings and funerals) gradually gained respect as part of the ethos in this African society.

However, the depth of commitment was brought into question whenever Christianity came into conflict with traditional worldviews. In this model we see a one-sided view of relevance—a view which often did not go far enough when measured by the challenges of kingdom living.

In contrast, I wish to present *transformation* as a response that involves total commitment. In this model, the work of grace takes place in people's lives to make them a new creation in Christ. It is important to note that this stage is not limited to a particular period in the mission history of Ghana. Neither does it necessarily sequentially follow the relevance model.

Transformation is uniquely a work of the Holy Spirit. It can take place in educated folk just as much as among uneducated people. When commitment and transformation are effected, those involved are owned by God. They become disciples who are praying and working for the transformation of others and the whole creation.

A visit to Ghana allowed me to witness transformation at work in a powerful way. I visited a youth camp where a number of Christian graduates were tutoring high school students in a Christian environment. Over two hundred students were involved in this intensive study camp. I found it interesting to observe that the leadership consisted of individuals who had been converted to Christianity through previous study camps. These students, who received positive experiences decades ago, were now in positions in which they were making disciples for Christ.

My visits in several congregations and institutions of learning in Ghana revealed a strong "lay" leadership in the sharing of the gospel and making disciples. The increasing number of young Christians who saw themselves as being in mission, both locally and outside the boundaries of the country, was encouraging. All these go to affirm transformation in progress.

CONCLUSION

There is a sense in which these models of convenience, relevance, and transformation cannot be confined to mission history. They can be observed in practical Christianity in all societies today. The motives for association and the level of commitment to Christianity vary. It is, however, better not to put people in boxes. God is always doing more in humanity than any of us can see. After all, it is beyond the human prerogative to judge the faith journeys of others.

Understanding responses to mission from the perspective of the nationals becomes important as we search for models and paradigms for mission in a postmodern world. All responses may be legitimate as far as they go, and perhaps each has its place in the history of mission. However, an authentic response is one that leads to commitment and transformation—one that is consistent with the vision of the kingdom of God.

The encounter between Jesus and the woman at the well is particularly instructive at this point. Here we get a glimpse of the mission of Jesus in operation. The woman's question and Jesus' response are pivotal for mission in our time and relevant to the question of global good news.

"How is it that you, a Jew, ask a drink of me, a woman of Samaria?" (John 4:9). The problem here is that the woman was placing priority on "dividing walls" and differences. The woman was pointing to a sore spot in mission strategies—the issue of "us" versus "them." This has been a major stumbling block to the mission of God. Emphasis on differences continues to sidetrack the purpose of God to reconcile humanity through Jesus Christ.

These differences may take other forms in the postmodern era. They include issues of race, class, gender, conservative/liberal theology, pluralism, and so on. Sometimes these issues have been taken out of the context of kingdom living and have become prerequisites for inclusion in the kingdom of God.

Jesus' answer to the Samaritan woman shifted the focus of the conversation back to transformation. Jesus said, "If you knew the gift of God, and who it is that is saying to you, 'Give me a drink,' you would have asked him, and he would have given you living water" (John 4:10). At the center of Christian mission is the offer of Christ. It is an offer that results not only in reconciliation but also in transformation.

This is the response that makes mission in all cultures credible.

Where does evangelism happen? By whom, and according to what model? Priscilla Pope-Levison says that Jesus is the "christological concentration" of the reign of God, the one through whom God's reign becomes visible. Yet the very life of Jesus points us to the importance of table fellowship as a locus of evangelism. Reminding us that table fellowship is a biblical image of the reign of God, she asks us to "imagine the impact on proclamation if the table, rather than the pulpit, became the central symbol" in our evangelization.

CHAPTER TEN

IS EVANGELIZATION LIBERATION?[1]
Priscilla Pope-Levison

INTRODUCTION: SPIRITUAL AND TEMPORAL DUALISM

In a pioneering 1981 article entitled "Evangelism and Liberation Theology," Norman Thomas of United Theological Seminary contended that "support for a holistic concept of evangelization and for creative new approaches based upon it may be the major contribution of liberation theologians to the church's mission."[2] Yet the so-called First World church has been reluctant to accept this contribution to evangelism that Norman Thomas portended.

We still struggle with the effects of a pervasive dualism that polarizes concepts in evangelism into either/or categories. There is an operative dualism in evangelism between the so-called spiritual and temporal spheres that affects both the Roman Catholic and Protestant traditions. The spiritual sphere includes faith matters and the church, while the temporal sphere includes everything else—including all political, economic, and social issues. It is important to investigate briefly this dualism, because it underlies the tendency to reject the contribution of liberation theology to evangelism.

Two specific examples from texts about evangelization will illustrate this dualism. The first is the Roman Catholic document *Evangelii Nuntiandi*, written in 1974. In this document Pope Paul VI devotes more than 10 percent of the content to the relationship between liberation and evangelism. The Pope employs an explicit dualism in arguing that evangelism has two constituent parts, the spiritual and the temporal. The first and the primary part of evangelization is the spiritual, which includes the proclamation of God's love in Jesus Christ and the proclamation of salvation in Jesus Christ.[3]

These two proclamations in the spiritual sphere, contends the Pope, are essential, for their absence "seriously dilutes the nature of evangelization itself."[4] The second and secondary part of evangelism is the temporal sphere, which includes "the rights and duties of every person, family life, life in society, international life, peace, justice, development, and liberation."[5] This list of issues in the temporal sphere is important, yet variable, depending on the situation. Being a secondary part of evangelism, in this case, means that as the circumstances change, emphasis on one temporal issue on the list could be replaced with another, more pressing temporal issue. Pope Paul VI thus argues that the spiritual part of evangelism is indispensable, while the temporal part is variable. Liberation, then, as a part of the temporal sphere of evangelism, may at times be included, and may at other times be superseded by other issues on the list.

In his definition of liberation, Pope Paul VI states clearly, however, that he understands liberation solely in the spiritual sphere and wants nothing to do with any other type of liberation. He writes, "It is hoped that all these considerations will help to remove the ambiguity which the word 'liberation' very often takes on in ideologies, political systems or groups. The liberation which evangelization prepares and proclaims is the one which Christ himself announced and gave to man by his sacrifice."[6] Thus, even though he considers liberation a part of the temporal sphere, the Pope defines liberation in spiritual terms.

Employing this spiritual/temporal dualism, the Pope argues that evangelism is primarily a spiritual endeavor that has little to do with liberation. What motivates his preoccupation to keep evangelism within the spiritual sphere is the fear that, otherwise, the church will devote its energies solely to liberation in the temporal sphere and neglect the spiritual. "Her activity, forgetful of all spiritual and religious preoccupation, would become initiatives of the political or social order. . . . Her message of liberation would no longer have any originality and would easily be open to monopolization and manipulation by ideological systems and political parties."[7]

In passing I would raise two questions about the relationship between evangelism and liberation in *Evangelii Nuntiandi*. First, why would a commitment to liberation consume the church's spiritual endeavors? The answer is hardly self-evident; yet the Pope never explains why he has this fear of an overzealous commitment to liberation. Second, can the spiritual and temporal spheres be so neatly packaged and separated from each other? Will not one spill over into the other, and vice versa? Certainly we have seen in the United States the spillover from the spiritual sphere into the political arena. Maybe this is etched in my mind because it was the first election year that I was old enough to vote, but I will never forget Moral Majority's impact in 1980 on selected Senate positions and perhaps even on the presidential race. Again I ask, can the spiritual and temporal spheres really be so separated from each other?

A second text that exhibits a similar—though less pronounced—dualism is Ben Campbell Johnson's book *Rethinking Evangelism*, published in 1987. Johnson espouses a spiritual/temporal dualism in his distinction between evangelism and mission. On the one hand, evangelism focuses upon the spiritual sphere and has as its goal "to awaken persons to their personal relationship with Jesus Christ and incorporate them into his body." On the other hand, mission focuses upon the temporal sphere with its goal of transforming "the culture in the direction of the kingdom of God."[8]

It is the priority he assigns to evangelism over mission that exposes Johnson's dualism. He gives evangelism the priority because of his view that changed persons in the spiritual sphere must precede a changed society in the temporal sphere. This is clear in his discussion of the kingdom of God. He indicates that it is evangelism that creates kingdom people; then, it is kingdom people who do mission.[9] With this statement, he clearly sets evangelism as a prior task to mission. Evangelism has an impact in the spiritual sphere on changing individuals who, through mission, have an impact on society in the temporal sphere.

Though I agree with much of Johnson's thinking, I would raise a question about his position. Doesn't his formulation, in the final analysis, make evangelism essential and mission optional? Even though he goes much further than many other writers on evangelism to integrate evangelism into social transformation, he still allows the dualism between personal conversion and societal commitment to stand. According to his framework, presumably one can become a Christian and fail, lamentably, to participate in transforming the culture in the direction of the kingdom of God.

This dualism restricts and hurts evangelism. Is there another model of evangelism that might eliminate dualisms? The purpose of this essay is to present another model—the model of evangelism from a liberation perspective.

Before presenting a new model, I want to state briefly two other reasons—in addition to transcending dualisms—why the proposed model is valuable. First, this model incorporates insights from those who are now among the majority of Christians but who have had, heretofore, little impact on the practice and theology of evangelism. The persons I am referring to are Third World Christians.

As Andrew Walls at the Centre for the Study of Christianity in the Non-Western World and others have pointed out, the center of gravity of Christianity has shifted from the First World to the Third World. Walls writes:

> One of the most important . . . events in the whole of Christian history, has occurred within the lifetime of people not yet old. It has not reached the textbooks, and most Christians, including many of the best informed, do not know it has happened. It is nothing less than a complete change in the centre of gravity of Christianity, so that the heartlands of the Church are no longer in Europe, decreasingly in North America, but in Latin America, in certain parts of Asia, and . . . in Africa.[10]

The movement in every arena—economic, political, and religious—has been largely one way, from the First World to the Third World. John Mbiti, an African theologian, poignantly questions this one-way movement in theology: "We have eaten theology with you; we have drunk theology with you; we have dreamed theology with you. . . . We know you theologically. The question is, do you know us theologically? Would you like to know us theologically?"[11]

Cannot the same be said about evangelism? Third World Christians can most assuredly say to First World Christians: "We have eaten evangelism with you. We have drunk evangelism with you. We have dreamed evangelism with you. We know you evangelistically. The question is, do you know us evangelistically? Would you like to know us evangelistically?" Is it possible that evangelism might be one arena in which there is a return trip of influence from the Third World to the First World? This model of evangelism from a liberation perspective endeavors to travel this return trip.

Second, this model of evangelism from a liberation perspective is valuable because it also incorporates insights from those who are among the voiceless in the First World. The persons I am referring to are women. In perusing five hundred computer data entries on recent books, articles, and book reviews on evangelism, I found fewer than twenty-five by women. Of that small number, the three articles on evangelism that I have written constitute more than 10 percent of the articles—that's a tragedy!

Undaunted and only slightly discouraged, I forged through a publication called "Teaching Evangelism: A Collection of Syllabi from North American Seminaries Compiled in 1989 for the Academy for Evangelism in Theological Education."[12] This collection contains 138 syllabi from more than fifty contributors. Among all the books on evangelism required on these 138 syllabi, only two were written by women. One book, *Out of the Salt Shaker and Into the World: Evangelism as a Way of Life*, was written by Rebecca Manley Pippert, and the other, *How to Share Your Faith Without Being Offensive*, was written by Joyce Neville. Looking through the syllabi, I noticed an assignment that was to focus on a leading personality and/or movement within evangelism. The professor included a list of 32 names from which the students were to choose. All 32 were men's names.

My hope for the proposed model is that, by its attempt to eliminate dualisms that plague evangelism, and by its attempt to incorporate over-looked insights from Christians in the Third World and women in the First World, it will contribute fresh perspectives to doing and thinking evangelism.

There are four steps in this model for evangelism from a liberation perspective.[13] The first three steps correspond to the methodology used in the Vatican II document *Gaudium et Spes*—fact, reflection, and recommendations.[14] In the first step, the purpose is to gather facts about the context of the marginalized. In the second step, the purpose is to reflect theologically on the reign of God and its bearing on the context. In the third step, the purpose is to act by choosing means of evangelism appropriate to steps one and two. And in the fourth step, which is added to the three steps from *Gaudium et Spes,* the purpose is to gather a community that will do evangelism from a liberation perspective.

My proposal follows this outline. For each step, I will first present a liberation perspective that reflects the Latin American context. Then I will suggest an adaptation for each step that arises from women's experience on the margins in North America. In this way, each step will have a two-part approach, first from a Latin American liberation perspective, and then from a North American woman's perspective.[15]

STEP 1: CONSIDER THE CONTEXT FROM THE PERSPECTIVE OF THE MARGINALIZED

In this step the evangelist asks two questions: Who are the marginalized, and what is their context? The first question requires looking to the periphery of society. The evangelist will encounter there those who are, according to Orlando Costas, "victims par excellence of a history of egoism, injustice, greed, alienation, and despair that has tragically characterized humanity."[16] I use the word "encounter" advisedly, for it is essential that the evangelist meet the marginalized personally, and not merely know the statistics and percentages of marginalization. However, this encounter is not purely empathy, for the evangelist must understand the encounter in the larger context of religious, economic, political, and social structures. In this way, the personal encounter and social analysis are held together.[17]

The difficulty in this step is that most evangelists or evangelizing communities will not choose to encounter the marginalized. In my first pastorate I served a church located right across the street from a low-income housing development. The marginalized were literally feet from our door. A few people from the development would drift in and out of our building, and one or two summers the church sponsored a swimming program for the children that was prompted by their loitering on church property, coupled with a theft or two. But we considered them intruders, outsiders, in our territory. We never encountered them, so we never had a reason to gather the facts about their marginalization.

As we look at the North American context, who might be the marginalized? No matter which oppressed group one chooses, women will be the oppressed within the oppressed. In other words, women on the periphery are doubly oppressed because sexism heightens the effects of socioeconomic, religious, or political oppression. Even in North America, this is the case. For example, the feminization of poverty in North America is a recognizable pattern. According to sociologist Virginia Sapiro, the feminization of poverty pattern is best illustrated by the evidence that families maintained only by women are much more likely to live under the poverty line than families maintained either by men or by a married couple. Sapiro showed that in 1986, 40 percent of white families maintained by women were impoverished compared with only 8 percent of families maintained by men or married couples. Poverty statistics are even more startling for nonwhite women who maintain families. Among blacks the percent of impoverished families headed by women rises to 58 percent, and for Hispanic women, the percentage increases again to 60 percent.[18]

However, to answer fully the question, what is the context of the marginalized, the evangelist must look beyond the statistics to the ideology that allows the statistics to exist and even to increase. Most women are victims of an ideology of domination.[19] An ideology can be defined as a "basic system of goals and values, plus the means to achieve them."[20] The goal of the ideology of domination is to suppress and control certain groups within the society. This ideology is effective because it structures society into subject/object dualisms, such as male/female, and then accords positive and negative values to opposing sides of the dualism.

The ideology of domination often has a story or myth that portrays the dominated group in a negative light, solidifying the subject/object dualism in the minds of most people. For women there is the sin of Eve (Gen. 3:13). The application of Eve's sin to all women explains why women are often labeled as easily tempted and fickle-minded. Then, in turn, any evidence of these qualities justifies the domination of women. The ideology of domination has been institutionalized in society within patriarchal structures; it hardly needs to be said that even the church is guilty of perpetuating it.

In step one, then, the evangelist must encounter the doubly oppressed and get to know them. In that personal encounter the evangelist will hear the myths whose ideological basis victimizes the doubly oppressed, and the evangelist will identify the systems and structures that institutionalize the ideology. It is this experience of personal encounter that leads the evangelist to ask larger questions and to analyze the context. Through the encounter and the analysis, the evangelist will be prepared to move on to step two and reflect on the context of the doubly oppressed in the light of God's reign.

STEP 2: COMPARE FINDINGS FROM STEP ONE WITH THE VISION OF GOD'S REIGN

Billy Abraham reminds us in his book *The Logic of Evangelism* that theology and evangelism must be partners. This is a two-way endeavor. Theology must include evangelism as a topic for serious reflection, and evangelism must operate from a theological foundation. According to Abraham, neither of these is happening at present. On the one hand, he criticizes theology for ignoring evangelism and begins his book with the statement, "One of the undeniable features of modern theology is the scant attention it has given to the topic of evangelism."[21] On the other hand, he criticizes modern evangelism for a "steady decline in the theological abilities of the better-known evangelists over the generations."[22]

Liberation theologians are addressing both lacunae. I have argued elsewhere that in evangelism, these theologians integrate theology and praxis. They are theologians who devote a great deal of attention to evangelism in their writings. And they are evangelists who ground their practice of evangelism in a theological foundation; that foundation is the reign of God.[23]

Liberation theologians understand the reign of God to be God's new order, which is an order of liberation in every realm. God's design is the liberation of the human creation and the cosmos "*from* every stigma (including suffering, division, sin, and death) and liberation *for* real life, for open-ended communication of love, grace, and plenitude in God."[24] The three most important characteristics of God's reign, from a liberation perspective, are God's preference for the poor, its present and future dimensions, and its visibility in Jesus Christ.

First, God has a preference for the poor. This preference is woven throughout Scripture, but perhaps is most evident in the covenant code in Exodus 20–23; in Jesus' explicit statement about the blessedness of the socioeconomically poor in the Lucan Beatitudes; and in the Lucan travel narratives in which Jesus' stories and teachings declare a preference for the poor. Because of their preferred status, the poor occupy the place of honor in God's reign. Following from this, Gustavo Gutiérrez suggests that evangelizers will find God's reign in history among the poor.[25]

Second, God's reign is both a present historical reality and an event yet to come within history. Evangelists proclaim its presence in history and labor for its final realization yet to come. This human labor has an impact on God's reign and furthers it within human history. Thus, "every act, action, or plan which, here and now on this earth, realizes God's plan, even if only partially, will have an eternal future."[26]

Third, because Jesus Christ is the key to understanding God's reign, he is "the christological concentration of the reign of God," as Jon Sobrino says.[27] Segundo Galilea concurs. Describing the relationship of Jesus and the reign of God, he says Jesus "is its origin and its concentration. He is its goal and its port of entry."[28] Throughout his ministry Jesus manifested the nature of God's reign when he preached good news to the poor, denounced oppressors, liberated through healings and exorcisms, and stood in solidarity with the poor and the marginalized. Through his death and resurrection Jesus inaugurated God's reign for all who would enter. In Jesus, the reign of God becomes visible.

Once the vision of God's reign has been established (which from a liberation perspective would include three characteristics: its preference for the poor, its present and future dimensions, and its visibility in Jesus Christ), then the evangelist questions the discrepancies between the reality of the context and the vision. For example, the evangelist might ask: Does the context of the marginalized give them a preference, as does God? Does the context encourage the marginalized to work actively in the present for God's reign? Do the marginalized understand that Jesus stood in solidarity with the poor of his day and desires as the risen Christ to stand in solidarity with them now? The evangelistic message in both word and deed should be tailored directly to eliminating the discrepancies between the context of the marginalized and the reign of God.

Evangelizing women among the marginalized in North America requires at least one adaptation in this second step. In particular, one element illustrates the kind of adaptation of the above vision of God's reign that is needed to evangelize the doubly oppressed. This adaptation is the *social reintegration* of those on the margins. In Jesus' ministry the table was the place where social reintegration happened. Jesus seemed always to be accused of eating with "tax collectors and sinners" and even commended an unnamed woman who caressed his feet while he was at table. Even his vision of the future is encapsulated in the image of the heavenly festive table: "Then people will come from east and west, from north and south, and will eat in the kingdom of God. Indeed, some are last who will be first, and some are first who will be last" (Luke 13:29-30).

Jesus' miracles also socially reintegrate people. The paradigmatic miracle in this respect is the healing of the hemorrhaging woman who was impoverished by unsuccessful visits to doctors and whose bleeding required social isolation according to Torah. By not only healing her but also addressing her directly as a "daughter" (of Abraham), Jesus reintegrated her into the social and religious world of early Judaism.[29]

The evangelist of women on the margins, in this second step, must consider the discrepancy between the social estrangement of women in the present context and the social reintegration in the reign of God exemplified in the ministry of Jesus. To encapsulate and concretize God's reign for the doubly oppressed, the evangelist might choose to portray the reign of God using the biblical metaphor of the table. With this image of the reign of God, the evangelist disavows a primarily individualistic interpretation of God's reign as something merely within the hearers' hearts and promotes instead a feast at the table with Jesus where the last are first. In light of the experience of exclusion that women have felt, the table as an inclusive, welcoming, celebrative image for God's reign can become a startling invitation to new life in God's reign.

STEP 3: CHOOSE THE MEANS OF EVANGELISM MOST LIKELY TO CHANGE THE CONTEXT

Once the evangelist has analyzed the discrepancy between God's reign and the contemporary context, he or she must choose the means of evangelism by which the context can become more consistent with God's reign. Several means of evangelism are appropriate to this model: proclamation, denunciation, calling to conversion, and witness. Each of these has an important place in traditional evangelism, but in evangelism from a liberation perspective, they are nuanced differently. Then, when we turn to the context of women among the marginalized in North America, each of these four means of evangelism is further adapted to reflect women's experience.

Proclamation of the good news is central, of course, to traditional evangelism. From a liberation perspective, proclamation declares the good news of God's liberating actions in human history. Proclamation recounts God's liberating actions in the past in creation, the Exodus, and ultimately in Jesus Christ. It also announces God's ongoing work in the present and future for liberation. Proclamation announces that God has acted, God does now act, and God will act within human history.

In adapting proclamation from a liberation perspective to women's experience on the margins, I suggest that the primary concern to women is not the content but the location. Where is the place of proclamation? Proclamation has traditionally occurred in the pulpit. However, many women are ambivalent about the pulpit, for historically the pulpit has been a symbol of exclusion within the church. Examples of this exclusion are manifold, but the most recent emerged in my research for this paper. I picked up the book *The Evangelistic Preacher*, published by Broadman Press in 1985, and on the cover was a pulpit occupied by a man in a suit and tie. One hand held an open Bible, and the other was poised in a gesture that resembled a pistol. The book's content reflected its cover. Sermon illustration after sermon illustration was taken from wars. What is a more powerful symbol of the exclusion of women in the secular sphere than war?

Males in the pulpit and male sermon illustrations coupled with the traditional strictures against women's preaching have compelled women to do their proclamation elsewhere. Women have circumvented the power centers of evangelism and have evangelized in informal settings, often around a table. The table as a place for proclamation coincides with the table as an image of God's reign and its concomitant social reintegration. Imagine the impact on proclamation if the table, rather than the pulpit, became the central symbol.

Some will say, though, that this is not evangelism from a liberation perspective because, once again, women are at the table and outside of the power centers. But that is precisely the point! Evangelism from a liberation perspective occurs on the periphery, far from the center of power. But it issues a challenge to those committed to evangelism: Will they recognize women's experience of proclamation at the table and allow it to challenge their thinking and practice of evangelism, or will they keep on sharing their war stories?

Denunciation, a second means of evangelism, is an element of traditional evangelism that typically focuses on individual sin. Speaking for the Latin American context (but I would suggest that it is often true for North Americans as well), Orlando Costas stated that most evangelistic denunciation concerned only individual ethics, such as the evils of liquor, tobacco, and drugs.[30] As an evangelist from a liberation perspective, Costas contended that limiting denunciation to such personal evils restrains the potential of denunciation. Instead, denunciation should focus primarily upon discrepancies between the present context and God's reign—that is, the findings of steps one and two.

These discrepancies may include false ideologies, unjust institutions that exclude the marginalized, and a person's own capitulation to these ideologies and institutions. As Mortimer Arias explains, "Part of the task of the Christian messenger is to criticize false gods and false prophets, to unmask the powers and principalities, to confront them, and to denounce anything that is against God's dream, against God's purpose."[31] Denunciation from a liberation perspective does not ignore the reality of individual sin; rather, it considers the larger ramification of that sin and the ideologies and institutions that support it.

In adapting denunciation to women's experience, evangelists must be careful to consider sin in light of the ideology of domination in which women are the objects in the subject/object dualism. The sins of the oppressed, or those who are objects, differ from the sins of the oppressor, or those who are subjects. In her groundbreaking article "The Human Situation: A Feminine View," written more than thirty years ago, Valerie Saiving argued that the definition of sin in contemporary theology as "pride, will-to-power, exploitation, self-assertiveness, and the treatment of others as objects rather than persons" reflects men's experience and men's sins; yet sin as pride has been universally applied to both men and women.[32] In contrast, Saiving recognizes that "the temptations of woman *as woman* are not the same as the temptations of man *as man*." She suggests that women's sins are "better suggested by such items as . . . lack of an organizing center or focus; dependence on others for one's own self-definition . . . in short, underdevelopment or negation of the self."[33] These sins are very different from sins of pride! If this is true, evangelists cannot continue denouncing sin in generic terms, for generic often equals male. Pride or self-assertiveness, often denounced as sin, may be precisely the qualities a woman on the margins needs to develop in order to break the ideology of domination.

A third means of evangelism, the *call to conversion*, is most often in traditional evangelism the point at which the individual is called to turn away from sin and enter into a personal relationship with Jesus Christ. Liberation theologians offer an important critique of any call to conver-

sion that stops there and goes no further. Emilio Castro considers inadequate an evangelism that strives to gain a convert's commitment to Jesus
first and then, at some later point, teaches the convert the importance of
loving one's neighbor. Yet this is precisely what Ben Johnson advocates.
In this kind of evangelism a commitment to Jesus is essential, but a commitment to neighbor is optional. Castro writes, "It appears to me an
erroneous theology which teaches that there is . . . a movement of love
to God first and a movement of love to neighbor after. . . . In [such] evangelistic preaching we call people to a vertical relationship and afterwards
we market Christian education to teach them the horizontal relationship
with the neighbor."[34]

In the liberation perspective, the evangelist recognizes that conversion
is a *simultaneous* turning toward God and neighbor. This evangelism
rejects a hierarchical dualism between the horizontal and the vertical,
between the temporal and the spiritual. Because conversion occurs within a sociohistorical context, even the interior, individual change has a
collective, societal impact. At the very least, conversion should create
new relationships. As Leonardo Boff writes, "Positively viewed, conversion is the implementation of altered relationships at every level of personal and social reality. These altered relationships will express concrete
forms of liberation and anticipate the kingdom of God."[35]

Earlier I suggested that an understanding of the reign of God for
women on the margins has as its center a vision for social reintegration
around the table. And if, as I have just argued, conversion is a commitment both to Jesus and to neighbor, then the call to conversion must be
understood as an invitation to join Jesus and those gathered with him at
the table. Jesus himself issued invitations to feast with him to those who
would not be scandalized by his controversial table habits. These habits
had gained him a reputation that must have been common knowledge,
for he referred to it himself in Luke 7:34: "The Son of Man has come eating and drinking, and you say, 'Look, a glutton and a drunkard, a friend
of tax collectors and sinners!'" Many were put off by Jesus' actions at
the table, but others responded to his invitation. Who are these who
accepted Jesus' invitation? Luke does not keep us in suspense. Three
verses later, after Jesus calls himself a friend of tax collectors and sinners,
we read of the first one who came to Jesus at the table. She was a woman
of the city, a sinner, who crashed an all-male dinner party to attend to
Jesus' feet with her tears, her hair, her kisses, and her oil.

The life of Jesus provides a further refinement of the call to conversion
from a liberation perspective. Jesus made different demands on different
groups of people in different contexts.[36] While some of what he said,
such as "the kingdom of God has come near; repent" (Mark 1:15),

applied to all people, the concrete nature of the conversion he required varied. Jesus called the poor to begin to believe that God could ameliorate their apparently hopeless situation. The poor must be converted from despair to hope in the recognition that the reign of God is theirs (Luke 6:20). In other words, the poor must be converted "so that they may *believe* in the good news, precisely because it is *so good*, so seemingly incredible, and so different from their accustomed situation."[37] In contrast, Jesus called the wealthy to evaluate critically their contribution to oppressive institutions, the very institutions that prevent them from being a neighbor to the poor. The Pharisees, for instance, by means of their interpretation of Torah, provided religious rationale for regarding poverty as the effect of sinfulness. In this way they helped to produce a class of oppressed people who were regarded as both socioeconomically oppressed and religiously impoverished. Consequently, Jesus called the Pharisees to a conversion that meant a move "from the oppressive security of the letter of the law to the liberating insecurity of having to opt for the poor, even in the face of God's very word."[38]

Thus, the evangelist within a liberation perspective must develop and practice a critical awareness of the context as he or she calls to conversion. For instance, the call to conversion at the table of a businessman's lunch in the downtown Hilton Hotel will be different from the call to conversion at the coffee break table of housekeepers who clean the hotel. Their sins may not be the same, and they certainly will have different life experiences. Therefore, the invitation to the table with Jesus and those gathered with him must reflect the context, which includes the intersection of such factors as class, race, and gender.

Witness, a fourth means of evangelism, traditionally has been understood as speaking about and doing deeds that show forth one's personal faith. In contrast, the evangelist from a liberation perspective defines witness as living a life of personal integrity in a context of injustice. Such integrity requires a realignment of one's commitments vis-à-vis oppressive structures and ideologies. Otherwise, without such integrity, a contradiction separates the evangelist's word and deed, the evangelist's proclamation and lifestyle.

Orlando Costas reminded those who would be evangelists of the thorough conversion necessary to be a witness to Jesus Christ. Being a witness "implies that it is impossible to bring good news of salvation . . . if one is allied to structures that disregard life and perpetuate injustice. . . . It would mean sharing the liberating message of the gospel with one hand and justifying domination and exploitation with the other."[39]

What does this mean for women's experience on the margins? If conversion is accepting the invitation to the feast, then witness involves bringing the feast to persons on the margins, especially to the doubly oppressed. Jesus told a story about such a witness: "When you give a luncheon or a dinner, do not invite your friends or your brothers or your relatives or rich neighbors, in case they may invite you in return, and you would be repaid. But when you give a banquet, invite the poor, the crippled, the lame, and the blind. And you will be blessed, because they cannot repay you" (Luke 14:12-14).

Tony Campolo tells a story about a night when he was unexpectedly a witness to the doubly oppressed. He threw a surprise birthday party at 3:00 A.M. in a Honolulu donut shop for a prostitute and invited her coworkers and the owner of the shop to the celebration. Campolo brought the feast to women on the margins and, in that act, witnessed to the one who was called "a friend of tax collectors and sinners."

In step three, then, the evangelist can employ any of these means of evangelism—proclamation, denunciation, call to conversion, and witness—in order to change the context in the direction of God's reign. The context, as well, will determine the order in which the means are employed. For instance, in a situation of extreme injustice, denunciation may be the initial means of evangelism, before proclamation.

STEP 4: CONVOKE A CONCERTED COMMUNITY EFFORT FOR EVANGELIZATION

Evangelism from a liberation perspective is not the sole responsibility of the individual evangelist, whether male or female. It is only in community that evangelism from a liberation perspective can be accomplished, and particularly with a very specific kind of community.

The community must be one whose majority members are the marginalized. It is they who understand firsthand the context of the margins. It is they who can interpret the disparity between their context and the vision of God's reign. It is the marginalized within the community who can extend the invitation to the table to those on the margins. As the document from the 1980 Melbourne conference of the World Council of Churches asks about the poor: "Might it not be that they have the clearest vision, the closest fellowship with the crucified Christ who suffers in them as with them? Might it not be that the poor and powerless have the most significant word for the rich and powerful: that Jesus must be sought on the periphery, and followed 'outside the city'?"[40]

In Latin America, communities of the poor and those in solidarity with them are called "base communities" to underscore their location at the grassroots of society. Base communities are especially significant in calling the institutional church to be converted, to turn from its sinful collusion with the powerful, and to turn toward the poor in solidarity. In this way, these communities evangelize the church anew by subverting its arrangement and status quo.[41] Leonardo Boff explains that base communities "are those principally responsible for the evangelization of the bishops and even of true conversion of the cardinals and bishops, priests and theologians."[42] The base communities subvert the arrangement and status quo of the cardinals and bishops, and through that subversion, many are converted!

In the same way, women could form communities similar to base communities to evangelize the institutional church by subverting its arrangement and status quo.[43] Even Jesus learned from women about going beyond the status quo. Jesus was educated in these matters by women and, not surprisingly, at the table. In particular, two women convinced Jesus to extend the reign of God from Jews to all people. In a conversation about food that took place at a meal, a foreign woman adroitly challenged Jesus to extend the bread of his table to non-Israelites (Mark 7:24-30). When this foreign woman, "a Gentile, of Syrophoenician origin," begged him to cast a demon out of her daughter, Jesus retorted, "Let the children [i.e., Israelites] be fed first, for it is not fair to take the children's food and throw it to the dogs." The woman's response, "Sir, even the dogs under the table eat the children's crumbs," convinced him to extend his power of exorcism beyond the borders of Israel. She who sought wholeness for her daughter is the "foremother" of all Gentile Christians.[44]

Another conversation with a woman provided the impetus for Jesus to extend his work beyond the confines of Judaism. This conversation also dealt with the topic of food. Jesus and a Samaritan woman conversed at a well about the topic of water while the disciples went away to provide food for the table. They returned, urging Jesus to "eat something." Jesus retorted, "I have food to eat that you do not know about." In typical Johannine irony, this comment indicates that the table at which Jesus ate was the conversation with this woman. As a result of this conversation, the woman brought many Samaritans to faith.

Just as women prompted Jesus' witness to persons beyond Judaism, so, in the same way, communities of women can extend the witness of the church to the oppressed and the doubly oppressed. These communities of women can evangelize the church anew by subverting its arrangement and status quo. After all, who knows better through experience about the church's collusion with patriarchal structures and ideologies? Who knows better what it feels like to be a new creature in

Jesus Christ, neither male nor female, and yet to be restricted as female in the church?

So there we have it—yet another model of evangelism. This model joins ranks with Robert Coleman's master plan, James Kennedy's evangelism explosion, Becky Pippert's salt shaker evangelism, Bob Webber's liturgical evangelism, and John Wimber's power evangelism. What we probably need least is one more model; what we need to be doing is evangelism itself.

But where? Where does evangelism occur in these other models? Is it on the periphery where the bulk of humanity lives? This model of evangelism from a liberation perspective begins there, on the periphery, and builds an evangelizing community there, on the periphery.

What we probably need least is one more model; what we need to be doing is evangelism itself. But who are the primary evangelists in these other models? Are they women? The poor? Third World Christians? This model of evangelism from a liberation perspective challenges evangelists to learn from those who have circumvented the power centers and who are evangelizing on the periphery, around a table. At the very least, this model of evangelism from a liberation perspective may help us begin to uncover blind spots, unmask biases, and most important, unleash the potential of unused resources in the unusual invitation to join with Jesus and those at table with him in the reign of God.

Cultures are diverse and complex. How can we communicate the love of Christ across deep cultural divides? Drawing on his many experiences around the world, Robert Tuttle explores several "cross-cultural common denominators" that can be of use when Christians and non-Christians from different cultural backgrounds meet each other.

CHAPTER ELEVEN

CROSS-CULTURAL COMMON DENOMINATORS: TOOLS FOR A MORE USER-FRIENDLY EVANGELISM
Robert G. Tuttle, Jr.

I need to be more of an anthropologist. For years I've been working on theology and technique, only to realize that I need additional tools to make evangelism more "user-friendly." Taking a page from Paul's "all things to all people," I began looking for transferable concepts in order to make communication between cultures and subcultures—and (for that matter) even across the dinner table—more effective.

Some years ago I began teaching a course entitled "Cross-cultural Evangelism." Right from the start I used several cases to illustrate the importance of being sensitive to cultural issues. One such case, the well-known "Peace Child"—in which two warring tribes are reconciled through the exchange of infants—sparked an interest.

Children are naturally cross-cultural. Around the world they laugh, cry, and even ridicule each other ("Nyah, nyah, nyah-nyah, nyah!") in the same language. So what about other cross-cultural common denominators? I decided to do some hands-on research. I set off around the world. Throughout Asia, the Middle East, North Africa, and Eastern Europe, I looked for concepts and even ideologies that communicate with more or less equal effectiveness across cultural boundaries. Then, after returning home, I continued my research in some of the largest urban centers in the United States. Here I briefly describe some of my findings.

THE CARE AND CONCERN FOR CHILDREN

Perhaps it is best to begin with the obvious. Children are of universal concern. Few things elicit more sacrifice than their care. Few things arouse more outrage than their abuse.

On a train from Yanji (Manchuria) to Beijing, I sat across from a couple taking their son to a hospital to be treated for cancer. Though I could understand no Mandarin, it was obvious to me that the boy was ill. At one point I simply pointed to the sky, folded my hands as in prayer, and then pointed to the boy.

The communication was instantaneous. Someone was summoned who could speak a little English. Smiles, handshakes, and eventually gifts were exchanged throughout the cabin. Although officially these parents may have been atheists, concern for a child opened the door to conversation about God.

If the care of children elicits sacrifice, then the abuse of children arouses outrage. Recently a man confessed to me at the communion rail following a worship service that he had molested his daughter, his granddaughter, and was now molesting his great-granddaughter. What I said to him surprised even me. With full conviction I said that one of two things was going to take place that very night. Either he was going to get help or he was going to jail.

Do we really know just how difficult it is to believe that God loves us if we were abused as children? Little wonder that in Asian cultures children must not be approached by a stranger unless the parent of the child initiates the contact.

God's gift of a son was genius. God was first revealed in the flesh not as a father or mother or even as an adult, but as a child. With growing awareness, that child came more and more to understand just who he was. As that child became a man, the realization of his mission was shared with others. Eventually that mission led to a cross—a sacrifice eternal in the heavens—and then culminated with the resurrection, that we too might live eternally.

It should be no surprise that that child himself speaks directly to the point: "Truly I tell you, unless you change and become like children, you will never enter the kingdom of heaven" (Matt. 18:3). And again: "Let the little children come to me, and do not stop them; for it is to such as these that the kingdom of heaven belongs" (Matt. 19:14).

In Bombay, India, I had an opportunity to get acquainted with a Muslim man in the airport where we were both waiting for a delayed plane. We decided to share a meal. I soon learned that he had been born in Kenya and was teaching at the University of London, and that he spent several months a year in India researching the growth of food crops.

Within minutes the conversation somehow turned to God. He confessed that his wife had recently had a religious experience and that she was teaching their seven-year-old daughter how to pray. Somewhat to his dismay, the child was asking him to pray with her as well, but he could not bring himself to do it.

I thought to myself, "You jerk, why don't you pray with your daughter?" Then I said out loud, "You believe in God—why won't you pray with your daughter?" He replied, "Yes, I believe in God, but why would God want to hear my prayers?"

In a flash I responded, "I'm going to tell you a story. On your return home your plane lands in London. You work your way through passport control and customs, and as you exit the security area you are hard to miss [he must have weighed over 400 pounds]. So she sees you before you see her. Suddenly you hear 'Daddy, Daddy!' as she works her way through the crowd. Then as she fights her way clear of the people she runs across the open space and jumps into your arms, hugging and kissing you, saying all the while, 'Daddy, Daddy, you are the most wonderful daddy in the whole wide world!' How would that make you feel?"

As I looked at him I could see tears beginning to form. He replied, "You know how that would make me feel. It would make me feel wonderful."

I simply added, "So why would God be any different?"

He concluded with a smile, "I can't wait to get home and pray with my daughter." The care and concern for children is cross-cultural—and a cross-cultural bridge for the good news of God's love.

COMPETITIVE SPORTS

The increasing number of U. S. major league baseball players recruited from Japan is evidence of that country's love of—and proficiency in—the sport. Latin America and Europe are consumed with soccer. I was amazed that in many Asian countries basketball is the craze. We were in parts of China where small villages seemingly had but one electric light and that was over a basketball hoop; and the kids played most of the night. On one trip I had a student with me who could slam-dunk a basketball. All he had to do was give a brief demonstration and the people would flock—it was instant communication.

Just the way one approaches a sport provides a transferable concept.

If a stronger player demonstrates courtesy and sportsmanship, the other players frequently respond in kind. Conversation between games can easily turn to Jesus without giving offense. If we had just had the stamina, evangelistic opportunities were available to us all night long on basketball courts all over that part of the world.

In Israel I was staying at a hostel at the foot of Masada. There were seventy-five to a hundred people sharing large dormitory-type rooms and common tables for eating. For several hours I attempted to engage people in conversation, but no one seemed interested. During the evening meal I found it difficult to communicate even with those who sat directly across the table from me.

After dinner a young Frenchman was challenging all comers to a game of chess. He was apparently the current champion and so intimidated the group that no one dared to take him on. Then, seeing me, he offered me the challenge. Since I've played a bit of chess and love an adventure, I accepted.

Immediately fifty to sixty people gathered round, cheering for the underdog—me. As the game developed the Frenchman became overconfident and careless, and I defeated him in thirty moves. The result: instant communication. Suddenly I was a celebrity. I was asked to speak. Somewhat embarrassed, I asked, "About what?" They replied, "Tell us your story." I have but one story—Jesus. They listened.

The next day I decided to climb to the top of Masada rather than take the cable car. On the trail I was approached by a young man who had heard "my" story the night before and was curious to know more. At the top of the mountain he accepted Jesus Christ as his Savior and Lord. We still correspond.

The psalmist writes: "In the heavens he has set a tent for the sun, which comes out like a bridegroom from his wedding canopy, and like a strong man runs its course with joy" (Ps. 19:5).

Even more to the point, Paul writes: "Do you not know that in a race the runners all compete, but only one receives the prize? Run in such a way that you may win it. Athletes exercise self-control in all things; they do it to receive a perishable wreath, but we an imperishable one. So I do not run aimlessly, nor do I box as though beating the air; but I punish my body and enslave it, so that after proclaiming to others I myself should not be disqualified" (1 Cor. 9:24-27).

"Let us run with perseverance the race that is set before us" (Heb. 12:1). That is a transferable concept. Often competitive sports constitute a cross-cultural language.

MUSIC

No surprises here. The church in Africa began to grow 10 percent a year the moment they brought drums into the church. I remember traveling in some of the most remote parts of the world and the only English I heard for weeks was the music of Madonna. How could "the Material Girl" be cross-cultural? The music—the beat perhaps more than the words—communicates.

Had I known I was to be an evangelist I would have taken my mother's advice and stayed with those piano lessons. Oh, to be a Levite! I've just finished rereading First and Second Chronicles, only to be reminded once again of just how crucial music is to the worship of God. Music gathers the people and pleases God.

A couple of years ago I asked God a question: How did King Hezekiah turn around a nation of "stiff-necked people" in less than one generation? King Josiah and his priests couldn't do it seventy-five years later, even though they rediscovered the Book of the Law in the Temple.

As I was meditating, I caught a vision. Since I do not consider myself particularly susceptible to visions, when I do have one I tend to remember it. In this instance I remember the sights, the sounds, and the smells. As I was praying I was suddenly outside the Temple in Jerusalem during the latter part of the reign of King Ahaz (735–715 B.C.). The nation had been spiritually and morally devastated. Ahaz had not done "what was right in the sight of the LORD" (2 Chron. 28:1). He had desecrated the Temple with idols, allowed the lamp to go out, and eventually nailed its doors shut.

As I watched, some of the people were wailing as Ahaz was sacrificing Hebrew babies in the Valley of Ben Hinnom to the pagan god Molech. Little wonder that Gehenna (an early word for "hell") literally means "out of the Hinnom."

As I continued to observe, a man and boy approached. It was Isaiah and Hezekiah—just before Hezekiah was to become co-regent with his father, Ahaz. Isaiah, holding on to Hezekiah with one hand and to a lamp with the other, stopped at the entrance to the Temple and forced open its doors. As they entered, I could see all sorts of strange shadows reflecting off the pagan gods. I could hear the pair's feet shuffling across the dusty floors. I could smell the musty odor of oil and incense, long since left to seep from cracks in some of the jars that lined many of the walls and terraces.

Isaiah led young Hezekiah to the only place not yet desecrated, the Holy of Holies behind the veil. As they entered I heard Isaiah whisper,

"Hezekiah, just look, don't touch." He then placed Hezekiah before the Ark of the Covenant and taught him how to worship God while singing:

Bless the LORD, O my soul,
    and all that is within me, bless his holy name.
Bless the LORD, O my soul,
    and do not forget all his benefits—
who forgives all your iniquity, who heals all your diseases,
who redeems your life from the Pit,
    who crowns you with steadfast love and mercy,
who satisfies you with good as long as you live
    so that your youth is renewed like the eagle's. (Ps. 103:1-5)

Who can doubt the significance of Hezekiah's first acts as king? During the first month of the first year of his reign he reopened the Temple, cleansed it, and raised up the priests and Levites. "Hezekiah appointed the divisions of the priests and of the Levites, division by division, everyone according to his service, the priests and the Levites, for burnt offerings and offerings of well-being, to minister in the gates of the camp of the LORD and to give thanks and praise" (2 Chron. 31:2). "When the burnt offering began, the song to the LORD began also, and the trumpets, accompanied by the instruments of King David of Israel. The whole assembly worshiped, the singers sang, and the trumpeters sounded" (2 Chron. 29:27-28).

Want to turn a church around in less than one generation? Worship and music will probably have to play a part in the revival.

Some years ago my wife and daughter began attending an independent Pentecostal church, although my wife was far from Pentecostal in temperament or theology. Why? For the music. Some of us know all too well just how boring church can be. I've been to some churches that made me go home and pray for an hour so I could get back to the spiritual place I was at before I went to church. Here, however, my daughter came home and said, "Gee, Mom and Dad, that was so much fun—I can't wait till next Sunday." The worship was lively and relevant. The kids danced, adults clapped, and the band played on to the glory of God. In my opinion there is absolutely no excuse for worship that is boring and irrelevant.

Years ago I served a small church on the South Side of Chicago. When I first arrived, there was only one church in the area that was more lifeless than mine—a huge Roman Catholic church around the corner. Fewer than a dozen people would show up for Mass on Sunday morning. I assumed that in just a few years the church would die. Recently, however, a student of mine asked me to accompany him to a worship service in a church that was making a significant impact on my old neighborhood. Curious, I tagged along. Imagine my surprise to find that the church, St. Sabina, was the same church that I thought had died years earlier.

We arrived at 10:30 A.M. for an 11:00 service and were fortunate to find a seat. Three and a half hours later the service ended and I still wanted more. This was one of the most significant worship experiences that I had had in several years.

So what had happened?

A few years earlier, a young white priest was appointed to St. Sabina. He decided to make the church lively and relevant to the community. Although the people were mostly African American, he carefully "exegeted" the neighborhood and devised a model for worship that would communicate. He brought in music and began to involve the local people. He learned the "language" and even adopted two African American children. Within months people began to attend the various services of worship.

Although the revival of St. Sabina involved more than music, music clearly played a significant part in turning the church around in less than one generation. Now, rather than a dozen or so at a single Mass each week, four different Masses are packed full week after week.

Music is cross-cultural.

THE NEED FOR COMMUNITY

People really do need each other. Some of my students have collected a book of "Tuttleisms." One of my favorites is far from profound but speaks a terrible truth: "You get singled out, you get picked off." I am convinced that the breakup of the family unit (especially among the poor) spawns the gang mentality. People are going to gather in an attempt to survive.

Geese fly in formation because they can fly 70 percent faster and further in formation than they can on their own. They also swap leadership. They honk to encourage each other. When one can no longer stay with the flock, its mate (for life) drops out with it and remains with it until it recovers or dies. They are on to something.

Richard Leaky's book *People of the Lake* suggests that there were four strains of humankind evolving simultaneously between 1.2 and 1.5 million years ago. The theory had been that the strain to survive would have to be the "macho" strain—the survival of the fittest. Leaky found, however, that the so-called macho strains were the first to become extinct. Why? They were loners and they got picked off. The only strain that survived to evolve into modern humankind was *homo sapiens*. Why? *Homo sapiens* was the only strain that dared to become community.

The world over, people are becoming more and more tribal. Recent trends toward nationalism and ethnic tribalism are evidence enough. People want an identity. They want someone to watch their backs. They even want something important enough to die for—a cause. I've always thought that Christians would be heard to the precise degree that they were willing to put their lives on the line.

The world over, people gather for protection and meaning. I've observed the kibbutz in Israel. I've seen monasteries in Egypt and Greece. I've spoken with gang warlords on Chicago's South Side. I've observed ashrams among the Hindus in India. I've seen Buddhist priests gather in Japan, in Korea, and in Thailand. I've watched Taoists in Singapore and Sikhs in Fiji. I've experienced the power of the Muslim community throughout Southeast Asia and the Middle East. I've seen gatherings of beggars, the homeless, prostitutes, street children, gays, lesbians, bikers, and secret societies, all looking for some sort of meaning and protection through community.

The same thing is true in the church. People want spiritual guides, not bureaucrats. They want shepherds, not butchers. Wonderfully, Jesus says: "Very truly, I tell you, I am the gate for the sheep. All who came before me are thieves and bandits; but the sheep did not listen to them. I am the gate. Whoever enters by me will be saved, and will come in and go out and find pasture. The thief comes only to steal and kill and destroy. I have come that they may have life, and have it abundantly. I am the good shepherd. The good shepherd lays down his life for the sheep" (John 10:7-11).

Community does not always have to be visible. The underground church in the former Soviet Union and in China is an example. The Spirit of God not only gives us to God but to each other. There were no Christians prior to Pentecost. To be a Christian is to be baptized by the Holy Spirit into the Body of Christ—a community. The world without the church will still find its community. Unfortunately, the ruler of this world is the devil. "We know that we are God's children, and that the whole world lies under the power of the evil one" (1 John 5:19). The gospel of Jesus Christ alone provides the kind of community that has weapons with "divine power to destroy strongholds" (2 Cor. 10:4). The church at her best is community. John Wesley insisted that converts without community are "children begotten for the murderer."

The flip side of community is loneliness. Since the need for community is universal, those without a significant community are lonely. Loneliness is rarely the result of our not knowing others. Usually it is the result of others not knowing us. And others do not know us because we do not want to be known. Furthermore, we do not want to be known because we do not trust. We are afraid of revealing who we are and making ourselves vulnerable to still more abuse.

At least three times a year I take six to eight students into local churches for a "Faith Renewal Weekend." The primary objective is to create community. At the conclusion of the first night we divide the entire congregation into groups of threes. I ask them to answer three simple questions among themselves and then to pray for each other, out loud if possible, though we will settle for silent prayer. With this simple exercise I've seen Christians lead non-Christians to Christ. The three questions?

1. Your name and something interesting about yourself.
2. What one thing has been an encouragement to you over the past two weeks to a month?
3. What one thing would you like God to do for you this weekend?

Admittedly, none of that sounds terribly profound. But the need to share is cross-cultural.

Obviously the church is the place where that kind of trust should be most available. Yet this is not always the case. The accusation that we shoot our own wounded is sometimes true. George Bernard Shaw said, "Leave Christians alone, they'll kill each other." God forbid! Surely the church has more to offer than does the local tavern. Let them know we are Christians by our love, one for another.

The church at her best has no equal in meeting the world's most basic needs. Establishing vital community is what we are all about. Little wonder that the author to the Hebrews exhorts, "And let us consider how to provoke one another to love and good deeds, not neglecting to meet together, as is the habit of some, but encouraging one another, and all the more as you see the Day approaching" (Heb. 10:24-25).

THE UNIVERSAL "OUGHTNESS"

One final cross-cultural common denominator is not as obvious, but it is absolutely crucial to the communication of the gospel. Within everyone there is some form of "oughtness"—a moral, ethical, or even religious form of *law* causing people to feel the need to measure up to some standard or some cultural imperative.

Paul writes, "When Gentiles, who do not possess the law, do instinctively what the law requires, these, though not having the law, are a law to themselves. They show that what the law requires is written on their hearts, to which their own conscience also bears witness; and their conflicting thoughts will accuse or perhaps excuse them" (Rom. 2:14-15). This is a bit more sophisticated than Kant's "categorical imperative" or even Calvin's "common grace."

I have found this oughtness to be strong enough in many people that they were receptive to the gospel. Almost without exception, whenever I have found persons who were completely serious about knowing God, they had become frustrated with their inability to measure up to this oughtness and were open and responsive to the good news of the power of the Holy Spirit available through faith in Jesus Christ for fulfilling such a law.

One day in London I met a Muslim man. Westerners often view Muslims as, en masse, far more ready to hate their enemies than to love their friends. Yet one-on-one, Muslims will frequently go to great lengths to help a stranger.

This was a one-on-one encounter. We were both walking up Edgeware Road, just north of Hyde Park. We began to chat and then sat down on a bench to continue the conversation. After some time we started to talk about God.

At one point I asked him about the Islamic law. He seemed pleased that I was interested. It soon became obvious to me that the law of Islam puts Judeo-Christian law in a whole new perspective. It seemed that in many ways the punishments for violating Islamic law were much harsher than those for violating Judeo-Christian law.

As soon as my new friend had completed his description, I asked him this question: "Do you really want to obey that law?" He said without hesitation, "You bet! I've been trying to obey that law all of my life." I said, "Get comfortable, I'm going to tell you a story." Here is a brief summary of the story I told him, and his response.

For Islam, Abraham is the archetypical Muslim. Allah for the Muslim is the Judeo-Christian God of Abraham, Isaac, and Jacob. I simply began with Abraham and talked about the covenant God established with him as the father of a nation of Semites, including both Jews and Arabs. I talked about the Law, a law that is in many ways similar to the one he had just described. I talked about sacrifice. I described the inability of the descendants of Abraham to fulfill that Law in spite of their sacrifices. I described a God of love and mercy—a God faithful to a "stiff-necked" people, often forgiving their disobedience. I then told him about Jeremiah 31:31 and the announcement of a new covenant. God speaks these words through the prophet: "But this is the covenant that I will make with the house of Israel . . . I will put my law within them, and I will write it on their hearts; and I will be their God, and they shall be my people. No longer shall they teach one another, or say to each other, 'Know the LORD,' for they shall all know me, from the least of them to the greatest . . . for I will forgive their iniquity, and remember their sin no more" (Jer. 31:33-34).

I described how the new covenant exchanged a law of sin and death for the law of the Spirit of life. The same law, once devoid of the Spirit (and therefore the power and inclination to obey it), was now empowered by the Spirit. In the new covenant a sacrifice was provided by God through the gift of God's own son, Jesus Christ, so that by virtue of our faith in him we could experience the indwelling power of the Spirit and thereby fulfill the law. I then said that the only way he could ever fulfill the Islamic law was by placing his faith and trust in Jesus Christ so that he too could experience the power of the Holy Spirit.

I shall never forget his response: "What you are telling me is that I must trust Jesus Christ in order to be a faithful Muslim." I simply nodded, and we prayed.

Once, on a train to Vladivostok, Russia, I engaged four fellow travelers in conversation. Well into the night, the Russians suddenly asked each other, "How is it that we have been talking about God for nearly four hours? None of us even believes in God." I then simply watched as they each bore witness to pious mothers who had had them baptized as babies. They all had a residual curiosity about God—and a need to measure up. They then listened to the gospel with interest and appreciation.

In Thailand I met an evangelist who recounted his testimony as one who had become frustrated with the inability of his family's religion to deliver him from drugs and alcohol. It was only in Jesus Christ that he experienced the power to overcome. John writes: "For the love of God is this, that we obey his commandments. And his commandments are not burdensome, for whatever is born of God conquers the world. And this is the victory that conquers the world, our faith. Who is it that conquers the world but the one who believes that Jesus is the Son of God?" (1 John 5:3-5).

A universal oughtness and the need for power to measure up is a cross-cultural reality.

CONCLUSION

There are obviously many more cross-cultural common denominators that can assist the church in the task of an evangelism that is more user-friendly. The evangelist must always be on the lookout for concepts that transfer from one culture to another.

George Gallup tells us that the whole world is incurably religious. Everyone is looking for meaning and purpose to life. The problem is that the church's witness is not always sufficiently clear. Frequently she vacillates between institutional self-interest and sacrificial giving, between sectarianism and ecumenical fervor, between obscurantism and moments of clarity and purpose, between introversion and all-out compassion, between irrelevance and poignancy, ignorance and wisdom, worldliness and godliness, impotence and power—incredible power, power to overcome sin in persons, power to overcome sin in systems, power to demolish strongholds, power to change the world.

Cross-cultural common denominators enable us to hear what people are really saying. They also teach us the kinds of things that alienate. Preaching to tribal peoples in parts of Africa without the approval of the tribal council is an offense and defeats the purpose of the gospel. Closer to home, gender references to God make it impossible for some feminists to hear the gospel. (In this paper, apart from biblical quotations I've not made one gender reference to God—yet the reader probably was not even aware of it.)

Communication is hard work. Too often the church has failed because we are simply not speaking the same language, even among ourselves. Evangelists often fail because they play to stereotypes, unaware of the images they conjure in the minds of the very people they have been called to evangelize.

The world has rubbed our noses in charges of torture (during the Inquisition), imperialism (during the colonial period), genocide (in Nazi Germany), and even fratricide (in Ireland and Latin America). Since the world delights in pointing out Christian hypocrisy (both real and imagined), I have attempted here to suggest some positive concepts that might possibly encourage us. I'm weary of being warned only of what *not* to do. There are many Christians who are doing it well.

Wherever there is revival, some universal need is being met. Psychologists who say that our most basic needs are sex and aggression are wrong. Our most basic needs are love and understanding. Cross-cultural common denominators can give us clues to a broader perspective on how to connect with these basic needs.

One day a student came to me for advice. A man in the nursing home where he was serving as a student intern had challenged him. As the student entered the man's room he could see that both his legs had been amputated just above the knees. The man looked at him and said, "God has a good list and God has a hit list, and I've been on God's hit list all of my life." (Actually, I've cleaned up his language a bit.)

Instantly I had a thought. God has no hit list and the world has no good list. Furthermore, we are all on God's good list and we are all on the world's hit list. Consequently, there "ain't no justice" according to this world's standards. Justice is in God alone, and if we wait until we receive what we deserve according this world's standards to be happy, we will *never* be happy.

Second Corinthians 4:18 states that "what can be seen is temporary, but what cannot be is eternal." I have found that few cross-cultural common denominators plumb the depths of the eternal. There is at least one exception, however—an interest (at some point) in things eternal. Something has to make sense of it all. There is simply too much injustice for this life alone to be all there is.

Some years ago my father and I were on a plane to New Zealand. A young man sat down next to me and introduced himself as a landscape architect. He asked me what I did for a living and I told him that I was a minister. He quickly responded that he was an atheist, almost as if he were proud of it.

I asked with genuine interest, "How does a man who gets to work with nature's beauty get to be an atheist?" He said, "Just lucky, I guess." My father immediately nudged me and whispered, "Son, this man is going to be tough."

The man then asked, "Why would anyone want to be a minister?" I replied, "Let me ask you a question. If you could know for sure that there really is a God who loves and cares for you and who makes a power available to sustain you in your life, would you be interested?" He said, "You bet." I said, "That's why I'm a minister. I want to help people just like you come to know that there really is a God who loves and cares for you and who makes a power available to sustain you in your life." He said, "Tell me more."

In less than five minutes I saw the man turn from resisting me to the point that he was actually helping me to tell him about God. What was the key? In spite of himself the architect was interested in things eternal. The existence of God, love, caring, power, even life after death—all are cross-culturally transferable concepts.

Perhaps the Holy Spirit sets the precedent. Look no further than Genesis 1–11. Did the Spirit of God use parts of a relatively unsophisticated Babylonian myth about creation as a transferable concept for communicating a truth about the origin of species? It's a thought.

Since "story" is also cross-cultural ("Once upon a time . . ." almost always draws attention), let me conclude with a story from the Bible as a word of encouragement.

In 2 Kings 6 the Arameans were at war with Israel. Elisha, by the

Spirit, knew where the enemy would strike and kept warning the king of Israel in advance. Eventually the king of Aram suspected a spy in his own camp, only to be informed that there was a prophet in Israel who knew his thoughts, even when the king was in his bedroom. The king of Aram demanded, "Bring him to me, now!"

The Aramean army surrounded Elisha's city of Dothan in order to capture him. When Elisha's servant saw the horses and chariots of a mighty army surrounding the city, he went to warn Elisha. But when Elisha saw the army he said, "Do not be afraid, for there are more with us than there are with them. . . . O LORD, please open his eyes that he may see" (2 Kings 6:16-17).

The Lord opened the servant's eyes and he saw chariots of fire on every hill. So be encouraged! Surely those who are with us are more than those who are with them. If we are loving and sensitive toward people, we can rest assured that the Spirit of God is even now preparing the hearts of people the world over to receive the gospel message. Now that's cross-cultural!

A member of the Lisu, a distinct people who have lived for centuries in what is now northeast Myanmar and western China, Yishey Latt is a first-generation Christian. He finds himself in the unique role of Christian evangelist among his people and also to Burmese Buddhists, and at the same time interpreter and preserver of his own Lisu culture. Here Latt shares his interpretation of the Christian good news within the Lisu context—an attempt at critical contextualization.

CHAPTER TWELVE

CROSSBOW THEOLOGY: CONTEXTUAL EVANGELISM IN MYANMAR

Yishey Latt

When I was about five years old, an historic event for Lisu people occurred in Pyaung Gaung, my native village in north-central Myanmar (Burma). It was the First Lisu Assembly. Colorful Lisu representatives from all parts of the country gathered for a week of joyful celebration. The program included discussions about culture, literature, unity, and future planning. I was too young to remember all the events, but I do clearly remember eating together, seeing varieties of Lisu dancing, and hearing beautiful music under the crossbow symbol of the Lisu flag.

Since my parents were among the leaders for that event, I have some pictures of it. In a sense the celebration was not a strange event in Myanmar, because a lot of tribal groups celebrate their own national days annually. But for the stateless Lisu people, whom missionaries sometimes call "Burma gypsies," it was a remarkable and historic event to meet peacefully under the crossbow flag.

When I was appointed General Secretary of the Lisu Baptist Convention, we developed a Lisu Baptist flag. This was accepted in the annual meeting and is still in use. We put the crossbow, the principal Lisu cultural symbol, on a heraldic shield centered on the cross of Christ. Since then, I have been trying to understand more fully the meaning of the crossbow symbol for the Lisu people.

In addition to Myanmar's Lisu, some seven hundred thousand to one million Lisu live in China.[1] There are some Lisu states, an annual Lisu

festival, and a Lisu monument in China. At the top of the monument
is a figure of a vigorous Lisu man shooting a crossbow. In January 1995, my home-
town celebrated its first Lisu Hunting Festival. The festival included a crossbow
shooting competition. Many were surprised that a young Lisu woman
(who had participated in crossbow competitions in Japan) won the
competition, beating the men.

As I studied Lisu culture and reflected on Christian evangelism
among the Lisu, I discovered that we Lisu Christians had misunderstood
our own culture and neglected our own worldview for many years. The
first generation of Lisu Christians believed they had to reject and forget
the old culture and must change to new Christian ways. These ideas
were being taught by the missionaries. The result was that Lisu
Christians and other Lisu people were separating from each other. We
had no effective bridges of communication between Christian and non-
Christian Lisus.

My missiological studies have led me to explore how the crossbow
might serve as a bridge among separated Lisu people (Christians, animists, and Buddhists). In this paper I consider the importance of the
crossbow in the identity and values of the Lisu people. I explore the
crossbow as a worldview symbol, as a bridge for understanding among
the Lisu, and as a powerful image of the cross of Jesus Christ useful for
holistic mission among the Lisu. Perhaps this pioneer effort will also help
other tribal groups as they search for and develop appropriate cultural
symbols for mission theology in Myanmar.

WORLDVIEW: SHAPER OF CULTURES

All people on earth are shaped in part by their worldviews. Cultures
and lifestyles vary, expressing different worldviews. Worldviews touch
every dimension of life—social, educational, economic, political, and
especially religious. Different worldviews account for varieties of living
styles, thinking, speaking, and images of society among cultures and in
different religious communities.

SOME DEFINITIONS AND FUNCTIONS OF WORLDVIEWS

"A worldview is our key to the universe. It is the lens through which
we see."[2] As Howard Snyder says in *EarthCurrents*:

A worldview is the grid we use to make sense of the cosmos. It is our set of silent assumptions as we navigate life's currents. It is our sense of the world, the framework that tells us what is true and important and what isn't. Worldviews answer questions of right and wrong and serve as the basis for countless daily decisions. Without a workable worldview, people are immobilized or else swept around like loose leaves, wherever the winds of events and the push of other people drive them.[3]

A workable worldview is very important for every person. Most people probably never evaluate their worldviews. As James Sire says, a worldview is "a set of presuppositions (or assumptions) which we hold (consciously or unconsciously) about the basic makeup of our world."[4] People simply accept worldviews unconsciously and follow them as their ancestors did.

"A world view is a world interpretation," Walter J. Ong says. It is "the person's way of organizing from within himself the data of actuality coming from without and from within."[5] It is difficult to interpret the mystery of the universe. This is the reason for worldviews. They become the key to the universe. John Wimber says, "Our worldview is like a lens—it colors, clarifies, classifies, warps, or partially excludes the world. It is, in Charles Kraft's words, our 'control box' of reality."[6] Charles Kraft, in his book *Christianity in Culture*, gives a more comprehensive definition:

Cultures pattern perceptions of reality into conceptualizations of what reality can or should be, what is to be regarded as actual, probable, possible, and impossible. . . . The worldview is the central systematization of conceptions of reality to which the members of the culture assent (largely unconsciously) and from which stems their value system. The worldview lies at the very heart of culture, touching, interacting with, and strongly influencing every other aspect of the culture.[7]

Kraft points out four functions of a worldview:

- A worldview provides "an *explanation* of how and why things got to be as they are and how and why they continue or change."
- A worldview serves as a basis for *evaluation,* for judging and validating experience.
- The worldview provides *psychological reinforcement* for a society's way of life.
- A worldview serves an *integrating function* for new information, values, philosophies, and experiences.[8]

In his discussion of worldviews, Paul G. Hiebert mentions five world-view functions. In his book *Anthropological Insights for Missionaries* he lists the following: (1) "Our world view *provides us with cognitive foundations* on which to build our systems of explanation, supplying rational justification for belief in these systems"; (2) "Our world view *gives us emotional security*"; (3) "Our world view *validates our deepest cultural norms*, which we use to evaluate our experiences and choose courses of action"; (4) "Our worldview *integrates our culture*"; and (5) "Our worldview *monitors culture change*."[9]

People hold particular worldviews for these and perhaps other reasons. For those who hold them, worldviews usually are self-evidently true and obviously believable. Snyder says that three things in particular make a worldview credible to us:

> How it squares with our own experience; the influence of other people who believe it, particularly people who are significant to us; and its ability to answer questions and provide meaning. A functional worldview is one that matches experienced reality, is believable to a large number of people, and suggests convincing answers to questions for which we otherwise have no clues. A worldview could be widely believable and answer our questions and still be wrong, of course. But worldviews must at least fulfill these roles.[10]

Since worldviews are the key to world-interpretation and form the heart of culture, it is important to study them if we are concerned about cross-cultural communication and with carrying the gospel to people of different worldviews. To evaluate one's worldview requires comparing it with other worldviews. Anthropologists and missiologists have done a lot of research on Western and traditional worldviews that is helpful here. I have drawn on some of this research in developing my vision of "crossbow theology."

A CHRISTIAN WORLDVIEW?

What is a Christian worldview? Christianity subscribes to or presupposes a theistic worldview. James Sire suggests that theism consists of eight basic worldview presuppositions:

• God is infinite and personal (Triune), transcendent and immanent, omniscient, sovereign and good.

- God created the cosmos *ex nihilo* to operate with a uniformity of cause and effect in an open system.
- Man [and woman are] created in the image and likeness of God and thus [possess] personality, self-transcendence, intelligence, morality, gregariousness and creativity.
- God can and does communicate with [human beings].
- Men [and woman were] created good, but through the Fall the image of God became defaced, though not so ruined as not to be incapable of restoration; through the work of Christ God redeemed [humanity] and began the process of restoring [humanity] to goodness, though any given [person] may choose to reject that redemption.
- For [humans] death is either the gate to life with God and his people or the gate to eternal separation from the only thing that will ultimately fulfill [human] aspirations.
- Ethics is transcendent and is based on the character of God as good (holy and loving).
- History is linear, a meaningful sequence of events leading to the fulfillment of God's purposes for [humanity].[11]

These presuppositions directly affect the ways we think and act. "Thinking Christianly is equated with holding a Christian worldview," says John Wimber in *Power Evangelism*. He quotes Harry Blamires's view: "To think Christianly is to accept all things with the mind as related, directly or indirectly, to [humanity's] eternal destiny as the redeemed and chosen child[ren] of God. . . . A prime mark of the Christian mind is that *it cultivates the eternal perspective*. . . . It is supernaturally oriented, and brings to bear upon earthly considerations the fact of Heaven and the fact of Hell."[12] A Christian worldview is determined by this supernatural perspective. It teaches the eternal destiny of humankind. "For Christians, then, there is objective truth, rational propositions about God, the creation, and morality that can be known and are eternal. We believe in transcendent moral standards to which we can submit every aspect of our thinking."[13]

But a Christian worldview is much more than rational propositions. Jack Rogers points out some basic characteristics of the Bible that are also important in articulating a Christian worldview. Rogers notes that: (1) "Scripture values the contemplative life"; (2) "Scripture is poetic"; (3) "the Bible employs vivid picture language"; (4) "Scripture accepts paradox easily," and (5) "religion in the Bible is a way of life."[14]

Christianity is rooted in God's revelation and in a highly developed sense of membership in the Body of Christ. Since it is grounded in God the Creator, Christian truth touches every area of life. This means that Christians can build distinctly Christian social environments and lifestyles. As followers of Jesus Christ, Christians should base their worldview and lifestyle on the life of Jesus and his worldview. Charles Kraft notes that while Jesus shared most of his worldview with the people of his society, there were some key differences. Jesus seems to have assumed:

- Two kingdoms—Satan's and God's.
- Authority of God's people over diseases and demons (Luke 9, 10; Matt. 10).
- Believing is seeing (Luke 8:9-10).
- Obedience brings knowledge (John 7:17).
- Confession brings forgiveness (1 John 1:9).
- God forgives us if we forgive others (Matt. 6:12).
- Don't fight back (Luke 6:29).
- Don't try to get ahead (Luke 9:25).
- Don't try to preserve your own life (Luke 17:33).
- Love your enemies (Luke 6:27-36).
- Refuse to judge/condemn others (Luke 6:37).
- Risk (parable of the talents).
- To be great, become a child (Matt. 18:1-5).
- To lead, serve (Matt. 20:25-28).[15]

This Jesus worldview or kingdom worldview shapes Christianity as a significant lifestyle among people and as the light of the world. It faces and clashes with other worldviews, yet it gives the world peace, justice, prosperity, and love.

WESTERN AND NON-WESTERN WORLDVIEWS

The Christian worldview is not the same as a Western worldview—as I discovered when I came to the United States to study. "Culture shock is the disorientation we experience when all the cultural maps and guidelines we learned as children no longer work," writes Hiebert. "Stripped of our normal ways of coping with life, we are confused, afraid, and angry. We rarely know what has gone wrong, much less what to do about it."[16] This was my experience when I came to America from Asia.

I saw and learned about the fabulous advancement of technology and the wonders of economic development. At the same time I sensed lots of cultural differences. I was "shocked" by such things as individualism (my culture is community-oriented), usually meeting only by appointment (we are happy to have unexpected guests), and the fact that money is much more valuable than friendship, loyalty, virginity, and so on. Here young people are proud of what we feel are shameful things in Asia, such as lack of respect for older people, professors, leaders, and so on. When I told an American friend about my family he said, "Aren't you bored to stay with the same woman for ten years?" I asked about his family. He was married and had two kids, and he has another two kids with his girlfriend, and another two girlfriends were pregnant. He said he was looking for another one. Yet he claimed to be a Christian. This was really culture shock for me.

America leads the world in science and technology, economics, and political power, but much of its family life is corrupt. I think this reflects the Western worldview. Note, for example, the contrasts between the American worldview and many more traditional worldviews, as listed in the chart beginning on the next page.[17]

These are some of the major differences between Western and other worldviews. It is difficult to fit either of these worldviews into a Christian worldview. Wimber says, "Western Christians have found it difficult to build distinctively Christian life-styles. Distilling Christian teaching down to a set of creeds and code of ethics, they are usually more concerned with personal conduct and assent to doctrine than with a Christian life-style."[18] Just as a Christian worldview conflicts with the secular mind, so it also conflicts with the Western worldview.

Non-Western Christians likewise have worldview difficulties. "[O]ne of the chief problems among the believers in the churches planted by evangelical missions in Africa was a frighteningly large number of Christian believers who still rely on the witch doctor whenever a serious problem comes into their lives," Peter Wagner notes.[19] This raises questions for adherents of other religions. What is an authentic Christian worldview? Is it that found among Western Christians, or that of Christians in non-Western countries? And Christian missionaries face the question of how to bring the message of Christ to both Western and non-Western people and disciple them into a Christian worldview.

In the Lisu context, authentic evangelism and discipling requires an understanding of the Lisu worldview.

American Worldview	Traditional Worldview
1. Individualism. Group interests usually subservient to individual concerns. Important decisions made by individuals of nearly any age or status.	1. The group is the reality. Individual interests always subservient to group concerns. Important decisions made as a group. Individualism is destructive. No person should "stand out" from others.
2. Equality of persons.	2. Different persons are of different value, according to status. Strongly hierarchical.
3. Freedom orientation.	3. Security orientation.
4. Competition is good (need to "get ahead").	4. Competition is evil; cooperation is good (wants everyone at same level).
5. Can validly generalize about others from one's experience.	5. Can't generalize; experience is always unique.
6. Human-centered universe.	6. God or spirit-centered universe; or tribe- or family-centered; or uncentered.
7. Humans can understand truth.	7. Humans can't understand truth.
8. Money/material things the measure of human value.	8. Family relationships, personal/family prestige, or spiritual power are the measure of human value.
9. Biological life sacred.	9. Social life supreme.
10. Time orientation.	10. Event orientation.

11. Start event with clock.

11. Start event when the right people have arrived.

12. Change is good (change = "progress").

12. Change is bad (= "destruction") or change is neither bad nor good.

13. Universe evolved by chance.

13. Universe created.

14. Orderly universe, like a machine.

14. Personal, unpredictable universe.

15. Material goods to be sought after (= wealth).

15. Material things bad, spiritual good.

16. Humans in charge of nature through science.

16. Supernatural beings in charge of most things. Humans have some control.

17. Scientific strategy and technique will give humans total power over all things.

17. Strategy and technique in the spiritual realm the source of whatever control we may achieve.

18. Humans in charge of other people through politics, economics, organizations.

18. Power over others structured by social patterns given by God.

19. No invisible beings with power in the universe.

19. Universe full of invisible, very powerful beings. Learning to control spirits through "spiritual technology" crucial.

THE LISU WORLDVIEW

The Lisu are one of the 135 tribal groups in Myanmar. They are spread throughout northern, eastern, and north-central Myanmar. About 70 percent of the Lisu live in rural villages and earn their living by farming, hunting, raising animals, and cultivating crops. Missionaries gave different names to the Lisu people based on dress and location, such as "Black Lisu," "White Lisu," and "Flowery Lisu," and the "Ruby Lisu" in the central part of the country. The first Christian conversion among the Lisu in Myanmar occurred in 1902.

The Lisu worldview was influenced by animist religion. The ancestors of today's Lisu were originally animists. As Gailyn Van Rheenen notes, animists perceive that "all of life is controlled by spiritual powers" and in various ways "seek to manipulate these powers."[20] Almost every area of life depends on spirits in the Lisu animistic culture.

Since I grew up in an animistic village, I saw and still remember some of the animist practices that were a part of the Lisu worldview. The first word for the charm used in spirit worship was "Sar-Wu-Sa," meaning "Three Gods." They call them gods, but actually they worship spirits, primarily the spirits of their ancestors. In every Lisu animist's home you can see the altar for the ancestor spirits hanging on the wall. The people burn joss-sticks (incense) on it, and put some local liquor, fruit, and paper money on it. They worship and bow down at times of special family events. Each morning they must offer the first cup of rice to the spirits.

At a high place in the village Lisu animists keep a special house for ancestor spirits called "ah pa mo hi," meaning "the house of Grandfather." Here the villagers worship the spirits. They believe they will be blessed if they worship the ancestor spirits and cursed if they fail to do so. Fear seems to be the dominant motivation for these practices. The Lisu also have diviners who conduct worship, heal the sick, do divination, exorcisms, and predictions, and lead special events.

The Lisu belief in sickness is especially interesting. If a person's soul goes out and wanders somewhere, the person will become sick. The soul can leave the body when the person is terribly scared or seriously injured, when there is a witchcraft curse, or when one does something the ancestor spirits dislike, thus causing illness. Then the family must invite a diviner to heal the sick person. The diviner will ask the family to buy some liquor or kill some chickens, cows, or water buffaloes as a sacrifice to the spirits.

I used to go with other children and watch these healings, and I remember them very well. The diviner would put sacrifices into a bamboo tray, bring them to the door, raise the tray, and call the soul of the sick person, something like this:

Sar-Wu-Sa, Sar-Wu-Sa! Oh, dear (name), come back, come back to your house. Your parents are waiting for you with tears day and night. Don't go to the forest, don't stay under the large stone, don't jump into the deep water, don't stay in the dark night, it is dangerous. Come back, come back. Lyio, Lyio.

They would also build some bridges on the village road for the returning soul, and post the heads of chickens on poles at the side of the road.

The Lisu belief in sin was based on obedience to ancestor spirits, parents, and teachers. If a person sins, the judgment will come within this life. The person will die by thunderstorm, earthquake, water, fire, or wild animals. He or she will then be reincarnated into an animal. To avoid such punishment, one must obey and respect one's parents. People took care of their parents and grandparents until they died and then after death worshiped their spirits.

To have many sons was therefore very important for animist families. If a couple had no children, then their ancestor spirit lines were finished. No one would worship them. Because of this belief, when a barren woman died her body was not brought out through the front door. The back of the house was destroyed and the body was taken out from there.

Diviners or sorcerers were consulted for every important event: weddings, beginning a journey, starting a new business, finding a gravesite, building a new house, and so on. The animistic Lisu worldview was inundated with these spirit beliefs. But the Lisu have always had one great hope for the future: the coming of Lisuwa (King of the Lisu). We Lisu have the traditional belief that a great Lisu king will appear one day on the earth—not a natural king, but a supernatural King of the Lisu.

These are some of the remarkable features of the traditional Lisu worldview, a worldview and set of practices that are still current with Lisu animists. And some elements and practices of the traditional Lisu worldview remain among Lisu Christian families.

Currently there are three religious groups among Myanmar's Lisu: Christians, animists, and Buddhists. Because of these different religions, we Lisu are now divided into three. A major problem behind this division is, I feel, the misunderstanding of culture. Converted Lisu Christians accepted the missionaries' Christian culture as their own and threw out Lisu culture because of the animistic influences. They looked upon the old culture as evil. Consequently, animist Lisus who wanted to maintain their culture did not like the Christians. They became enemies. Animists saw the Christians as destroyers of the culture, and Christians thought that animists were totally controlled by Satan. Meanwhile, Lisu Buddhists began participating in the dominant Burmese culture (which is strongly Buddhist) and thus became rivals of the Christians. Lisu Buddhists get along with the animists without problems. All this presents a great challenge for authentic evangelization among the Lisu, requiring us to find new mission strategies.

As I pondered this challenge, I had a vision of using the Lisu crossbow as the bridge among the Lisu people. Perhaps the gospel could be brought to them through the crossbow, the symbol of the Lisu people. As I mentioned earlier, all Lisu people gather together under the crossbow flag, whether Christian, animist, or Buddhist. It is already the bridge for the Lisu people. But my vision is not just seeing the crossbow as a symbol or as a goodwill bridge. I want my people to see the past, the present, and the future of Lisu destiny pictured in the crossbow. I see the crossbow not as a weapon, but as the bridge to carry the holistic salvation of Jesus to the Lisu people. This is "crossbow theology"!

THE CROSSBOW AND THE CROSS OF JESUS

The crossbow is a very simple traditional weapon for the Lisu. It is a piece of wood fixed crosswise to a bamboo bow with a string. It is a cheap weapon, using bamboo arrows. But Lisu people love the crossbow very much. All Lisu people around the world honor it as the symbol of their people. Almost every family has a crossbow hanging on the wall. As noted earlier, there is a Lisu crossbow monument in China, and we are using the Lisu crossbow flag in Myanmar. Lisu in Thailand, Laos, and other countries also use this symbol. The crossbow represents the Lisu, and the Lisu represent the crossbow.

The cross of Christ is a simple crucifixion pole made of two pieces of wood. It was an ugly symbol of death before Christ died on it. But the cross became a symbol of victory and identity for Christians. Christians around the world love the cross because the Lord Jesus gave his life on it to win salvation for the whole world. Christians love the cross because there is the powerful Lord behind the symbol. The cross represents Christians, and Christians represent the cross.

The cross of Christ and the Lisu crossbow are made in similar ways: a vertical pole and a horizontal pole fastened together. The main difference is that one is a weapon (the crossbow) and the other is a crucifixion device. Jesus used the cross to draw together all people beneath it.

The crossbow draws all the Lisu people together under the crossbow flag. If all Lisu people can look at the crossbow and feel the cross of Christ, then God's holistic salvation will reach the Lisu people. By holistic salvation I mean not only spiritual redemption but also liberation from the bondage of poverty, illiteracy, suffering, disease, oppression, and separation.

THE ORDER AND THE BEAUTY
OF UNITY IN THE CROSSBOW

Even though the crossbow is a simple weapon, it is difficult to make a perfect one. The quality of the pieces of wood, bamboo, string, and ivory, and the balance and the order of construction are critical for making a perfect crossbow. We choose aged wood and bamboo, make the frame, and keep it for years. We search for thin tree bark, twist it tightly to make the bowstring (it must be guaranteed for at least five years), and use ivory or horn to make the trigger. We build it very carefully, getting balance between the right and left sides of the bow. Then we can have a perfect crossbow. We can see the beauty of its unity. The unity of high-quality elements and the skill of the construction make the crossbow perfect. If the wood or the bamboo is flawed, or the string is not strong, or the bow is not in balance, then the crossbow will be broken after a week.

The Lisu people learn from the crossbow. They value its qualities. Like their symbol, the colorful Lisu must also have strong unity and balance. Then the beauty and the fruits of this unity will blossom.

One can make theological and worldview connections at this point. The Bible is also about unity, beauty, and balance. Psalm 133:1 says, "How very good and pleasant it is when kindred live together in unity." First Peter 2 tells us, "Like living stones, let yourselves be built into a spiritual house" (v. 5).

Howard Snyder speaks about "order, surprise, and beauty" as worldview elements in his book *EarthCurrents: The Struggle for the World's Soul.* Snyder suggests:

Order suggests a coherent pattern in which all the parts stand in nonchaotic relationship to each other and to the whole. *Surprise,* as I use it here, means the element of freedom and unpredictability that may appear in a system and that yet turns out to be compatible with the order. *Beauty* in relation to worldviews means symmetry and balance and the ability to invoke in human beings a sense of attraction and aesthetic appreciation—

a sense of wonder. . . . All three must, therefore, be taken into account in any valid and credible worldview. Together these qualities may give us clues for discerning a sustainable worldview.[21]

"What makes something beautiful?" Snyder asks. In answering the question, he points to poetry and music. "Poetry and music give good examples. Orderly music has a certain beauty. Add the element of surprise, and the result (if done skillfully) is much greater beauty."[22] This applies also to the Lisu crossbow. The unity of quality elements and skillful construction makes the crossbow perfect. Likewise, the unity of each member helps make the beauty of the society. The beauty of the society is its life as a peaceful community. I see this in the correspondence between the symbol of the crossbow and Lisu identity.

How can the crossbow—a weapon—be the symbol of peace? Is it possible to find peace with a weapon? This leads to my next step: developing a crossbow theology for *shalom*.

THE CROSSBOW AND THE PEACEFUL COMMUNITY

Trying to win peace with weapons usually means violence. But God is powerful and he can change the situation, bringing peace. A three-step process is illustrated on the next page.

Critical contextualization is represented by the crossbow in the cross of Jesus Christ. Here the crossbow represents a peaceful existence for the individuals and the community of Lisu people. The weapon is not a weapon anymore. It becomes the symbol of love, like the cross. It is the symbol of peace—like the cross, a vertical bridge between the people and God, and a horizontal bridge among the people. The crossbow becomes the image of the cross of the Savior, Jesus Christ.

This transformation can happen through the process of critical contextualization as outlined by Paul Hiebert. "Critical contextualization takes the Bible seriously as the rule of faith and life," says Hiebert. "Contextualized practices, like contextualized theologies, must be biblically based. This may seem obvious, but we must constantly remind ourselves that biblical revelation is the standard against which all practices are measured."[23] The "crossbow in the cross" position is grounded in the biblical understanding of the gospel and in the world's need to reduce and destroy weapons (including nuclear weapons) for the sake of a peaceful world. The cross is the symbol of the obedience of Jesus Christ. It is the place of reconciliation, the place of expiation, the place where all can find the love of God.

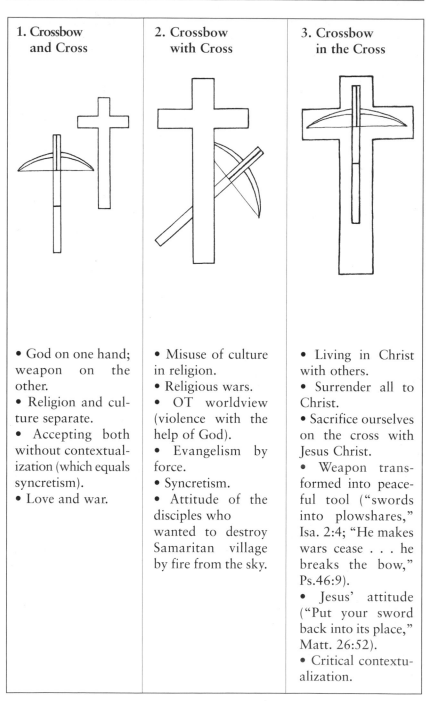

1. Crossbow and Cross	2. Crossbow with Cross	3. Crossbow in the Cross
• God on one hand; weapon on the other. • Religion and culture separate. • Accepting both without contextualization (which equals syncretism). • Love and war.	• Misuse of culture in religion. • Religious wars. • OT worldview (violence with the help of God). • Evangelism by force. • Syncretism. • Attitude of the disciples who wanted to destroy Samaritan village by fire from the sky.	• Living in Christ with others. • Surrender all to Christ. • Sacrifice ourselves on the cross with Jesus Christ. • Weapon transformed into peaceful tool ("swords into plowshares," Isa. 2:4; "He makes wars cease . . . he breaks the bow," Ps.46:9). • Jesus' attitude ("Put your sword back into its place," Matt. 26:52). • Critical contextualization.

THE CROSSBOW AND ECONOMICS

Crossbow theology has an economic dimension. The first priority of the purpose of the Lisu crossbow is economic. We used the crossbow as the weapon for hunting. Wild animals such as monkeys, deer, birds, bears, lions, tigers, and boars cannot escape the poisonous arrows of the Lisu crossbow. Sometimes even elephants were caught. We sold the animals' meat, skin, and bones for money. Thus the crossbow made lots of money for Lisu families. It gave us prosperity. The symbol of Lisu people gives prosperity to Lisu people. It is one reason we love it so much.

The cross of Christ also has an economic meaning. It is the sign of liberation from poverty and a door to prosperity. Jesus came and used the cross to give people abundant life in all its dimensions (John 10:10). He came to take our poverty and to give us his riches (2 Cor. 8:9). The cross brings us blessing from God, happiness for both body and spirit.

The crossbow cannot really make the Lisu people rich or assist them to develop economically. Traditionally, Asian people in general have seen wealth as evil. Economic success creates social disturbance. But the cross of Christ can point the way to a balanced view. Like a well-constructed crossbow, orderly and skillfully made, crossbow theology proposes to thoughtfully use the materials and techniques of economics to build a prosperous society, one marked by positive surprise and beauty.

God loves the poor but he doesn't want his sons and daughters to remain poor. He wants us to be blessed materially as well as spiritually (Mal. 3:8-10; Eph. 3:8-9; 1 Pet. 2:9-10). This creates the challenge of a proper biblical understanding of economics and stewardship, one that is faithful to the values and priorities of the kingdom of God.

It is crucial for the Lisu people to develop a more adequate way of thinking and living. Our people are satisfied if they have daily food and are not thinking much about the future and the need for economic betterment. Crossbow theology must develop this longer-term economic worldview dimension. We must learn how to open the economic meaning of a Christian Lisu worldview in order to receive God's blessing on the Lisu people. On the crossbow monument in China the vigorous Lisu man points his crossbow upwards, ready to shoot. So today the Lisu must aim for greater economic achievement and well-being. This is a task yet to be accomplished. But I see the crossbow in the cross as opening up new possibilities.

THE CROSSBOW AS SECURITY AND VICTORY FOR US

"The Cross . . . is an eschatological event, because it brings forward into time a partial realization of the judgment of God," writes David Wells. "For those who stand in Christ, the judgment is already past. For them there is now no condemnation. For those who stand outside of Christ, however, the Cross is a somber and awesome revelation of God's relationship to sin and of the judgment to come."[24]

The cross of Christ gives us security for the present and for the future. I believe in the power of the cross because there is a powerful Lord behind it. As the blood of the lamb on the doorposts saved the Israelites from the death angel, so the blood of Christ on the cross saves us from eternal death. We dwell safely under the cross of Christ.

The crossbow as a weapon provides physical security for Lisu families. We use it to protect us from enemies, robbers, wild animals, and so on. Enemies know that Lisu are adept in crossbow shooting and that they use strong poison for their arrows. So they dare not attack the Lisu people. The crossbow gives us physical security, and the cross of Christ gives us spiritual security. What shall we fear? With the understanding of the "crossbow in the cross" model, we Lisu people will feel both physical and spiritual security whenever we see the cross or the crossbow. But we know that fundamentally our security lies in Jesus Christ and his gospel.

The crossbow represents victory for the Lisu people. It gives us security, prosperity, and unity, and leads us to victory. Maybe with time we can develop the traditional crossbow into a more scientifically advanced form. This will require more education, both secular and religious.

About a million Lisu people live in China, as noted above. They are China's largest ethnic minority. What will become of them as China goes through deep transition in coming decades? "The long-term direction of China is uncertain. A trend toward broader democracy seems likely, either throughout China or in major sections, should the nation break into smaller pieces," suggests Snyder.[25] Can we envision someday a "new Lisu country" with a seat at the United Nations? This is my secret dream for the Lisu, even though we have no Lisu state in Myanmar. This would require developing the political dimensions of a Christian Lisu worldview. Maybe the utopian dream of a traditional Lisu king will appear in reality on this earth. Then the Lisu crossbow flag will be one of the flags among the world's religious organizations and among the United Nations.

Yet the true King of Lisu is Jesus Christ. The traditional Lisu hope of a coming king is much like the Jewish expectation of a coming Messiah. Lisu people are looking for a supernatural king with a unique, charismatic personality and mighty power. Only under such a king, they feel, can there be true Lisu unity. As a Christian, however, I see the coming king as Jesus Christ, the King of Kings. My aim in developing crossbow theology is to draw the Lisu together under the cross of Christ, the crossbow serving as the bridge. The goal is to draw the Lisu into the kingdom of God.

These are some of the dimensions of crossbow theology—good news for the Lisu people. "In the Jesus-based worldview, each new discovery [of truth] shows further the wisdom and glory of the Divine Mind."[26] A cross of Christ-based crossbow theology has to discover a new worldview of wisdom and glory for the Lisu people—yet one that is, above all, faithful to the Lord Jesus Christ. And then finally, "Every tongue [including Lisu, will] confess that Jesus Christ is Lord, to the glory of God the Father" (Phil. 2:11).

How do we understand the power of the gospel, and the "principalities and powers" that oppose God's purposes? North American Christians are accustomed to economic, political, and military power but—at least until recently—often dismissed demonic power as superstition. Yet in most cultures of the world demons and evil spirits are taken with deadly seriousness. Out of her missiological research and her years of evangelistic and counseling work in Brazil, Neuza Itioka reflects on the struggle with demonic powers and particularly the forms of Brazilian low spiritism called Macumba and Candomblé. "Evangelism and mission are warfare," she writes. Itioka reflects a perspective that is increasingly common among "Third Wave" Christians today whohave been influenced by the Pentecostal and Charismatic movements.

CHAPTER THIRTEEN

EVANGELIZATION AND THE POWERS
Neuza Itioka

A certain church was full of vitality but then, all of a sudden, it began to experience bitter division among its members. Leaders who used to love and respect each other began to fight. The church was almost destroyed. In a final effort to avoid a split, the pastor called the leadership together to fast and pray.

As these leaders studied the Bible, prayed, and fasted, they began to understand that the struggle they were engaged in was not really against each other, but rather "against the rulers, against the authorities, against the cosmic powers of this present darkness" (Eph. 6:12). These were powers that promoted confusion to the point of creating hatred in order to separate people by magnifying their differences.

After deep repentance and genuine reconciliation, these leaders humbled themselves as individuals and as the church before God. With spiritual authority they declared the Lordship of Christ over the area where the church was located, challenging the powers and making a covenant among themselves that they would resist such powers until they retreated. Shortly thereafter a new convert, an ex-priestess and witch of Macumba[1] in that area, came to tell these leaders that thirteen spiritist centers in that

208

area had conspired to destroy that church. They were determined to bring division through witchcraft.

That confession opened the church's eyes to the seriousness of spiritual warfare. These Christians became, as it were, overnight experts in spiritual battle. They immediately took the offensive, counterattacking the powers, and soon many people in their area came to confess Jesus as Lord. Within a year, this church organized a citywide interdenominational evangelistic crusade in which more than seventy thousand people made public confessions of faith.

If the church of Jesus Christ wishes to be effectively evangelistic and positively impact an area through its presence, it can never bypass the need to confront spiritual oppression.[2] As the apostle Paul makes clear, the church's very calling implies a struggle against the powers.

The church is the product of Jesus' work of redemption. A Savior was promised at the beginning of human history. When Adam and Eve relinquished to the serpent their right and privilege to become the governors of the earth with the Creator, the Lord said: "I will put enmity between you and the woman, and between your offspring and hers; he will strike your head, and you will strike his heel" (Gen. 3:15).

Without the Fall, there would have been no need for redemption; and there would have been no Fall had Satan not rebelled against God. Because Satan conspired to be similar to Almighty God, desiring his position and lusting for his rights and privileges, he was expelled from his ancient habitat and fell to the earth, losing his place as a guardian cherubim. From that point on, Satan became God's adversary, just as his name implies, becoming malignant, destroying, killing, and robbing.[3] The adversary purposed to oppose all that Almighty God is, does, and loves. He hates the truth that human beings are the target of the greatest love of God and that they were created to enjoy his love.

This is why the target of Satan's hatred was Adam, Eve, and God's creation. When Adam and Eve succumbed to the serpent's lies, the holiness of God was compromised and his authority was challenged, opening an enormous abyss between the Creator and his creatures. Death became an inevitable ingredient of human life as man and woman lost the right to live eternally with their creator. Fellowship and friendship with God, which were so vital to human beings, were abolished as the result of God's wrath.

This wrath could not be appeased by any human sacrifice or ritual. There was only one solution, provided by God himself. God brought redemption through Calvary's cross, through the descendant of the woman, Jesus Christ, who was sacrificed there. The cross is central to the work of redemption, for through the cross God not only redeemed humans from their sins, nullifying the power of death, but he also rescued them from the hands of the devil, destroying his work.[4]

This was Jesus' mission. When he called the twelve to discipleship before sending them to preach the gospel, he showed them concretely the *sine qua non* condition for following him: intimate fellowship with him. He did not fail to equip them for their task, giving them the power to heal the sick and cast out demons and showing them that the gospel included a concern for both spirit and body (Matt. 10:8). In the Great Commission, the Master ordained his apostles and followers to "make disciples of all nations, baptizing them in the name of the Father and of the Son and of the Holy Spirit, and teaching them to obey everything" that he had commanded them to do (Matt. 28:19-20).

EVANGELIZATION AND SPIRITUAL WARFARE

The church of Jesus Christ was called to continue the work of the Son, Jesus Christ, in destroying the work of the devil, transferring people from the empire of darkness to the reign of the kingdom of light. The church is called to participate in building a new spiritual order, rescuing humanity from the old system that is under the domain of the adversary. This task involves the supernatural work of a triune God in the persons of the Father, the Son, and the Holy Spirit. It is only through their active involvement that people will be rescued to become a new creation.

The old system commanded by Satan has been overthrown by the Son. Today we participate in the same task, preaching, teaching, healing, and liberating people from the bondage of the evil one. In this sense evangelism is warfare. Mission is warfare. This is why evangelism depends so heavily upon how much we take the spiritual realms seriously.

In the world, which in many respects is becoming worse every day, we are obliged to face all kinds of manifestations of the evil one making war against the church. Yet the church will one day judge the powers. Angels and demons will be forced to come to know the multiple facets and aspects of the wisdom of God, to see a display of the most diverse variety of shades, tonalities, and colors of the truth of God put into practice in the lives of the redeemed under his greatness, mercy, and faithfulness. The principalities and powers will be obliged to see in the church a display of the many diverse forms and expressions of the power and authority of God (Eph. 3:10).

THE POSITION AND AUTHORITY OF THE CHURCH

The church of Christ is called "the Body of Christ" since it is the presence of the resurrected Son of God on earth and is the executive agent of his work. The church exists to give continuity to the work initiated by Christ. It exists to realize the work of the Lord. Jesus said, "The Spirit of the Lord is upon me, because he has anointed me to bring good news to the poor. He has sent me to proclaim release to the captives and recovery of sight to the blind, to let the oppressed go free, to proclaim the year of the Lord's favor" (Luke 4:18-19).

When Jesus gave the authority to expel demons, he gave the church the necessary power to confront spiritual oppression. No other organization or group of men and women has this authority to confront the powers. Jesus Christ, the Lord of the church, was the only one who could defeat the principalities and powers. As Paul wrote, "He disarmed the rulers and authorities and made a public example of them, triumphing over them" by the cross (Col. 2:15).

Jesus said to Peter, "On this rock I will build my church, and the gates of Hades will not prevail against it. I will give you the keys of the kingdom of heaven, and whatever you bind on earth will be bound in heaven, and whatever you loose on earth will be loosed in heaven" (Matt. 16:18-19). Here Jesus was giving a charge to the only agency on earth that was capable of confronting the powers. This agency, however, is also a body formed by human beings with frailties and limitations. It is formed by men and women who acknowledge their vulnerability and depend entirely upon the one who conquered the enemy on the cross, Jesus Christ.

Anticipating what would happen at the cross Jesus said, "I have given you authority to tread on snakes and scorpions, and over all the power of the enemy; and nothing will hurt you" (Luke 10:19). In spite of the church's failures, problems, struggles, sins, apostasies, and spiritual prostitution, it maintains a unique position won for it by Jesus Christ. For God "raised us up with him and seated us with him in the heavenly places in Christ Jesus" (Eph. 2:6). This position earned at the cross is "far above all rule and authority and power and dominion, and above every name that is named, not only in this age but also in the age to come" (Eph. 1:21). With the authority won by the Lord, the church, walking in holiness, is able to assume a position to confront Satan.

In God's sight the church is the most important body in the universe. It is the most cherished and beloved, bought by the blood of Jesus Christ at the highest cost. This is why the church is also the principal target of the hatred of the adversary. In an aggressive "war on the saints" (Rev. 13:7), the evil host attacks the church of Jesus Christ. The adversary opposes the expansion of the church and the growth of the kingdom of God.

This is why evangelism and mission are warfare. The powers use all kinds of tricks to deceive the people of God, from advocating their own supposed nonexistence to inciting an insatiable obsession with the occult. Satan and his dominion suggest other subtle lies, such as the myth that, once converted, a person cannot be reached or harmed by demons. Referring to the ignorance of the church on this subject and its refusal to be informed about the enemy, Penn-Lewis and Roberts state:

> Through lack of knowledge, the majority of even the most spiritual people, do not carry out a full and perpetual war upon this army of wicked spirits; and many are shrinking from the subject, and the call to war against them, saying that if Christ is preached it is not necessary to give prominence to the existence of the devil, nor to enter into direct conflict with him, and his hosts. Yet large numbers of the children of God are becoming a prey to the enemy for lack of this very knowledge, and through the silence of teachers on this vital truth, the Church of Christ is passing on into the peril of the closing days of the age, unprepared to meet the onslaught of the foe.[5]

But today there are healthy signs of change. Throughout the world the church is perceiving that it is engaged in a war against spiritual darkness. Like it or not, ever since we affirmed our faith in Christ, we as the church of Christ are, and always have been, at war with the powers.

THE WORLD IN WHICH THE CHURCH IS PLACED

Brazil is an example. Today Brazil is passing through one of the most mystic periods in all of its existence. Brazilian High Spiritism has nearly seven million adherents.[6] Folk spiritism, the spiritism of the masses, is growing in its dominant Brazilian forms of Candomblé and Umbanda. Many other Latin American countries are importing aspects of Brazilian folk spiritism.[7] Mysticism grows in the shadow of Catholicism, which gives it the veneer of an official religion.

The phenomena of Satanism and the occult are also a part of the so-called First World. American youth are no longer being seduced simply by drugs or the yuppie lifestyle. Many have fallen prey to Satanism with its promise of power and control in their own lives and in the lives of others.[8] Rumors persist of satanic human sacrifice and occult-related abductions.[9] In Europe, spiritism and occult mysticism also abound. One

American missionary estimates that in France, for example, the number of witches and wizards exceeds the number of evangelical Christians.[10] England, long considered a Christian nation, reportedly is experiencing rapid growth in Satanism and witchcraft.

The church in Latin America finds itself in a context in which the occult (spiritism, New Age mysticism, Satanism) is growing. Meanwhile, the society is witnessing escalating social violence, permissiveness, the destruction of the family, and the death of youth through crime. The need for orphanages grows as more and more babies are abandoned.

The consequences of escalating occultism in the so-called First World are many and diverse. The high rate of suicide among the rich, the vacuum of materialism, the illusions of technology, the violence of children and teenagers against their parents, the marginalization of the disabled, and the exploitation of the poor are all evidence of the power of evil. Expressions of spiritual oppression can vary from one place to another, but the burden of sin and of godlessness are there, from the "belt of misery or poverty" running across many Third World nations to the palaces of gangsters and powerful economic czars in the world's rich countries.

Occultism tempts people to control their destinies through magic and divination as well as through negotiations with the powers for one's own benefit. The only true God is left unconsidered, since human beings resist submission to him. Enthroning itself as god, the idolatrous heart turns to magic, communication with the dead, and seeking after other "gods" in an attempt to manipulate and exercise control. In reality, however, he or she will end up being manipulated by the evil one.

Those committed to evangelization and the deliverance of captives of the empire of the enemy must understand the extent to which those in darkness live without God. An amazing amount of money is spent each year on astrology, the occult, and Satanism in order to seek help with problems in finances, love, health, and relationships. People wander as "sheep without a shepherd," looking for comfort and for peace, "deceiving others and being deceived" (2 Tim. 3:13).

Today many people who seek counseling are suffering the results of having sold themselves to Satan, giving themselves to him in exchange for power,[11] perhaps seeking material prosperity, social position, marriage, property, and happiness. Power may also be employed to harm others, for people who are upset by the happiness and prosperity of their neighbors may place curses upon them. Through occult practices they may seek to destroy the health, position, marriage, fame, wealth, and even life of their enemies. Idolaters, according to Paul, begin to trust in their own craftiness; they create "gods," making themselves proud, but becoming fools instead. Thus enslaved, they become like their own "gods" (Rom. 1:18-27).

People become like what they worship. This truth is illustrated with deep insight by Dr. Koissuke Koyama. Commenting on the moment when the Japanese people declared their emperor divine, Koyama said the people became similar to their idol: blind, deaf, and speechless. They lost their perception by making their emperor absolute. This resulted in a kind of megalomania, leading to a suicidal war. When we trust in idols, says Koyama, our idols begin to speak, see, hear, smell, feel, and walk for us. We then become "like them"—dumb and mute. Thus, a vicious exchange takes place. The idols become eloquent, while the human worshipers become dumb. In this sense, idolatry is one of the most "dynamic" situations that the human mind can create. But it produces paralysis and destruction, not creativity.[12]

The apostle Paul says that "what pagans sacrifice, they sacrifice to demons and not to God" (1 Cor. 10:20). What is the reality behind our idols? Evangelicals in Latin America may question the power behind the Virgin of Guadalupe or Senhora Aparecida or Rosario. But all Christians may ask themselves: Who really are our gods? Who are the "gods" of Brazil, of the United States, of Europe?

When we analyze the nature of the gods that we as nations worship, we find they are perverse, corrupt, and evil. Modern society reflects these gods. All of them have the satanic tendency to destroy, rob, and kill. What then can we expect from people who seek direct and open communication with those gods? As peoples and nations, we are giving them legal right to exercise their activities, not only in our personal lives, but also in the life of society as a whole. The people become similar to the image of the god that they adore.

Brazil is a good example. According to the national periodical *Veja* (meaning "Look"), Brazil was the world's fourth largest food producer and its seventh greatest economic power. But now the nation faces tremendous debt and mounting social problems. Many people lack money for even their most basic needs, such as education, health, housing, and work. Brazil and other countries that have embraced spiritism by openly communicating with demonic powers now reflect the disastrous consequences of such unhealthy alliances in the familial, social, political, and economic arenas of national life.

WAR AGAINST THE POWERS

"The ruler of this world" is one of the names of Satan (John 12:31). The apostle John calls the world system "the cosmos" (John 12:31 and many other passages). According to René Padilla, "the world" is a system in which evil is organized in opposition to good. But it is the world's connection with Satan and his forces that gives it its evil character. Satan is "the god of this world" (2 Cor. 4:4). His forces are the powers that rule the world.[13]

The church of Jesus Christ was sent into the world, but does not belong to it. The church cannot agree with the world's methods or use its strategies and resources of manipulation in order to reach its purposes. If it were to do so, it would be declaring its own suicide, giving place to the devil and denying its own nature. It would lose its authority and become powerless to struggle against the principalities and powers.

The church was called to struggle against the world system. If it refuses to fight and resist the devil's actions, its enemies will keep on using their "worldly" ways in order to enslave and bind millions of people. In fact, the powers are fed by the repeated practice of satanic abominations forbidden by God in Deuteronomy 18:9-14, as well as by the works of the flesh (Gal. 5:19-21) and the continuous transgressions of God's law. Godlessness in all its forms, idolatry in its every expression, and immorality and perversion of any sort all strengthen the powers.

These powers exercise control not only over human lives but also over the social, religious, and political structures of districts, cities, and geographical areas. Through his fasting and prayer, Daniel provoked intense warfare between God's angel and the "prince" of Persia (Dan. 10:12). This suggests what can happen spiritually in a country when a man or woman of God prays, invoking the name of the Almighty.

In the same passage the "Prince of Greece" is mentioned (Dan. 10:20). Such Old Testament texts may imply that there are powers designated over nations and other geographical regions. In the words of Michael Green:

> Frequently God is called *Yahweh Sabaoth*, "Lord of the powers," and here the gods of polytheism are seen as captives under his suzerainty. And we read of the *bene elohim* or "sons of God" in Job, the Psalms, and Genesis 6:3. But perhaps the most important passage of all is Deut. 32:8 where the best texts read that the God "fixed the bounds of all the peoples according to the number of the *bene elohim*, the sons of God. For the Lord's portion is his people, Jacob his allotted heritage." The meaning is well brought out elsewhere: Deut. 4:19 speaks of the moon, stars and hosts of heaven which the Lord has allotted to all the peoples under heaven, with the exception of Israel whom he has appointed for himself. Thus "He appointed a ruler for every nation, but Israel is the Lord's own portion" (Ecclus. 17:7).
>
> In this way the Jews resolved the problem of the one and the many. There was only one God, and he was their God for ever. All other spiritual

forces, be they good or bad, were ultimately of his creation, under his control and assigned as tutelary deities to other nations.[14]

The expulsion of the demons from the Gadarene in Mark 5 is an interesting New Testament example. The demons pled with Jesus not to be sent out of the country (Mark 5:10). If they were sent to another location, they feared they would be expelled from there because they would be invading another authority's territory.

The powers will be strengthened or not, depending upon what we human beings purpose and do in feeding them or rebuking them. Are the powers over regions or cities good or evil? Some scholars suggest that demons often take on the nature of the area where they have been placed, and that human behavior is directly related to their actions. Humans and the powers mutually influence each other. When the church is inserted into the context, it has as its fundamental role the stopping of the evil actions of the powers. There is no halfway: either the church chooses to use its authority, repudiating diabolical actions through its prophetic ministry and living out the ethics of Christ, or it loses itself in the deep sleep of indifference or compromise, becoming a cooperator with the powers of destruction.

Walter Wink comments on Ephesians 6:12 in this connection. The passage says that our struggle is against "rulers" *(archas),* "authorities" *(exousias),* "cosmic powers" *(kosmokratoras),* and "spiritual forces" *(pneumatika).* Wink says:

> Here once again we have what is essentially a series, a heaping up of terms to describe the ineffable, invisible world-enveloping reach of a spiritual network of powers inimical to life. The very intention of series such as this, as we have seen repeatedly, is to be comprehensive. We must include here, then, all the *archai* and *exousiai* we have encountered, not only divine but human, not only personified but structural, not only demons and kings but the world atmosphere and power invested in institutions, laws, traditions and rituals as well, for it is the cumulative, totaling effect of all these taken together that creates the sense of bondage to a "dominion of darkness" presided over by higher powers.[15]

What Wink intended to expose in his books on the powers[16] is that whatever social, political, religious, or economic structures exist are under the rule and manipulation of the powers. John Dawson, analyzing the history of Uganda, discovered that the peculiar behavior and attitudes that marked the administration of ex-president Idi Amin had been repeated over the generations. What caught my attention was an account of a tribal king who once dominated Uganda. He was proud, sexually depraved, and extremely cruel. The description was remarkably similar to the newspaper reports of the modern dictator who ruled Uganda. Idi Amin and his regime of death seemed to match his predecessor in every detail. I have since studied the history of Uganda in greater depth. The cycle of a bloodbath followed by revival followed by bloodbaths is evidence of the ebb and flow of a battle. The national church has come against the evil spirit, thus prevailing over this nation.[17]

Behind the peculiar attitudes of political regimes and social structures there may exist a personality that perpetuates its characteristics, generation after generation. This power may go unchecked if it is not challenged by the church of Jesus Christ. Perhaps movements like Communism, Nazism, Pan-Nipponism, and apartheid would be better understood if we could identify the powers behind them.[18] On the other hand, there are certain powers that are continually present and they have been much more influential in human history. Is not Mammon still manipulating many today through materialism, consumerism, illicit businesses, the love and worship of money, and the exploitation of the poor? The annual disappearance of thousands of children and babies, the killing of millions of lives through abortion, the institutionalization of innumerable boys and girls who, in fact, do not live but simply survive in halfway houses and detention centers, the indignity of children and others making the streets their home—are not all these manipulated by the god Moloch and his minions? This god, feared since the time of Moses, required the bloody sacrifices of children. Is he not still with us today, marking his presence in modern society, albeit with new sophisticated clothing that better fits our century?[19] Some writers believe that even today, in both the so-called First and Third Worlds, the god Moloch has had sacrificed on his altar thousands of children through Satanism,[20] religious rituals of power, and the denial of fatherhood and motherhood by killing and abortion.

MISSIOLOGICAL IMPLICATIONS

This ongoing struggle, this declared war between the saints and the powers, has several important missiological implications. If the church of Jesus Christ is to faithfully and fully live out its calling, genuinely expressing its God-ordained nature, then ongoing warfare with the powers is inevitable. At times this war will take dramatic forms. The church must be a community that really knows how to worship the Lord of Lords, that invests its time and efforts in a life of prayer and contemplation of God, and that proclaims the gospel in its all dimensions.

The church is the only community that worships and exalts the true God in Spirit and truth (John 4:23). True worship in and of itself, by confessing who God is and by exalting his glory, his great deeds, and the depths of the richness of his wisdom, mercy, and love, is also a facet of war against the powers. The church becomes a community of worship when we invest time enough to intercede and pray.

Through prayer we fight and struggle against the powers. In Ephesians 6, after describing the nature of spiritual armor, God calls the church to be strong against the enemy. "Pray in the Spirit at all times in every prayer and supplication. To that end keep alert and always persevere in supplication for all the saints" (Eph. 6:18). Prevailing prayer by the people of God is at the heart of the war against Satan and his hosts. Through prayer, the church is enabled to bind and immobilize "the strong man" in the life of an individual, a family, a church, and even a city and nation (Matt. 12:29), forbidding his devastating action.

Through prayer one is also able to satisfy one's own hunger for God and for his righteousness. Battles are fought with the sword of the Spirit, as suggested by the picture of the Lord Jesus in the book of Revelation, a sharp two-edged sword in his mouth (Rev. 1:16). It is the verbal proclamation of the gospel together with the "demonstration of the Spirit and of power" (1 Cor. 2:4) that overcomes. It is not intellectualized and intelligent discourse that convicts the captive of Satan of his or her need. It is the Holy Spirit who convicts the person enslaved by the world system, by the work of the flesh, or by the devil. John reminds us that it is the Holy Spirit himself who convicts the world of sin, of judgment, and of righteousness (John 16:8).

The word transmitted by Jesus was spirit and life (John 6:63). Gospel proclamation enlivened and activated by the Holy Spirit brings life to the dead. Authentic proclamation and the power of the Living Word break the power of sin. But the proclaimed Word must be saturated with true, sincere prayer.

Jesus Christ was the evangelist par excellence. He spoke "as one having authority" (Mark 1:22). This same authority is available to the church today through the Holy Spirit, who is the living and working Lord here and now. The Word of God must also be communicated and received through the empowering of the Holy Spirit. What makes the difference is time invested in prayer by the speaker and the church.

Exercising authority over demons does not mean simply expelling them from a demonized person. It also implies wielding influence over the powers of evil that incite sins—powers such as vices, materialism, violence, sensuality, misery or poverty, and social injustice. It also means resisting and dethroning the principalities and powers over cities and geographical areas. A number of authors are presently researching this subject both in the Bible and in the practicum of life.[21]

God has given the church the ability to identify the powers over cities in order to cast them out and dethrone them. The church, as the extension of Christ, can commit certain geographical areas to the true Lord's control. The consequences of such an action are unprecedented gospel receptivity. The commitment of a city or region to the Lordship of Christ and the dethroning of the strong man of the area must be followed by the proclamation of the gospel.

There are many cases that could provide examples, especially in mission contexts and in the evangelization of large cities and nations. In the Philippines, for example, when Lester Sumrall expelled a demon from a certain medium (in one of the most horrendous spiritual/physical encounters ever witnessed), the immediate result following the liberation of that woman was the conversion of 150,000 people to Jesus Christ as Savior. Significantly, during the five months of preaching prior to this encounter, only five people were converted.[22]

Some Argentinean evangelists have discovered other forms of confronting the powers, subduing them and then preaching the gospel. They have been successful in integrating traditional evangelization with spiritual warfare. Many Argentine cities, once under the control of the powers and completely closed to the gospel, have become open to the message of salvation. A significant example was the rapid multiplication of churches in the one hundred-kilometer area surrounding the city of Rosario after Edgard Silvoso broke the authority of the power controlling this area. The area had been under the dominion of an internationally known spiritist healer until 1985. Similar experiences have been reported in Uruguay, the United States, Brazil, Korea, Greece, and Papua New Guinea.

To evangelize—to present the gospel—is to give impetus to the transfer of men and women from the empire of darkness to the kingdom of the light of the Son. It is to deal with the powers in spiritual realms. If we want take evangelization seriously, we have to face the powers and all the implications of an ongoing battle for the family, the church, personal lives, and also for cities and entire nations. God wants the church to experience the reality of the spiritual realm so that it might not only win people as individuals, but also fulfill his desire to subdue cities and even nations in the name of the Lord Jesus Christ. Only the church of Jesus Christ can do it!

Serving as a Free Methodist missionary in Brazil from 1968 to 1975 prompted Howard Snyder to rethink his understanding of the church and its mission. Since that time he has continued to develop and articulate a biblical theology of mission, using a variety of models. This chapter, based on Snyder's inaugural lecture as Heisel Professor of Evangelization and Church Renewal at United Theological Seminary, argues that the gospel is genuinely good news for all cultures and suggests the basic elements of an authentic evangelization for today.

CHAPTER FOURTEEN

THE GOSPEL AS GLOBAL GOOD NEWS
Howard A. Snyder

INTRODUCTION

One day I received a letter from my daughter, Jerilyn. She was having long discussions with a friend. In the letter she asked me several questions: "Is Jesus Christ really the *only* way to salvation? If so, what about the Scripture passages that speak of 'sheep of another fold' and the examples of Melchizedek and Cornelius? What happens to the people who really don't know or understand or never hear of the Way of Christ?"

Good questions. Though perhaps slightly embarrassing to many postmodern minds sharply aware of cultural pluralism, these are questions many sincere Christians ponder. And they deserve, in fact, serious consideration. What of the millennia-old claim, the heartbeat of the first Christians, that the news about Jesus Christ is the great good news for all times and peoples?

From various angles the contributors to this book have wrestled with the claim that the gospel is global good news. In this chapter I argue the case that the gospel of Jesus Christ is, in fact, good news—not only for individual persons, but for the whole cosmos; not only for North Americans, but for everyone; not only for the past or present, but also for the future.

Is such an audacious claim credible today?

I will show that it is. The message of Jesus Christ is good news to the whole earth—in fact, to the cosmos. In an age of newly emerging global society, the gospel of Jesus Christ is in fact *the* good news for all creation.

Of course, this has been the gospel's own claim from the beginning. The gospel is an announcement of "peace on earth" (Luke 2:14). It is good news to all creation, to all people and nations, to the whole earthly environment, and to the whole cosmos. This is the claim of Scripture. Instead of suggesting that this claim is now outmoded, I will argue that it is true in some new ways as we enter the twenty-first century. At this hinge between millennia, this transition between modernism and postmodernism, this closing of almost seventeen hundred years of Christendom, we must know what we mean when we say the message of Jesus Christ is good news.

I begin with five affirmations that will in turn structure the chapter. Speaking of the gospel as good news involves these claims:

1. The good news is, first of all, Jesus Christ and the mission of God.
2. The gospel is good news to the whole creation.
3. The gospel is good news in a postmodern, post-Christendom age.
4. The gospel calls for radical renewal in the church.
5. The gospel calls us to the task of evangelization.

THE GOOD NEWS IS JESUS CHRIST AND THE MISSION OF GOD

Jesus Christ is the good news. The gospel is good news first of all because of who Jesus Christ is, and of what God has done and is doing through him. Essentially the gospel is not about what Christians believe, or even about what the Bible says. It is about what God has done historically in Jesus Christ. It centers in the life, death, resurrection, and continuing ministry of Jesus Christ.

The Gospel Story

In all our theologizing, the essential story, the essential good news, can get lost. Two thousand years ago in an obscure Middle Eastern village, a baby was born whose mother was a young Jew and whose father was God. This child grew up and lived a life utterly remarkable in its simplicity, directness, compassion, and authority. He was executed on trumped-up charges but returned to life a couple of days later. He spent a month or so with a group of his followers, and then ascended into the sky, beyond human sight.

He was never physically seen again, but his followers later claimed he was with them in the form of his Spirit, and that someday he would return to earth. They showed such remarkable certainty about this that thousands of people believed in Jesus as Savior, Lord, and the meaning of all history. For nearly twenty centuries this circle of believers has expanded so that today the body of those who believe in Jesus Christ is now a great multitude that no one can count, from nearly every nation, tribe, people, and language (see Rev. 7:9).

Now plainly, this interpretation of Jesus Christ is incredible. Is it credible that God would take on human form, or that a crucified man would come back to life? Certainly it is not credible in the modern age of science and reason, or in this postmodern time of rejection of "meta-narratives," denial that we can know "facts," and suspicion about the ideological nature of all belief systems.

This story was no more credible two thousand years ago, however, in the first-century Roman world. The account of Jesus was not credible to Greeks because they knew that the eternal, perfect, changeless Deity could not exist in imperfect, corruptible, material form. It was incredible to Jews that the Messiah could be crucified and die without restoring the Davidic kingdom to Israel. It was incredible to scientists and medical people who knew that "dead men don't rise" (hardly a modern discovery). It was incredible to adherents of other religions, for these and a variety of other reasons. It was too simple a story—not sophisticated enough.

In other words, the gospel of Jesus Christ wasn't any easier to believe in the first century than it is today. It was "a stumbling block to Jews and foolishness to Gentiles" (1 Cor. 1:23). Probably all the objections to Christ's uniqueness raised today were heard in the first-century world. The story of Jesus clashed with people's worldviews as well as with their personal commitments.

It is no surprise that the same is true today. Perhaps the only real surprise is that today many people who consider themselves Christians stumble over the bare essentials of the gospel message.

Here we face a remarkable paradox. That which is plainly incredible—that is, unbelievable—is believed today by more and more people worldwide at the rate of several thousand a day. And these are not "primitive" or superstitious people given to believing incredible things. They are people like Tatiana Goricheva, who had a strange experience while studying philosophy in Leningrad. She had rejected dialectical materialism and embraced existentialism, yet found that unsatisfying. She turned to yoga, but still found no answer to her despair. She tells what happened next:

In a yoga book a Christian prayer, the "Our Father," was suggested as an exercise. . . . I began to say it as a mantra, automatically and without expression. I said it about six times, and then I was suddenly turned inside out. I understood . . . that he exists. [God], the living, personal God, who loves me and all creatures, who has created the world, who became a human being out of love, the crucified and risen God.[1]

The world today provides thousands of such stories from around the globe. Among the Sawi tribe of West Irian, Jesus is discovered to be the "Peace Child" who brings reconciliation to warring tribes.[2] Among the Masai of Tanzania, Jesus Christ is found to be the one who brings hope and a new sense of community, as recounted in the remarkable book *Christianity Rediscovered* by the Roman Catholic missionary Vincent Donovan.[3] The story of Jesus Christ is still proving to be "the power of God for salvation to everyone who has faith" (Rom. 1:16).

Certainly the gospel has never won points for being easy to believe when it clashes with other worldviews and commitments. But it *has* brought unspeakable joy and confidence and meaning to those who *have* believed. And, when honestly and openly examined, it has often been found to give more satisfying and coherent answers than competing worldviews.

The gospel is good news not only about Jesus as a person, however. It also concerns God's purpose to bring reconciliation or *shalom* to all creation through Jesus Christ. Scripture expresses this sense of overall purpose and direction in a variety of ways. In both Testaments it is frequently called "the kingdom of God." Missiologists often speak of it as "the mission of God." This theme is expressed nowhere more profoundly than in Ephesians 1:10 and Colossians 1:15-20. God is carrying out a plan, an "economy," through Jesus Christ "to gather up all things in him, things in heaven and things on earth" (Eph. 1:10). "For in him all the fullness of God was pleased to dwell, and through him God was pleased to reconcile to himself all things, whether on earth or in heaven, by making peace through the blood of his cross" (Col. 1:19-20).

Missiologists debate how this central theme can best be expressed in our emerging global context. The term "kingdom of God" has certain limitations, as many have pointed out.[4] A variety of models and paradigms for the church's mission have been suggested.[5] The term "mission of God" is useful, for it grounds this aspect of God's overarching purposes in God's own nature. Any mission that the church may have is to be measured by the mission of God as seen in Jesus Christ.

Scripturally, to speak of Christ is to speak of Jesus. "Christ" is not some abstract, indefinite cosmic principle or generic divine spirit. "Christ" means "Messiah." To say "Jesus Christ" is to say "Jesus Messiah." It is to affirm that Jesus is the promised Servant of God who brings deliverance, liberation, and salvation to Israel and to all nations.

Jesus Christ is the same Jesus who rose from the dead. If Jesus Christ is not raised, then our hope is only in hope. As Paul says in Acts 26, in Jesus is fulfilled what the prophets foretold: "that the Messiah must suffer and that, by being the first to rise from the dead, he would proclaim light both to our people and to the Gentiles" (Acts 26:23).

THE GOSPEL IS GOOD NEWS TO THE WHOLE CREATION

The gospel is *global* good news. Thinking globally, God acted locally.

The gospel is good news about personal, social, ecological, and cosmic healing and reconciliation. It is God's good news to the whole creation—to the whole earth and, in fact, to the cosmos. This is clearly what the "all things in heaven and on earth" of Paul's letters implies. But this claim is grounded in a broad range of scriptures in both Testaments, as well.

The gospel is good news to people, tribes, nations, and ethnic enclaves, to culture, and to nature itself. It is good news *globally* and *locally*. It is good news *personally* and *socially*. It is good news for time and for eternity. It is, as William Booth of the Salvation Army said over a hundred years ago, "salvation for both worlds."[6] Or, as we perhaps might prefer to say today, it is salvation for the universe in all its dimensions, in all its multi-dimensionality.[7]

The good news addresses God's creation on at least four levels:

1. *It is directed to the individual human person,* "calling for the conversion of heart and mind,"[8] so that life is lived after the pattern of Jesus Christ. While the gospel is addressed to all people everywhere, it is especially a mission to the poor, the masses, and the underclasses of the world. Though it excludes none who come to God with a "humble and contrite heart," the primary direction of its energy is toward the poor. The gospel message is incoherent if it is not a message for all peoples in all times and places. Its most central claim concerns what God has done and is doing in history to bring *shalom* to the whole creation. Remove this, and you may still have Christianity, but you no longer have the gospel of Jesus Christ.

2. *The gospel is addressed to society,* to social life, "the structures of public life, calling for the righting of wrong and the liberation of the oppressed."[9] It is good news to the social order.

3. *The gospel is addressed also to the underlying patterns and assumptions of culture,* the "root paradigms" that form worldviews and govern definitions of truth and reality. It calls for their transformation away from partial or ideological truths to a cosmic worldview in which each particle and particular has its proper place.

4. *The gospel is addressed also to the whole cosmos*—"the rocks and the mountains," the earth and the planets. God speaks through God's Word to the whole created order. This is the basis (in part) for what we might call "ecological evangelism."

In Scripture, the word of God is at times directed to the material environment itself. Jeremiah 22:29 says, "O land, land, land, hear the word of the LORD!" In Ezekiel 20:47 God tells the prophet, "Say to the forest of the Negeb, Hear the word of the LORD." And again in Ezekiel 36:1, 8-9: "Prophesy to the mountains of Israel, and say: O mountains of Israel, hear the word of the LORD. . . . You, O mountains of Israel, shall shoot out your branches, and yield your fruit to my people Israel; for they shall soon come home. See now, I am for you; I will turn to you, and you shall be tilled and sown."

Another way of stating this is that the gospel proposes and offers *healing* or reconciliation at the four levels of hurt and alienation in our world: between the human person and God; between the human person and herself; between and among people (the interpersonal, social level); and between human beings and the whole cosmos—the total environment.

But as the good news, the gospel may first be heard as bad news, for it also confronts the world's idolatries and self-deceptions. It exposes our idolatries of ideology, nation, religion, technology, power, the self, and nature. Ideology can be oppressive, whether in political, economic, or religious form. Whenever we put anything in the place of Jesus Christ—theology, church structures, the Bible, or any political or social cause—this is idolatry and must be exposed. For many of us the danger is to put our nation or our ethnic group, rather than Jesus, at the center. Technology, for all its positive powers, can become our god. So can nature, or the earth, when we worship the creation rather than the Creator, or make the fatal assumption that the two are the same.

As we hear what God is saying to us through Jesus Christ in all these areas, we learn what it means for the gospel to be good news for the whole cosmos. This must shape our understanding and practice of an authentic, winsome evangelization for today.

THE GOSPEL IS GOOD NEWS IN A POSTMODERN, POST-CHRISTENDOM AGE

The gospel of Jesus Christ is good news specifically in the postmodern, post-Christendom age we are now entering. In fact, this may be the time of the gospel's greatest power and opportunity. It was made for such a time as this.

Part of today's good news is that Christendom is dead and modernism is dying. A new age is coming. We are entering a global marketplace of worldviews and ideas. It is a time, as we hear constantly, of new models and paradigms. But this is no threat to the gospel.

We do not yet know fully what the "new paradigms" of understanding the gospel and the church's mission in a postmodern age will look like. It is interesting to see the growing theological interest in the Trinity today, however. It may be that the "old" doctrine of the Trinity holds new power for setting forth the dynamism of the gospel in a postmodern age.

The good news can certainly be proclaimed with vigor and conviction in such an age, even while it is proclaimed and lived with humility and compassion. Jesus' own life is the obvious proof of this. But thousands of other faithful witnesses through the centuries can be cited as corroborating evidence, from Peter at Cornelius's house, to many Christian slaves in early America, to Mother Teresa in the twentieth century.

This is also a time of religious pluralism, as well as pluralism of other kinds. In this regard, our age is much like the first century. The question is: What do we do with this pluralism?

One answer—not a new one, but newly posed in recent years—is the suggestion of a "pluralistic theology of religion."

As a fact, religious pluralism must be recognized and respected. It can even be welcomed by those who are confident that Jesus Christ is "the way, the truth, and the life" and thus have no fear of competing claims. But as a worldview in itself, religious pluralism is incoherent and self-contradictory, as Andrew Kirk shows in his book *Loosing the Chains*.[10]

Authentic evangelization does not mean a quixotic quest for some theoretical pluralistic theology of religion—as though all religions at heart taught the same thing or led in the same direction. Such a view would be unfair to the world's religions.

It is interesting that thoroughgoing advocates of religious pluralism (as a worldview) believe rather dogmatically that any religion's dogmatic claim to be the only way to salvation is necessarily false. The view seems to be: All religions may be true, or contain truth. But if any religion claims to be the only way, that claim is false. Yet this claim of absolute pluralism is true.

The significance of this view (in part) is twofold: (1) This claim in effect cancels beliefs that are central and essential to the religious system in question. (2) This assertion becomes a dogmatic claim utilized to deny other dogmatic claims.

It is not "good news" to the Buddhist, the Muslim, the Hindu—or even the secularist or New Ager—to say: *You have only a partial understanding of the truth. You give up your absolutist claims, and I'll give up mine, and together we'll believe in "religion in general," or "religion altogether," a lowest-common-denominator faith that relativizes all the historic claims of our traditions.* This is not good news. In fact, it is presumptive and imperialistic. It is arrogant to suggest to a Muslim or a Hindu that the "real" truth lies not in the truth they claim, but in some deeper or higher or broader truth they haven't yet perceived. We must take non-Christian beliefs and worldviews more seriously than that.

Christian witnesses must always have a profound respect for other beliefs and worldviews, because the Christian worldview calls Christians to respect every person. Christians must be tolerant. I speak, however, of a tolerance that is based on a profound conviction of transcendent truth, not a disregard for or denial of truth.

For Christians, the way forward lies not in a pluralistic theology of religion but in the recognition that we all operate out of particular worldviews, or what sociologist Peter Berger calls "plausibility structures." The challenge for the Christian is to "inhabit" the plausibility structure that finds its central meaning in Jesus Christ as attested in Scripture.

Bishop Lesslie Newbigin is particularly lucid on this point. In *Truth to Tell* Newbigin writes, "We have to offer a new starting point for thought. That starting point is God's revelation of his being and purpose in those events which form the substance of the Scriptures and which have their center and determining focus in the events concerning Jesus."[11] Newbigin argues that "it is . . . possible to indwell the Bible story so that you do not so much look *at* the Bible from without as look at the world from within the Bible, through the lenses that the Bible gives you. . . . Our use of the Bible is analogous to our use of language. We indwell it rather than looking at it from outside."[12]

Here the role of Scripture is crucial, for clearly it is our primary source of information about Jesus Christ. The Bible functions as the Book of the Covenant, an always revolutionary force in the church whose chief function is to reveal Jesus Christ to us.[13]

The Postmodern Jesus

When we begin with *this* starting point and then interact with postmodernism, Jesus appears in a startling new light. Jesus is not made obsolete by postmodernism. Rather than making Jesus irrelevant, postmodern sensibilities make Jesus look all the more remarkable.

In many respects, Jesus fits postmodern sensibilities better than he does modern or premodern views. The premodern worldview locked Jesus in a box of static order and changelessness, as in much medieval Christian theology and other forms of Christian orthodoxy. The modern worldview in its various forms remade Jesus in its own image—philosopher, poet, philanthropist, or lawgiver. Postmodernism helpfully shatters these earlier worldviews, just possibly making Jesus accessible and understandable as never before.

Here is true irony—perhaps the strangest irony of all: The most postmodern person of history lived not in the twentieth century but in the first century A.D. The irony of Jesus is that he embodies and transcends the postmodern sensibility.

One of the startling ironies of Jesus Christ is that this person whom millions of people throughout history have seen as the most selfless and self-giving of persons was also the most self-centered. In the New Testament records Jesus constantly speaks of himself, even making faith in him the door to truth. This is the great irony and the great conundrum of the person of Jesus. The claims he made about himself suggest that he was either deluded, mentally ill, or insufferably vain and self-centered. Yet his life shows the opposite. He was remarkably compassionate, self-giving, and humble, "the man for others." What kind of man is this? How does one solve the mystery of Jesus?

One way is to say that he was the ultimate postmodern, incarnating in his person the very concerns of postmodernism. And then, most pointedly, he transcends the postmodern critique, standing it on its head. Jesus Christ carries the ironic and self-referential elements of postmodernism to new dimensions of meaning. Ironically, Jesus transforms irony into meaning and self-reference into self-identity and therefore self-giving.

It is remarkable how Jesus embodies and anticipates postmodernist concerns. In Jesus we find self-reference that, however, is not selfishness. We find the ultimate irony of an irony that transcends irony. Ironically, Jesus lived a transitory life on Earth of only thirty years and yet is the most abiding figure of all history. No one's life appears freer, more contingent, or more open-ended. And yet he said he came into the world to fulfill God's purposes and spoke as though the very events of his life were preplanned. He claimed, in fact, to be the Messiah, the Christ, the promised one through whom God would fulfill his promises to save Israel and bring justice and peace on earth.[14]

Building on Jesus' own words, the writers of the New Testament found the explanation for Jesus to be that he was unique among all human beings who ever lived. Their explanation is that Jesus is both God and human, the incarnation of God in human form, "the Word made flesh."

If this claim is true, it answers the riddle of Jesus. The reason Jesus is unlike every other human being is that he is God incarnate. Yet the reason he is like every other human being is that he is God incarnate—fully and in every way human, God doing the philosophically impossible: assuming the dimensions of space, time, and matter.

This, of course, still leaves us with a great mystery—how Jesus Christ could be both divine and human. No one has ever figured that out. No creedal formula is adequate. But if that mystery is accepted by faith or as a hypothesis, or as the basis of a worldview, it provides plausible answers to every other human question.

Here is, in fact, the basis for a coherent worldview: Jesus, the source and goal of history. He is the pivot, the meaning of the story, the one on whom all else turns. He is history's end, not as terminator but as *telos,* the goal that opens into new life, new levels, and new dimensions and meanings of existence in the limitless realm of the spirit.

The bottom line is that postmodernism—in whatever form it takes—is an opening, not a threat, to the good news.

THE GOSPEL CALLS FOR RADICAL RENEWAL IN THE CHURCH

The good news of Jesus Christ calls for the radical renewal of the church.[15] An authentic evangelization today requires recentering the gospel in Jesus Christ as attested in Scripture.

Today there are three revolutions that must happen if the global church is to be faithful to Jesus Christ and to world need in the twenty-first century. Perhaps these revolutions are already beginning in "the fullness of time."

First, the church must really come to see itself as a *missionary community* in the world, existing for the sake of the mission of God—or, as Greg Leffel says, a mission *movement.*

Second, the church must come to see itself as the community of aliens who are *in* but not *of* the world—aliens, not to the physical world or to other people, but to the exploitive world systems. There is a tension to be maintained here, of course. We are not called to withdraw from the world, but we are called to take our key cues for living from the gospel, not from society's reigning values.

Jesus Christ himself provides the model. He was fully *in* and *with* the world, but lived by a contrasting set of realities. His life was marked by integrity and love. A life so lived will always be, at one and the same time, winsome and alien.

Third, ministry must be understood as the privilege and responsibility of *all* Christian believers. This means thoroughly reconceiving the pastoral role. It means an affirmation of the gifts and calling of all believers.

One step in this direction is to begin using inclusive language when we speak of ministry. Christians don't usually speak inclusively when they refer to the ministry of God's people. The New Testament distinguishes between different kinds of ministries and callings, based on the diversity of personalities and spiritual gifts. God calls and the church recognizes, in particular, equipping ministers whose task it is "to equip the saints for the work of ministry" (Eph. 4:12). This is simply part of the diversity of total ministry, however, not a distinction between some who are ministers and others who are not.

It is time to begin using inclusive language when referring to ministry. In fact, the unbiblical use of the terms "ministry" and "laity" is the most extensive and oppressive form of exclusive language in the church. When we use gender-exclusive language, we exclude about 50 percent of all Christians. But when we use the minister/layman distinction, we exclude 90 or 95 percent of all Christians! It is time to be truly inclusive by referring to all Christians as ministers and banning the term "layman" whenever it means Christians who are not ministers.

Evangelization and church renewal are interrelated. A vital church is an evangelistic magnet, even as it is a river of love and service in the world. And a church that evangelizes effectively and holistically lives off a spring of perpetual renewal.

THE GOSPEL CALLS US TO THE TASK OF EVANGELIZATION

Finally, the gospel of Jesus Christ calls us to an authentic evangelization. This is part of our calling, our "vocation" *(vocatio)* as followers of Jesus. The One who calls us to Jesus Christ calls all men and women everywhere, and sends us into the world as Jesus was sent into the world (John 20:21).

The task of evangelization is, most basically, simply the living out of the command to love God with all our heart, soul, strength, and mind, and to love our neighbor as ourselves. We want what is best for everyone, and therefore want everyone to experience the love of God as expressed in Jesus Christ. But because of love, we approach that desire and impulse humbly, recognizing that often others will see matters differently. So we are willing to listen, to hear, to try to understand, and to recognize that God is already ahead of us, already working in those to whom we would witness. Evangelization grows from love, energized by the Holy Spirit in our lives and faith communities.

Authentic Evangelization

The book of Acts provides us with many key insights for an authentic Christian evangelization. We can learn much from the first Christian evangelists. In Acts we see several key themes emerging:

- Jesus of Nazareth was sent by God as God's unique instrument.
- Jesus fulfilled the prophecies about the Messiah.
- Jesus was crucified, but God raised him from the dead.
- The apostles were witnesses of these events.
- Everyone who believes in Jesus receives forgiveness of sins.[16]

Now the gospel in Acts, and certainly in the New Testament, is broader than this. It includes the whole message and hope of the kingdom of God. But here is its heart. At its center are the life, death, and resurrection of Jesus. In Acts, the gospel is the good news of "peace by Jesus Christ—he is Lord of all" (Acts 10:36). It is "the good news about Jesus and the resurrection" (Acts 17:18). It is the message of "the kingdom of God and . . . the Lord Jesus Christ," as the very last verse in Acts says (28:31).

Evangelization is more than sermons or "verbal summaries" of the gospel story, of course. It is about life lived; about community; about everyday discipleship that is so marked by Jesus Christ that people say things like, "Look how they love one another; look how they meet human need. Look: these are the people who have been with Jesus" (see Acts 4:13 and John 13:35). We see this also in Acts, and sense the link between what the first Christians lived and proclaimed and what Jesus himself said and did in the gospel accounts.

As we seek for an authentic evangelization, the account of Peter's

encounter with Cornelius is particularly instructive. The key passage is
Acts 10:34-43. Note especially the first two things Peter says: "I truly
understand that God shows no partiality, but in every nation anyone
who fears him and does what is right is acceptable to him. You know the
message he sent to the people of Israel, preaching peace by Jesus Christ—
he is Lord of all." Two things are happening here: Peter learns something
about God, and he proclaims something about Jesus Christ. In this situation Peter is both evangelizing and being evangelized. He proclaims
good news, and he learns good news.

Here is a two-way evangelization, or what we might call the *double
action* or reflexivity of evangelism: its action on Peter and on Cornelius.
Evangelization acts on the church and on the non-Christian seeker for
God.

Peter's encounter with Cornelius shows us several things:

First, Peter needed to learn something. Peter learned that "God shows
no partiality, but in every nation anyone who fears him and does what is
right is acceptable to him." This was a new lesson for Peter—it was
clearly a paradigm shift. Here *Peter* is evangelized. He learns what is, in
fact, good news: God accepts people anywhere who worship God and
live just lives, even if they are Gentiles! We might call this the *first action*
of evangelization: what the Christian learns when sharing her or his faith
with someone from a different perspective.

But we see here also what *Cornelius* needed to learn. This is found in
the next several verses, and particularly in the very next sentence: "the
message [God] sent to the people of Israel, preaching peace by Jesus
Christ—he is Lord of all." Cornelius needed to know that this God
whom he had worshiped sincerely and uprightly had sent Jesus Christ,
the "Lord of all," into the world. He needed to know and believe the
central story about Jesus Christ. Peter relates this, and the result was that
the Holy Spirit came upon Cornelius and his household. They received
the Holy Spirit just as did Peter and the others on the day of Pentecost.

This incident thus teaches us multiple lessons about authentic evangelization. We learn, first, that in evangelizing we are evangelized. Second,
we learn that God is at work among all nations, hearing and accepting
those who worship God and lead just lives. And third, we learn that we
are to share the story of Jesus Christ, the Lord of all, with all people of
all nations who are willing to hear.

This and other New Testament examples give us the basis for a faithful evangelization—an evangelization that is both audacious and humble. Christians do not claim that Christianity is simply one religion
among many, or that of the world's many belief systems, this just happens to be ours. They claim rather that God has acted in Jesus Christ

decisively, once for all in human history. God has *acted*. He is not simply or passively present in "events" or "happenings." God is seen in the self-conscious, willing, acting life of Jesus Christ.[17]

Now, this claim may sound audacious and even arrogant. How do we respond? The modern and postmodern tendency is to say: Arrogance is wrong, so it must be that this claim for Christian uniqueness is wrong. But such either/or logic is faulty. It is not necessarily arrogant to tell the truth.

But is the Christian message inherently arrogant? No. It is inherently audacious, but also inherently humble, just like Jesus—if it is in fact the good news of and about Jesus Christ.

The problem is that the proclamation of the gospel has often been wed to social or political power and divorced from humility and compassion. This is the problem not of the gospel, however, but of Christianity or Christendom. Christianity has often taken on powerful institutional form, and in the process betrayed the very gospel it claims and proclaims. The church comes to feel it *owns* the gospel, rather than *being owned by* the gospel. And so Christianity itself becomes a stumbling block to the good news. It converts the good news into bad news.

Whenever this happens, the gospel must be freed from the religion of Christianity in order truly to be good news. This should not seem surprising; it is precisely what prophets and effective evangelists have shown us repeatedly in history. This is the situation we face today in any cultural setting in which Christianity is allied with the power structures and is visible principally in institutional form.

Evangelization can be done with conviction and humility when it isn't caught up in defending Christianity as an organized religion. Christians really have no business defending Christianity, for at least three reasons. First, to the degree that Christianity has been unfaithful to the gospel, it deserves critique and correction, not defense.

Second, to the degree that Christianity has been *true* to the gospel, it needs no defense, for its faithfulness is its own witness and defense. It needs no *defense*, but it does call us to faithful witness.[18] Third, Christians cannot defend Christianity without at least *sounding*, and probably actually *being*, defensive.

What would a faithful, authentic, postmodern evangelism look like? It would exhibit an unbounded, joyous confidence in Jesus Christ and in what God has done through him for the salvation of the world. It would spring from the profound conviction that Jesus is the answer to the longing of every human heart and to the highest aspirations of every human culture.

Such a winsome telling of the good news can and should be done.

Most important, such an authentic postmodern evangelization will:
- reclaim the importance of history,
- serve in a listening, hearing mode in encountering other people and religions,
- be global in perspective,
- center in Jesus Christ as revealed in Scripture,
- combine word and act,
- be empowered by the Holy Spirit,
- be based in community,
- seek the renewal and unity of the whole church,
- elaborate a credible Christian worldview, and
- be ecological in perspective.

More succinctly, we might say that an authentic Christian evangelization today will be *trinitarian, Christocentric, incarnational, ecclesial,* and *ecological.*

It will be *trinitarian* in that it will affirm and explore the power of the doctrine of the Trinity as a paradigm for authentic, faithful witness today. A. H. Matthias Zahniser has explored this helpfully in his essay "The Trinity: Paradigm for Mission in the Spirit." Zahniser suggests that in God the Father we find the *motivation* for "mission without boundaries"; that in God the Son we see the *model* for world evangelization; and that in God the Spirit, "the Spirit of self-effacement," we find the *mode* of Christian mission.[19]

Starting with the Holy Trinity as ultimate reality means affirming *community,* not individualism or autonomy or the annihilation of personal identity. It means *mutuality,* not hierarchy or anarchy. And it affirms *personality,* not impersonal energy or mere personalism.

Authentic, faithful evangelization will certainly be *Christocentric,* centering in the life, death, resurrection, and ongoing reign of Jesus Christ that we see in the New Testament.

Authentic evangelization will also be *incarnational.* It will take seriously Jesus' words, "As the Father has sent me, so I send you." Faithful evangelization "incarnates" the love of Jesus Christ in self-giving human life, serving others in their need and also being ready to tell the story of what God has done in Jesus Christ.

Faithful evangelization will be *ecclesial.* It will be the good news incarnated not just in individual lives, but also in community. It will be ecclesial in the sense that it is grounded in shared life, in a vital expression of the Body of Christ. It will be ecclesial not only in the sense of each local community of believers, but also in the broader sense of a visible people of God scattered throughout the earth.

Finally, authentic evangelization will be *ecological* in the biblical sense. It will be concerned with the "all things" of God's creation, and with the interrelationship between human life, economics and society, nature, and the physical environment. It will be a demonstration of the *shalom* that God is bringing to all creation. It will take seriously not only the cycles of nature, but also the currents of history. If it remains biblically faithful, the church can engage in ecological evangelism without compromising personal evangelism, for the two are intertwined. Demonstrating in the physical environment the reconciliation that Jesus Christ is bringing is an integral part of the good news.

We are called to an authentic, faithful sharing of the good news of Jesus Christ. And share it we will, if in fact God is at work in us, making us the church Jesus called us to be.

CONCLUSION

Properly understood and incarnated, the gospel of Jesus Christ really is global good news. It is the best possible news for the whole cosmos and for every person and culture in it.

At the beginning I mentioned my daughter's letter. I responded, telling her what I think and what it seems to me that Scripture teaches. I said there are many things we don't yet know, particularly about just what God will or won't do in the future. Above all, I affirmed that God is reconciling the world to God's self in Jesus Christ, and that whoever is in Christ is "a new creation: everything old has passed away; see, everything has become new!" (2 Cor. 5:17).

NOTES

1: Mission in the Valley of Postmodernity

1. Neil Postman, *Technopoly: The Surrender of Culture to Technology* (New York: Alfred A. Knopf, 1992), pp. 52, 70, xii.

2. Dr. Ibrahim Abu-Rabi'; unpublished lecture to a planning group in Richmond, VA.

3. Harry Alpert, *Emile Durkheim and His Sociology* (New York: Russell & Russell, Inc., 1961), p. 206.

4. Quoted in Alpert, *Emile Durkheim and His Sociology*, p. 206.

5. Bassam Tibi, *The Crisis of Modern Islam: A Preindustrial Culture in the Scientific-Technological Age* (Salt Lake City: University of Utah Press, 1988), p. 47.

6. William A. Henry III, "Ready or Not, Here It Comes," *Time* Special Edition: *Beyond the Year 2000*, Fall 1992), p. 34.

7. Peter Drucker, *The New Realities* (New York: Harper & Row, 1989), pp. 131-32.

8. Abu-Rabi; unpublished lecture.

9. Gerald H. Anderson, James M. Phillips, and Robert T. Coote, eds., *Mission in the 1990s* (Grand Rapids, Mich.: William B. Eerdmans Publishing Company; New Haven, Conn.: Overseas Ministries Study Center, 1991).

10. George Land and Beth Jarman, "Future Pull: The Power of Vision and Purpose," *The Futurist* (July-August 1992), p. 25.

11. Lesslie Newbigin, *Mission in Christ's Way* (New York, N.Y.: Friendship Press, 1987), p. 11.

12. Charles Malik, "Christian Responsibility," *Together* (February 1961), p. 13.

2: The Mystery of Evangelism: Mission in an Age of Cosmic Discovery

1. Philip Doddridge, *The Correspondence and Diary of Philip Doddridge, D.D. Vol. 4*, ed. John Doddridge Humphrey (London: Henry Colburn and Richard Bently, 1829), pp. 274-75; *Philip Doddridge 1702–51: His Contribution to English Religion*, ed. Geoffrey F. Nuttall (London: Independent Press Ltd., 1951), pp. 83, 93-94.

2. John Wesley, *The Works of John Wesley, Volume 7: A Collection of Hymns for the Use of the People Called Methodists*, eds. Franz Hildebrandt and Oliver A. Beckerlegge with the assistance of James Dale (Oxford: Oxford University Press, 1983), pp. 350-51.

3. I have addressed this issue in *God Does Not Foreclose: The Universal Promise of Salvation* (Nashville: Abingdon Press, 1990), pp. 28ff., 99ff.

4. For example, when the church in North America was beginning to take an interest in small group dynamics, a history of encounter groups had already been written. See Kurt W. Back, *Beyond Words: The Story of Sensitivity Training and the Encounter Movement* (New York: Russell Sage Foundation, 1972).

5. Ludwig Feuerbach, *Principles of the Philosophy of the Future* (New York: Bobbs-Merrill, 1966), p. 5; *Lectures on the Essence of Religion* (New York: Harper & Row, 1967), p. 17ff.

6. Henry Fairlie, *The Seven Deadly Sins Today* (Notre Dame, Ind.: University of Notre Dame Press, 1979), p. 5.

7. Matthew Fox, *The Coming of the Cosmic Christ: The Healing of Mother Earth and the Birth of a Global Renaissance* (San Francisco: Harper & Row, 1988); Leonard I. Sweet, *Quantum Spirituality: A Postmodern Apologetic* (Dayton, Ohio: Whaleprints, 1991).

8. David B. Barrett, *Cosmos, Chaos, and Gospel: A Chronology of World Evangelization from Creation to New Creation* (Birmingham, Ala.: New Hope, 1987), p. 73. Barrett is the editor of *World Christian Encyclopedia: A Comparative Study of Churches and Religions in the Modern World*, A.D. 1900–2000 (Nairobi, Kenya: Oxford University Press, 1982; 2nd ed., 2001).

9. C. S. Lewis, *Out of the Silent Planet* (New York: Macmillan Publishing Co., Inc., 1965), p. 121.

10. Barrett, *Cosmos, Chaos, and Gospel*, p. 73.

11. Ibid., pp. 73-74. Stephen Hawking, *A Brief History of Time* (New York: Bantam Books, 1988).

12. Ibid., p. 74.

13. Elie Wiesel, *Night* (New York: Bantam Books, 1982), pp. 61-62.

14. Barrett, *Cosmos, Chaos, and Gospel*, p. 74.

15. Ibid., p. 75.

16. Hans Margull, *Hope in Action: The Church's Task in the World* (Philadelphia: Muhlenberg Press, 1962); Alfred C. Krass, *Five Lanterns at Sundown: Evangelism in a Chastened Mood* (Grand Rapids, Mich.: William B. Eerdmans Publishing Company, 1978); Mortimer Arias, *Announcing the Reign of God: Evangelization and the Subversive Memory of Jesus* (Philadelphia: Fortress Press, 1984); William J. Abraham, *The Logic of Evangelism* (Grand Rapids, Mich.: William B. Eerdmans Publishing Company, 1989); Howard A. Snyder, *Models of the Kingdom* (Nashville: Abingdon Press, 1991).

17. Arias, *Announcing the Reign of God*, p. 8ff.

18. M. Douglas Meeks, *God the Economist: The Doctrine of God and Political Economy* (Minneapolis, Minn.: Fortress Press, 1989), p. 120.

19. Quoted in Watson, *God Does Not Foreclose*, pp. 118, 155n.

20. For a definitive treatment, see Van Harvey, *The Historian and the Believer: The Morality of Historical Knowledge and Christian Belief* (New York: Macmillan Publishing Co., 1966).

21. Richard R. Niebuhr, *Resurrection and Historical Reason: A Study of Theological Method* (New York: Charles Scribner's Sons, 1957), pp. 4-23; Jürgen Moltmann, *Theology of Hope: On the Ground and the Implications of a Christian Eschatology* (New York: Harper & Row, 1967), pp. 172-90.

22. As, for example, during the evening news in San Antonio, Texas, on October 20, 1992. The commercial was aired by a United Methodist church in the city.

23. Quoted in Robert W. Lind, *From the Ground Up: The Story of "Brother Van," Montana Pioneer Minister 1848–1919* (Missoula, Mont.: Published by the author, 1961).

24. Robert E. Cushman, "Biblical Election as Sacred History: A Study in the Ancient History of Ecumenism" in John Deschner, Leroy T. Howe, and Klaus Penzel, eds., *Our Common History as Christians: Essays in Honor of Albert C. Outler* (New York: Oxford University Press, 1975), p. 210. J. C. Hoekendijk, *The Church Inside Out* (Philadelphia: Westminster Press, 1966).

25. David Lowes Watson, "Christ All in All: The Recovery of the Gospel for North American Evangelism," *Missiology* Vol. XIX, No. 4 (October 1991), p. 449.

26. Jacques Ellul, *The Presence of the Kingdom* (New York: Seabury Press, 1973); Juan Luis Segundo, *The Community Called Church* (Maryknoll, N.Y.: Orbis Books, 1973).

27. Albert C. Outler, "The Place of Wesley in the Christian Tradition" in Kenneth E. Rowe, ed., *The Place of Wesley in the Christian Tradition* (Metuchen, N.J.: Scarecrow Press, 1976), p. 25ff.

28. This is due in large measure to the widespread influence of the church growth movement, particularly in North America. While there is much of value to be culled from the work of scholars and practitioners in this field, the cumulative effect of church growth has been to foster a self-preoccupation of the church marked by inappropriate triumphalisms and unnecessary defeatisms. For contrasting approaches, see Priscilla Pope-Levison, *Evangelization from a Liberation Perspective* (New York: Peter Lang, 1991).

29. Barrett, *Cosmos, Chaos, and Gospel*, p. 74.

30. *A Collection of Hymns for the Use of the People Called Methodists* (London: Wesleyan Conference Office, 1831).

3: The Gospel Among the World Religions

1. David Barrett, "Annual Statistical Table on Global Mission: 1995," *International Bulletin of Missionary Research* 19:1 (January 1995), p. 25.

2. International Missionary Council, *Minutes of the Ad Interim Committee of the International Missionary Council*, Jordans, England, 4-8 June 1936 (London and New York: The Council), p. 15.

3. Hendrik Kraemer, *The Christian Message in a Non-Christian World* (New York: Harper & Brothers, 1938), p. 296; IMC, *The Authority of the Faith: The Madras Series Vol. I* (New York: International Missionary Council, 1939), p. 185; pp. 172-99 contain the Conference findings.

4. Stanley Samartha, "Mission in a Religiously Plural World: Looking beyond Tambaram 1938," *International Review of Mission* Vol. 78 (July 1988), p. 320; Jean Stromberg, "Christian Witness in a Pluralistic World: Report on a Mission/Dialogue Consultation," *International Review of Mission* Vol. 78 (July 1988), pp. 414, 421, 424.

5. Paul F. Knitter, *No Other Name? A Critical Survey of Christian Attitudes Toward the World Religions* (Maryknoll, N.Y.: Orbis Books, 1985); John Hick and Paul F. Knitter, eds., *The Myth of Christian Uniqueness: Toward a Pluralistic Theology of Religions* (Maryknoll, N.Y.: Orbis Books, 1987). See also Ken Gnanakan, *The Pluralistic Predicament* (Bangalore: Theological Book Trust, 1992).

6. Quoted in Knitter, *No Other Name?* p. 121.

7. 1910 World Missionary Conference, *Report of Commission IV: The Missionary Message in Relation to Non-Christian Religions* (London and Edinburgh: Oliphant, Anderson and Ferrier, 1910), p. 268. See Kenneth Cracknell, *Justice, Courtesy and Love: Theologians and Missionaries Encountering World Religions 1846–1914* (London: The Epworth Press, 1995), pp. 181-260, for a full analysis of the variety of responses at Edinburgh.

8. "The Lausanne Covenant" in *Let the Earth Hear His Voice: International Congress on World Evangelization, Lausanne, Switzerland. Official Reference Volume: Papers and Responses*, ed. J. D. Douglas (Minneapolis, Minn.: World Wide Publications, 1975), pp. 3-4.

9. Alan Race, *Christians and Religious Pluralism: Patterns in the Christian Theology of Religions* (Maryknoll, N.Y.: Orbis Books, 1982), p. 24.

10. Karl Rahner, *Theological Investigations Vol. 5: Later Writings* (Baltimore: Helicon Press, 1966), pp. 121, 125; Knitter, *No Other Name?* pp. 125-30.

11. Carl F. Hallencreutz, *Dialogue and Community: Ecumenical Issues in Inter-religious Relationships*, Studia Missionalia Upsaliensia XXXI (Uppsala: Swedish Institute of Missionary Research; Geneva: WCC, 1977).

12. *The Documents of Vatican II*, ed. Walter M. Abbott, S.J. (New York: The America Press, 1966), pp. 660, 662.

13. Joseph Neuner, ed., *Christian Revelation and World Religions* (London: Compass Books, 1967), pp. 21-22.

14. The Jerusalem Meeting of the International Missionary Council March 24-April 8, 1928, *Vol. I: The Christian Life and Message in Relation to Non-Christian Systems of Thought and Life* (New York: International Missionary Council, 1928), p. 410.

15. J. H. Bavinck, *The Church Between Temple and Mosque: A Study of the Relationship Between the Christian Faith and Other Religions* (Grand Rapids, Mich.: William B. Eerdmans Publishing Company, 1966), p. 125.

16. Ralph R. Covell, "The Christian Gospel and World Religions: How Much Have American Evangelicals Changed?" *IBMR* 15 (January 1991), p. 13.

17. Paul F. Knitter, "Preface" in *The Myth of Christian Uniqueness*, p. viii.

18. John Hick, *God Has Many Names: Britain's New Religious Pluralism* (London: The Macmillan Press, 1980), pp. 5-6; Paul F. Knitter, *No Other Name?*, pp. 146-52.

19. Krister Stendahl, "Notes for Three Bible Studies" in *Christ's Lordship and Religious Pluralism*, eds. G. H. Anderson and T. F. Stransky (Maryknoll, N.Y.: Orbis Books, 1981), pp. 11-15.

20. S. J. Samartha, *One Christ—Many Religions: Toward a Revised Christology* (Maryknoll, N.Y.: Orbis Books, 1991), pp. 118, 124-30, 131.

21. Ibid., pp. 86-89.

22. See Karl Rahner, *Foundations of Christian Faith* (New York: Seabury Press, 1978), pp. 176-320, and Carl E. Braaten, *No Other Gospel! Christianity Among the World's Religions* (Minneapolis: Fortress, 1992), pp. 65-102, for Christologies of this type. Unfortunately, David Bosch in *Transforming Mission* (Maryknoll, N.Y.: Orbis Books, 1991) omits the Gospel of John, which undergirds much of this argument from his New Testament models of mission.

23. Paul Devanandan, *I Will Lift Up Mine Eyes to the Hills* (Bangalore: CISRS, 1962), p. 126; quoted in M. M. Thomas, "A Christ-Centered Humanist Approach to Other Religions in the Indian Pluralistic Context" in *Christian*

Uniqueness Reconsidered: The Myth of a Pluralistic Theology of Religions, ed. Gavin D'Costa (Maryknoll, N.Y.: Orbis Books, 1990), p. 56.

24. Joachim Wietzke, ed., *Paul D. Devanandan Vol. II* (Madras, India: Christian Literature Society, 1987), p. 164.

25. Ibid., p. 26.

26. See "M. M. Thomas" in *Dictionary of the Ecumenical Movement*, eds. N. Lossky et al. (Geneva: WCC Publications, 1991), pp. 1006-7.

27. M. M. Thomas, *Man and the Universe of Faiths* (Madras: Christian Literature Society, 1975), pp. 147, 138.

28. M. M. Thomas, *The Acknowledged Christ of the Indian Renaissance* (Madras: CLS, 1970); "A Christ-Centered Humanist Approach," p. 58; Ken Gnanakan, *The Pluralistic Predicament*, pp. 118, 88.

29. Raimundo Panikkar, "The Jordan, the Tiber, and the Ganges: Three Kairological Moments of Christic Self-Consciousness" in *The Myth of Christian Uniqueness*, p. 110. Introductions to Panikkar's christology are found in Knitter, *No Other Name?*, pp. 152-57, and M. M. Thomas, *Risking Christ for Christ's Sake* (Geneva: WCC, 1987), pp. 29-35.

30. Raimundo Panikkar, *The Unknown Christ of Hinduism: Towards an Ecumenical Christophany* (Maryknoll, N.Y.: Orbis Books, 1981), pp. 67-68.

31. Ibid., pp. 81-86.

32. Ibid., pp. 2, 58-61, 65.

33. Michael Amaladoss, "Interreligious Dialogue: A View from Asia," *IBMR* 19:1 (January 1995), p. 5; "The Pluralism of Religions and the Significance of Christ" in *Asian Faces of Jesus*, ed. R. S. Sugirtharajah (Maryknoll, N.Y.: Orbis Books, 1993), p. 99.

34. Amaladoss, "Interreligious Dialogue," p. 5.

35. Amaladoss, "The Pluralism of Religions," p. 99.

36. Ibid., pp. 92-96; "Interreligious Dialogue," p. 5.

37. Lesslie Newbigin, *The Gospel in a Pluralist Society* (Grand Rapids, Mich.: William B. Eerdmans Publishing Company, 1989), p. 171.

38. *The San Antonio Report—Your Will be Done: Mission in Christ's Way*, ed. Frederick R. Wilson (Geneva: WCC Publications, 1990), pp. 31-32.

39. Ibid., pp. 31-33, 36.

40. Arne Sovik, *Salvation Today* (Minneapolis: Augsburg Publishing House, 1973), pp. 72-73.

4: Global and Local: A Critical View of Mission Models

1. Carlos Fuentes, *The Buried Mirror: Reflections on Spain and the New World* (Boston: Houghton Mifflin Company, 1992), p. 10.

2. Salvador de Madariaga, *Vida del Muy Magnifico Señor Don Cristobal Colon* (Buenos Aires: Editorial Sudamericana, 1991).

3. See David J. Bosch, *Transforming Mission: Paradigm Shifts in Theology of Mission* (Maryknoll, N.Y.: Orbis Books, 1991).

4. Columbus used the Franciscan habit when he returned as prisoner after his second trip, and was wrapped with it for his burial at his request.

5. See Gardiner Davenport, ed., *European Treaties Bearing on the History of the United States and Its Dependencies to 1648* (Washington, D.C.: Carnegie Institution of Washington, 1917).

6. See David Bosch, *Transforming Mission*, chapter 8; Stephen C. Neill, *A History of Christian Missions* (London: Lutterworth, 1966).

7. Gisbertus Voetius (1588–1676) is credited as the first Protestant to develop a theory of mission including the conversion of the Gentiles, the planting of the church *(plantatio ecclesiae)*, and the glory and manifestation of divine grace. See Bosch, p. 256ff.

8. See Donald McGavran's classic work *Understanding Church Growth*, rev. ed. (Grand Rapids, Mich.: Eerdmans, 1980).

9. Bosch, *Transforming Mission*, pp. 277-91.

10. See Arthur F. Glasser, "The Evangelicals: Unwavering Commitment, Troublesome Divisions" in *Mission in the 90s* (Grand Rapids, Mich.: Eerdmans/Overseas Ministries Study Center, 1991). Compare the report of the Consultation on the Relationship Between Evangelism and Social Responsibility, *Evangelism and Social Responsibility: An Evangelical Commitment* (Wheaton, Ill.: Lausanne Committee for World Evangelism, 1982).

11. Eugene L. Stockwell, "Mission Issues for Today and Tomorrow," *International Review of Mission* Vol. 78 (July/October 1989), p. 305.

12. It is remarkable that the Roman Catholic Church is beginning to qualify some of her understandings of global salvation and mission. John Paul II, in his missionary encyclical, while reaffirming the unique role of the church as being "the ordinary way of salvation," does not exclude the possibility that "the followers of other religions can receive God's grace and be saved by Christ." See "Redemptoris Mission" in Joseph G. Donders, ed., *John Paul II: The Encyclicals in Everyday Language* (Maryknoll, N.Y.: Orbis Books, 1996), pp. 143-72. Protestant churches in the newly pluralist Western world are also struggling with the question of a global claim of salvation in Christ. See J. Andrew Kirk's suggestive bibliography in his book *Loosing the Chains: Religion as Opium and Liberation* (London: Hodder & Stoughton, 1992), pp. 202-10.

13. Bosch, *Transforming Mission*, p. 298ff. See also Martin E. Marty, *The Righteous Empire: The Christian Experience in America* (Chicago: University of Chicago Press, 1970).

14. See the ecumenical literature around these missiological emphases in successive conferences and assemblies: Uppsala 1968, Bangkok 1973, Nairobi 1975, Melbourne 1980, Vancouver 1983, Seoul 1990, Canberra 1991.

15. Lewis Hanke, *The Spanish Struggle for Justice in the Conquest of America* (Philadelphia: University of Pennsylvania Press, 1949), pp. 31-36.

16. Leonardo Boff, *Nueva Evangelizacion* (Caracas, Venezuela: Ed. Paulinas, 1991), p. 8ff. ("Decimate" means to reduce by 10 percent; the reduction in this case was 90 percent!)

17. Fuentes, *The Buried Mirror*, pp. 88-89.

18. The Franciscan Luis de Bolaños is considered the founder of the "reduction" model in Spanish South America about 1580 near Asunción in Paraguay. These Christian settlements were developed by the Jesuits in Paraguay, Brazil, Bolivia, Argentina, and Uruguay beginning in 1610. The movement reached its peak by 1767 when the Jesuits were expelled from America due to the resistance of the Spanish landowners, the Portuguese slave-traders, and conflicts of the Iberian monarchies with the Jesuits. The movie *The Mission* is a powerful portrayal of this conflict. See Antonio de Egaña, S.J., *Historia de la Iglesia en America Española: Hemisferio Sur* (Madrid, Spain: La Editorial Católica, 1966), pp. 189-98, 761-72.

19. See Egaña on the Jesuit model and Ed Sylvest, *Motifs of Franciscan Mission Theory in Sixteenth Century New Spain* (Washington, D.C.: Academy of American Franciscan History, 1975), chap. 4, for a critical evaluation of the Franciscan paternalistic model.

20. Boff, *Nueva Evangelizacion*, p. 144, my translation.

21. Stephen Neill, *A History of Christian Missions*, pp. 322-96, deals with this issue on a global scale, and Martin E. Marty, among others, points to this cultural imperialism of Christians missions in North America itself in his book *The Righteous Empire: The Christian Experience in America* (Chicago: University of Chicago Press, 1970), p. 48ff ("the evangelical empire").

22. See Mortimer Arias, "Crisis in Motivation: The Twilight Between the Old and the New" in *Perkins Journal* 32:2 (Winter 1979), pp. 24-25.

23. David B. Barrett, "Annual Statistical Table on Global Mission: 1990," *International Bulletin of Missionary Research*, 14:1 (January 1990), pp. 26-27; 15:1 (January 1991), pp. 24-25.

24. David B. Barrett and James W. Reapsome, *Seven Hundred Plans to Evangelize the World: The Rise of the Global Evangelization Movement* (Birmingham, Ala.: New Hope, 1988).

25. See David Stoll, *Is Latin America Turning Protestant?* (Berkeley, Calif.: University of California, 1991); David Martin, *Tongues of Fire: The Explosion of Protestantism in Latin America* (Oxford, England: Basil Blackwell, 1990); C. René Padilla, ed., *De la Marginacion al Compromiso: Los Evangelicos y la Politica en America Latina* (Buenos Aires, Argentina: Fraternidad Teológica Latinoamericana, 1991); *Boletin Teologico* 23 (September 1991), pp. 42-43; *Consulta "Teología y Vida"* 23 (1991), p. 44, "Los Evangélicos y la Política en América Latina."

26. Valdir R. Steuernagel, "Social Concern and Evangelization: The Journey of the Lausanne Movement," *International Bulletin of Missionary Research*, 15:2 (April 1991), p. 55, emphasis added.

5: Churches in the Mode of Mission: Toward a Missional Model of the Church

1. See, for example, sociologist Rodney Stark and economist Laurence Iannaccone's "A Supply-Side Reinterpretation of the 'Secularization' of Europe" in *Journal for the Scientific Study of Religion* 33 (1994): pp. 230-52. Stark and Iannaccone attribute the decline of churches in the West to their failure to perform competently in the "market of religion," not in a competing trend toward secularization. Regarding secularization as a myth masking the truly religious character of Western society, they argue that churches competing freely as "religious firms" in the marketplace can, by radical adjustment to conditions as they are, grow successfully.

2. See Charles Trueheart, "Welcome to the Next Church" in *The Atlantic Monthly* 278 (August 1996), for a thorough analysis of the trends of successful contemporary churches.

3. Avery Dulles, *Models of the Church*, Revised edition (New York: Image Books, 1987).

4. Ibid., p. 204.

5. Ibid., p. 207.

6. Gregory P. Leffel, *Intuitive Barriers to Growth: The Role of Semantic*

Structures in Limiting Vision, and a Process-oriented Methodology for Overcoming Them. Unpublished paper, 1995.

7. Thomas C. Oden, *Life in the Spirit—Systematic Theology: Volume Three* (San Francisco: HarperSanFrancisco, 1992), p. 260.

8. F. J. Verstraelen, gen. ed., A. Camps, L. A. Hoedemaker, and M. R. Spindler, eds., *Missiology: An Ecumenical Introduction—Texts and Contexts of Global Christianity* (Grand Rapids, Mich.: William B. Eerdmans Publishing Company, 1995), p. 4.

9. Rodney Stark, *The Rise of Christianity: A Sociologist Reconsiders History* (Princeton, N.J.: Princeton University Press, 1996), p. 7.

10. Ibid., p. 18. Also see Rodney Stark, "The Rise of a New World Faith" in *Review of Religious Research* 26 (1984): pp. 18-27.

11. Stark, "The Rise of a New World Faith," p. 22.

12. Stark notes that if Mormon growth in the period from A.D. 1980 to 2080 (beginning 250 years after its birth) fits a range of from 30 to 50 percent per decade, the Church will grow to between 63 and 265 million members. We are witnessing, in Stark's opinion, the birth of the first world religion since the rise of Islam. See Stark, "The Rise of a New World Faith"; see also Gordon Shepherd and Gary Shepherd, "Mormonism in Secular Society: Changing Patterns in Official Ecclesiastical Rhetoric" in *Review of Religious Research* 26 (1984): pp. 28-42.

13. In his construction of a model of the spread of innovations, Everett M. Rogers notes the most rapid diffusion in the center of the economic strata. See Rogers, *Diffusion of Innovations*, 4th ed. (New York: The Free Press, 1995). Similarly, missiologist Eugene Nida notes the strength of Latin American church movements among the lower-middle and upper-lower classes, which he dubs the "creative class" operating in relative freedom from both poverty and a necessary conservatism based on preserving accumulated wealth. See Nida, *Customs and Cultures: Anthropology for Christian Missions* (New York: Harper & Row, 1954).

14. See Rodney Stark and William Sims Bainbridge, "American-Born Sects: Initial Findings" in *Journal for the Scientific Study of Religion* 20 (1981): pp. 130-49, and "Secularization and Cult Formation in the Jazz Age" in *Journal for the Scientific Study of Religion* 20 (1981): pp. 360-73.

15. See Rodney Stark, "Epidemics, Networks, and the Rise of Christianity" in *Semia* 56 (1992): pp. 159-75.

16. Stark, *The Rise of Christianity*, p. 153.

17. Ibid., pp. 161-62.

18. Stark and Iannaccone, in "A Supply-Side Reinterpretation of the 'Secularization' of Europe," note that religious vitality is strongest where political and religious structures permit a "free market." In such conditions, the performance of each religious "firm" is critical to its domination of "market share." Christianity in the ancient world performed as a "firm" without peer, especially on the level of daily communal life, allowing it within a short time to create a "monopoly."

19. Stark, *The Rise of Christianity*, p. 213.

20. Edward Schillebeeckx, *The Church with a Human Face: A New and Expanded Theology of Ministry* (New York: Crossroad, 1985).

21. Ibid., pp. 48ff.

22. L. Michael White, "Finding the Ties That Bind: Issues From Social

Description" in *Semia* 56 (1992): pp. 3-22; "Social Networks: Theoretical Orientation and Historical Applications" in *Semia* 56 (1992): pp. 23-36.

23. Schillebeeckx, *The Church with a Human Face*, p. 73.

24. Ibid., p. 122.

25. Ibid., pp. 257-58.

26. Ibid., p. 39.

27. Lothar Coenen, "Church, Synagogue" in Colin Brown, gen. ed., *The New International Dictionary of New Testament Theology Vol. I: A-F,* English trans. (Grand Rapids, Mich.: Zondervan Publishing House, 1975), pp. 291-307.

28. Walter Kaiser, "Israel's Missionary Call" in Ralph D. Winter and Steven C. Hawthorne, eds., A-25-33, *Perspectives on the World Christian Movement: A Reader*. Revised ed. (Pasadena, Calif.: William Carey Library, 1992), A-29.

29. Oden, *Life in the Spirit*, p. 283.

6: The Case for Culturally Relevant Congregations

1. The metaphor of circumcision is fortunate, because it illustrates that changing one's culture is not a superficial act, like changing one jacket for another, because a person's basic identity is involved. The circumcision metaphor also illustrates that a person feels vulnerable when considering culture change.

2. This principle of indigeneity was to become one of Christianity's towering differences with Islam. Muslims believe that the Koran cannot really be translated, that its full meaning can be apprehended only within the original Arabic language and culture. But Christians have discovered that the Christian scriptures can be translated into any tongue on earth, and that Christianity's essential meaning can be apprehended through any culture.

3. See Martin Robinson, *A World Apart: Creating a Church for the Unchurched* (Tunbridge Wells, England: Monarch Publications, 1992), especially chapter 2, "Secularisation and the Contemporary Church."

4. Martin Robinson, *A World Apart*, pp. 36-7.

5. Ibid., p. 37.

6. Bishop Richard Wilke, "Out of the Depths" in *The World Forever Our Parish*, ed. Dean S. Gilliland (Lexington, Ky.: Bristol Books, 1991), pp. 24-25.

7. C. Peter Wagner, *Church Growth and the Whole Gospel: A Biblical Mandate* (San Francisco: Harper & Row, 1981), pp. 177-78.

8. See David Burnett, *Clash of Worlds* (Nashville: Thomas Nelson, 1992), especially chapter 14, "Transforming Worldviews."

9. *Lausanne Occasional Papers No. 2: The Willowbank Report—Gospel and Culture* (Wheaton, Ill.: Lausanne Committee for World Evangelization, 1978), p. 13.

10. John Wesley, "The Character of a Methodist," *The Works of John Wesley Vol. 9: The Methodist Societies—History, Nature, and Design*, ed. Rupert E. Davies (Nashville: Abingdon Press, 1989), p. 34.

11. Steve Rabey, "Big-band Fan Turns Missionary to Metal Heads" in *Christianity Today* (February 10, 1992), pp. 10-11.

7: The Mission of Theology and Theology as Mission

1. I take the word "reinvent" from the subtitle of Leonardo Boff's celebrated book *Ecclesiogenesis: The Base Communities Reinvent the Church* (Maryknoll,

N.Y.: Orbis Books, 1986) because of its evocative sense of an exciting new project.

2. I use the term in preference to either "Third World" or "Two-Thirds World" to denote all parts of the world that, from the fifteenth century onward, became the object of the European (and later the North American) aspiration to conquer new territories and new markets.

3. David Kelsey elaborates this ideal model at some length under the nomenclature of "Berlin": "The overarching and organizing goal of the university was to be research and teaching students how to do research; its goal was to be inquiry that aims to master the truth about whatever subject is studied." See *Between Athens and Berlin: The Theological Education Debate* (Grand Rapids, Mich.: William B. Eerdmans Publishing Company, 1993), p. 13.

4. The definition given by the *Concise Oxford Dictionary* of the word "academic" is quite instructive: "1. scholarly. 2. abstract, unpractical, theoretical, cold, merely logical."

5. See Hans-Georg Link, ed., *Apostolic Faith Today* (Geneva: World Council of Churches, 1987).

6. See Margaret Hebblethwaite, *Base Communities: An Introduction* (New York: Paulist Press, 1994), pp. 44-76.

7. See J. A. Kirk, "Liberation Theology and Local Theologies" in Anthony Harvey, ed., *Theology in the City* (London: SPCK, 1986).

8. This was in connection with a lay-training institute, known originally as The London Institute for Contemporary Christianity and now called Christian Impact.

9. Robert J. Schreiter, *Constructing Local Theologies* (London: SCM Press, 1985).

10. David Bosch gives an excellent summary of the various interpretations of the meaning of theology in *Transforming Mission* (Maryknoll, N.Y.: Orbis Books, 1991), pp. 489-490.

11. See Kelsey, *Between Athens and Berlin*, pp. 12-27.

12. Charles M. Wood, *Vision and Discernment: An Orientation in Theological Study* (Atlanta: Scholars Press, 1985), p. 21.

13. Orlando E. Costas, "Theological Education and Mission" in C. René Padilla, ed., *New Alternatives in Theological Education* (Oxford, England: Regnum Books, 1988), p. 6.

14. I fully recognize the inadequacy of attempting to set down any one description of theology. Sometimes the most interesting insights into the various ways of doing theology come through an analysis of what is done in practice! My own statement is not a refined definition. It is intended, rather, as a working model.

15. The "compare and contrast" kind of question so beloved by examiners!

16. The same can be said for certain other texts that make similar claims as to their origin, similar demands upon the reader, and a similar impact in concrete historical situations—most notably the Qur'an.

17. See Ian Barbour, *Religion in an Age of Science* (London: SCM Press, 1990), chapter 2.

18. Kelsey, *Between Athens and Berlin*, p. 25.

19. It is, perhaps, one of the consequences of the current tendency to treat all cultures as relative and conditional that the separation between rationalistic cultures and "wisdom" cultures has become a commonplace.

20. Of course, this describes the ideal. In reality social and personal circumstances intervene to make the processes less straightforward, sometimes causing theories to be held for a long time against what seems to be the prevailing evidence. Nevertheless, scientific work would not proceed if the ideal did not remain in place.

21. Kelsey, *Between Athens and Berlin*, p. 27.

22. Since approximately the 1960s, theologians have begun to discover the importance of the social science disciplines to aspects of their work. This has led, in some cases, to a certain naiveté about their efficaciousness. Thus Wood maintains that theological inquiry is made rigorously critical by incorporating the relevant "secular" disciplines of history, philosophy, or the human sciences (see Kelsey, *Between Athens and Berlin*, p. 206). The truth is that all these disciplines may also be impregnated by ideological presumptions that require just as much disentangling. They cannot, therefore, be used as value-free tools to judge the ideological commitment of theological inquiry.

23. However, much more sophisticated ways of understanding God's interaction with the world are opened up by the new physics. See Ian Barbour, *Religion in an Age of Science*, chapter 4.1.

24. The assertion that any claims to events being caused other than by phenomena in principle measurable and testable have to be disqualified from rational inquiry.

25. Eric Ives, "The Gospel and History" in *The Gospel and Contemporary Culture*, ed. Hugh Montefiore (London: Mowbray, 1992), pp. 19-20.

26. Micheal O'Siadhail, *Hail! Madam Jazz: New & Selected Poems* (Newcastle upon Tyne, England: Bloodaxe Books, 1992), p. 123.

27. Though the historical context in which it has arisen may be different, this approach has much in common with the romantic strain of modern thought since the Enlightenment that came to its denouement in existentialism. See Basil Mitchell, *Morality: Religious and Secular* (Oxford, England: Clarendon Press, 1980), chapters 1 and 3.

28. "One might say generally that modern liberal theology is that kind of theology that speaks of God under the conditions laid down by the theory of natural liberty and the laws of the modern market." M. Douglas Meeks, "Global Economy and the Globalization of Theological Education" in Alice Frazer Evans, Robert A. Evans, and David A. Roozen, eds., *The Globalization of Theological Education* (Maryknoll, N.Y.: Orbis Books, 1993), p. 249.

29. Kelsey, *Between Athens and Berlin*, pp. 224-25.

30. Theo Sundermeier, "Missiology Yesterday and Tomorrow" in *Mission in Creative Tension: A Dialogue with David Bosch*, eds. J. N. J. Kritzinger and W. A. Saayman (Pretoria, Republic of South Africa: South African Missiological Society, 1990), p. 263.

31. Costas, "Theological Education and Mission," p. 15.

32. Jane I. Smith, "Globalization as Ecumenical/Interfaith Dialogue" in Evans, Evans, and Roozen, *The Globalization of Theological Education*, p. 96.

33. "In the social sphere evil occurs when a group's self-absolutizing of its particularity violently utilizes other groups." The notion of the equal validity of the many voices cuts away the grounds for censuring "the absolutizing of particularity." Meeks, "Global Economy and the Globalization of Theological Education," p. 257.

34. For an account of the subject matter of the thesis, see Walter Riggans,

"Messianic Judaism: A Case of Identity Denied," *International Bulletin of Missionary Research* 16:3 (July 1992), pp. 130-32.

35. Michael Polanyi, *Personal Knowledge: Towards a Post-Critical Philosophy* (London: Routledge and Kegan Paul, 1958).

36. I have tried to explore some of the major aspects of its impact upon the whole theological scene in J. Andrew Kirk, *Theology and the Third World Church* (Exeter, England: Paternoster Press; Downers Grove, Ill.: InterVarsity Press, 1983).

37. Karl Marx, "Theses on Feuerbach, No. 11" in Karl Marx and Frederick Engels, *Collected Works Vol. 5* (New York: International Publishers, 1976), p. 8.

38. "Robert Heilbroner says that the nature of our society is accumulation of wealth as power, and that the logic of our society is exchange of commodities." Meeks, "Global Economy and the Globalization of Theological Education," p. 250.

39. Lesslie Newbigin, *The Gospel in a Pluralist Society* (Grand Rapids, Mich.: William B. Eerdmans Publishing Company, 1989); *Truth to Tell: The Gospel as Public Truth* (London: SPCK, 1991).

40. If, on the basis of historical hindsight, it is legitimate to draw a fairly clear distinction between the abiding apostolic gospel and the doctrinal and practical accretions often promoted by the church—and generally accepted in society as a whole—it is probably true to say that there never was such a time.

41. In an unpublished paper given to a group of missiologists in Paris, January 1992.

42. Lamin Sanneh elaborates and criticizes the principle of territoriality that is deeply embedded in the European Christian heritage in his book *Encountering the West—Christianity and the Global Cultural Process: The African Dimension* (London: Marshall Pickering, 1993).

43. See, for example, R. Munoz, *The God of Christians* (Maryknoll, N.Y.: Orbis Books, 1991), pp. 3-14.

44. See Richard Shaull, *The Reformation and Liberation Theology: Insights for the Challenges of Today* (Louisville, Ky.: Westminster/John Knox Press, 1991).

45. John Milbank, *Theology and Social Theory: Beyond Secular Reason* (Oxford, England: Blackwell, 1990), p. 261.

46. Allan Bloom, *The Closing of the American Mind* (New York: Simon and Schuster, 1987), p. 143.

47. I have myself explored the nature, extent, and consequences of modern concepts and experiences of freedom in secular societies in *The Meaning of Freedom: A Study of Secular, Muslim and Christian Views*.

48. See Carver T. Yu, *Being and Relation: A Theological Critique of Western Dualism and Individualism* (Edinburgh: Scottish Academic Press, 1987), pp. 115-43.

49. A pointed example is that of the American indigenous cultures, largely liquidated through the expansion of the European powers beginning five hundred years ago. The denial of full human equality to those vanquished militarily was without excuse. However, to lay a justified blame on the attitudes and actions of the *conquistadores* should not be confused with a certain modern tendency to view the pre-Columbian cultures through romantic, rose-tinted spectacles. Some of them were also mightily oppressive and vicious with regard to minorities.

50. See particularly the essays by Jane Smith and Robert Schreiter in Evans,

Evans, and Roozen, *The Globalization of Theological Education*, pp. 90-103 and 122-33.

51. Robert J. Schreiter, "Globalization as Cross-Cultural Dialogue" in Evans, Evans, and Roozen, *The Globalization of Theological Education*, pp. 127-28. I would personally prefer to use "pluralism" of the ideology, and "plurality" of the reality of cultural, religious, and moral multiplicity.

52. See "Theology, Drugs and Zen," *The Listener*, November 5, 12, 19, 1970, British Broadcasting Corporation, London.

53. J. Andrew Kirk, *Loosing the Chains: Religion as Opium and Liberation* (London: Hodder & Stoughton, 1992), p. 156.

54. See Kirk, *The Meaning of Freedom*, chapter 9.

55. William E. Lesher, "Living the Faith Under the Conditions of the Modern World" in Evans, Evans, and Roozen, *The Globalization of Theological Education*, p. 44.

56. Meeks, "Global Economy and the Globalization of Theological Education," p. 257.

8: "The Wisdom of God in Creation": Mission and the Wesleyan Pentalateral

1. John Wesley, *The Works of John Wesley Vol. 18: Journals and Diaries I (1735–1738)* eds. W. Reginald Ward and Richard Heitzenrater (Nashville: Abingdon Press, 1988), p. 276.

2. Donald Thorsen, *The Wesleyan Quadrilateral: Scripture, Tradition, Reason & Experience as a Model of Evangelical Theology* (Grand Rapids, Mich.: Zondervan Publishing House, 1990), p. 16.

3. Hugh T. Kerr, *Readings in Christian Thought* (Nashville: Abingdon Press, 1990), p. 190.

4. Thorsen, *The Wesleyan Quadrilateral*, p. 17.

5. Leslie D. Wilcox, *Profiles in Wesleyan Theology* (Salem, Ohio: Schmul Publishing Co., 1983), pp. 1-13.

6. Sidney I. Landau, ed., *The Doubleday Dictionary for Home, School and Office* (Garden City, N.Y.: Doubleday, 1975), p. 763.

7. Albert C. Outler, "Introduction," in *The Works of John Wesley Vol. 1: Sermons I (1-33)*, eds. Albert C. Outler and Richard Heitzenrater (Nashville: Abingdon Press, 1984), pp. 60-61.

8. Thorsen, *The Wesleyan Quadrilateral*, p. 15.

9. Ibid.

10. Wesley, *Works of John Wesley Vol. 1*, pp. 302-03.

11. Quoted in Robert W. Burtner and Robert E. Chiles, eds., *John Wesley's Theology: A Collection from His Works* (Nashville: Abingdon Press, 1982), pp. 19-20.

12. John Deschner, *Wesley's Christology: An Interpretation* (Dallas: Southern Methodist University Press, 1960), p. 5.

13. Thorsen, *The Wesleyan Quadrilateral*, p. 15.

14. Ibid., p. 169.

15. Ibid., p. 199.

16. Howard A. Snyder, *The Radical Wesley and Patterns for Church Renewal* (Eugene, Ore.: Wipf and Stock Publishers, 1996), p. 146.

17. Wesley, *The Works of John Wesley Vol. 1*, pp. 120, 124.

18. Thorsen, *The Wesleyan Quadrilateral*, p. 201.

19. Tércio Machado Siqueira, "O Jeito de Wesley Interpretar a Bíblia" ("Wesley's Way of Interpreting the Bible"), *Em Marcha* magazine (1995), p. 15, my translation.

20. Ibid.

21. Burtner and Chiles, *John Wesley's Theology*, p. 17 (italics added).

22. Ibid., pp. 17-40.

23. Ibid., p. 40.

24. Ibid., p. 37.

25. John Telford, ed., *The Letters of the Rev. John Wesley, A.M., Vol. IV* (London: The Epworth Press, 1931), p. 91.

26. Quoted in Burtner and Chiles, *John Wesley's Theology*, p. 38.

27. Ibid., p. 36.

28. See Stephen B. Bevans, *Models of Contextual Theology* (Maryknoll, N.Y.: Orbis Books, 1992), p. 17.

29. Stanley J. Grenz and Roger E. Olson, *Who Needs Theology? An Invitation to the Study of God* (Downers Grove, Ill.: InterVarsity Press, 1996), p. 116.

30. Ibid., p. 115. Though it is true that Wesley was not a systematic theologian as that term is generally understood, yet clearly his thought did have coherence and system, if not consistency in every detail.

31. Personal letter from Howard Snyder, May 18, 2000.

32. Mildred Bangs Wynkoop, *A Theology of Love* (Kansas City, Mo.: Beacon Hill Press of Kansas City, 1972).

33. Personal letter from Howard Snyder, May 18, 2000.

34. Howard Snyder, "Summary of Wesley's Theology of Redemption." Class handout, Wesleyan Theology of Mission, Asbury Theological Seminary, 1997.

35. Theodore Runyon, *The New Creation: John Wesley's Theology Today* (Nashville: Abingdon Press, 1998), pp. 8-9.

36. See Tore Meistad, "To Be a Christian in the World: Martin Luther's and John Wesley's Interpretation of the Sermon on the Mount." Ph.D. dissertation, University of Tronthein, Norway, 1989, p. 244.

37. Runyon, *The New Creation*, p. 12.

38. Bevans, *Models of Contextual Theology*, p. 16.

39. John Wesley, *A Survey of the Wisdom of God in the Creation; Or A Compendium of Natural Philosophy Vol. 1*, 3rd American ed. (New York: N. Bangs and T. Mason, 1823), p. 313.

40. William Ragsdale Cannon, *The Theology of John Wesley* (New York: Abingdon-Cokesbury Press, 1946), p. 172.

41. Ibid.

42. Ibid., p. 197 (referring to Wesley's Sermon LX, part i, sect. 2).

43. Ibid., p. 172.

44. Wesley, *Works of John Wesley Vol. 1*, p. 359.

45. Wesley's Sermon LX, sec. 3, quoted in Cannon, *The Theology of John Wesley*, p. 197.

46. Wesley, *Works of John Wesley Vol. 1*, p. 405.

47. Wynkoop, *A Theology of Love*, pp. 16-17.

48. John Wesley, *The Works of John Wesley Vol. 2: Sermons II (34-70)*, ed. Albert C. Outler (Nashville: Abingdon Press, 1985), p. 39.

49. John Wesley, *The Works of John Wesley Vol. 4: Sermons IV (115-151)*, ed. Albert C. Outler (Nashville: Abingdon Press, 1987), p. 356.

50. Ibid., p. 307.

51. Wesley, *Works of John Wesley Vol. 1*, pp. 213-14.

52. Wesley, *Works of John Wesley Vol. 2*, pp. 188-89.

53. These six points are adapted from Snyder, "Essential Elements of a Wesleyan Theology of Mission." Class handout, Wesleyan Theology of Mission, Asbury Theological Seminary, 1997.

9: Convenience, Relevance, and Transformation: An African Response to Christian Mission

1. Mortimer Arias's original paper was "Global Mission in the Columbus Quincentenary," presented at the Consultation on Evangelization in the Postmodern World, United Theological Seminary, Dayton, Ohio, October 28-30, 1992.

2. David J. Bosch, *Transforming Mission: Paradigm Shifts in Theology of Mission* (Maryknoll, N.Y.: Orbis Books, 1991).

3. Lesslie Newbigin, *The Gospel in a Pluralist Society* (Grand Rapids, Mich.: William B. Eerdmans Publishing Company, 1989).

4. David Barrett, "Annual Statistical Table on Global Mission: 1992," *International Bulletin of Missionary Research* (January 1992), pp. 26-27.

5. Maxie D. Dunnam, *Congregational Evangelism: A Pastor's View* (Nashville: Discipleship Resources, 1992), p. 12.

6. Lamin Sanneh, *West African Christianity* (Maryknoll, N.Y.: Orbis Books, 1983).

7. Stephen Neill, *A History of Christian Missions* (New York: Viking Penguin, 1964).

8. Lamin Sanneh, *Translating the Message: The Missionary Impact on Culture* (Maryknoll, N.Y.: Orbis Books, 1989), p. 125.

10: Is Evangelization Liberation?

1. The author is deeply indebted to Dr. John R. Levison for his contributions to this article. He supplied ideas, critiques, and refinements as well as many hours of both editing and attending to our daughter Chloe. This essay is reprinted from *Theology & Corporate Conscience: Essays in Honor of Frederick Herzog* (1999), with permission of Kirk House Publishers, Minneapolis.

2. Norman Thomas, "Evangelism and Liberation Theology" in *Missiology: An International Review*, Vol. 9 (October 1981), p. 483.

3. Pope Paul VI, *Evangelization in the Modern World: Apostolic Exhortation* Evangelii Nuntiandi, trans. by Vatican Polyglot Press (London: Catholic Truth Society, 1975), pp. 26-27.

4. Ibid., p. 25.

5. Ibid., p. 29.

6. Ibid., p. 38.

7. Ibid., p. 32.

8. Ben Campbell Johnson, *Rethinking Evangelism: A Theological Approach* (Philadelphia: The Westminster Press, 1987), p. 78.

9. Ibid., pp. 120-21.

10. Andrew Walls, "Towards an Understanding of Africa's Place in Christian History" in John Pobee, ed., *Religion in a Pluralistic Society* (Leiden: E. J. Brill, 1976); quoted in William A. Dyrness, *Learning About Theology from the Third World* (Grand Rapids, Mich.: Academie Books, 1990), p. 13.

11. John Mbiti, "Theological Impotence and the Universality of the Church" in Gerald H. Anderson and Thomas F. Stransky, eds., *Mission Trends No. 3: Third World Theologies* (New York: Paulist Press, 1976), pp. 16-17.

12. The collection was compiled by Kenneth Parker, Richard Peace, and James Singleton, and was published by MARC, a division of World Vision International, 1990.

13. For more on this model, see Priscilla Pope-Levison, *Evangelization from a Liberation Perspective*, American University Studies, Series VII, Theology and Religion, Vol. 69 (New York: Peter Lang, 1991), pp. 167-73.

14. Edward Cleary, *Crisis and Change: The Church in Latin America Today* (Maryknoll, N.Y.: Orbis Books, 1985), p. 22; Priscilla Pope-Levison and John Levison, *Jesus in Global Contexts* (Louisville, Ky.: Westminster/John Knox, 1992), p. 29.

15. I recognize that there exists no one North American woman's perspective or experience. See our discussion in Pope-Levison and Levison, *Jesus in Global Contexts*, p. 132. However, very little of any North American woman's perspective has been integrated into evangelism. This article is an initial attempt. My hope is that many North American women from many perspectives will bring their experiences to the discussion of evangelism.

16. Orlando Costas, *Evangelizacion Contextual: Fundamentos teologicos y pastorales* (San José, Costa Rica: SEBILA, 1986), p. 85, my translation.

17. Social analysis is nothing new to evangelism; the church growth movement generously utilizes analysis, statistics, and data gathering. As Eddie Gibbs writes in his book *I Believe in Church Growth*, "Only by painstaking research are we able to paint an accurate picture of what is really happening." Eddie Gibbs, *I Believe in Church Growth* (Grand Rapids, Mich.: William B. Eerdmans Publishing Company, 1981), p. 132. Though Gibbs is referring specifically to research in church membership and attendance and homogeneous unit totals, the same scrutiny for data gathering is necessary for this model.

18. Virginia Sapiro, *Women in American Society*, 2nd. ed. (Mountain View, Calif.: Mayfield Publishing, 1990), p. 26.

19. For a fuller discussion of the ideology of domination, see Pope-Levison and Levison, *Jesus in Global Contexts*, pp. 128-31.

20. Alfred T. Hennelly, *Theologies in Conflict: The Challenge of Juan Luis Segundo* (Maryknoll, N.Y.: Orbis Books, 1979), p. 123.

21. William J. Abraham, *The Logic of Evangelism* (Grand Rapids, Mich.: William B. Eerdmans Publishing Company, 1989), p. 1.

22. Ibid., pp. 8-9.

23. Pope-Levison and Levison, *Jesus in Global Contexts*, pp. 160-61.

24. Leonardo Boff, *Jesus Christ Liberator: A Critical Christology for Our Time* (Maryknoll, N.Y.: Orbis Books, 1978), pp. 280-81.

25. Priscilla Pope-Levison, *Evangelization from a Liberation Perspective*, American University Studies Series VII, Theology and Religion, Vol. 69 (New York: Peter Lang, 1991), pp. 44-47.

26. José Miguez Bonino, *Room to Be People: An Interpretation of the*

Message of the Bible for Today's World (Geneva: World Council of Churches, 1979), p. 55. Bonino adds, "But God has invited us to begin to create the future and has promised to guarantee and certify for eternity what we create through personal and collective love" (p. 57).

27. Jon Sobrino, *The True Church and the Poor* (Maryknoll, N.Y.: Orbis Books, 1984), p. 42. "We know how the kingdom is to be proclaimed and brought to fulfillment from [Jesus'] words, his attitudes, his acceptance of the destiny that this proclamation and fulfillment brought upon him. His predilection for the poor tells us for whom the kingdom is meant and in what way it is meant for them. We know what the reign of God demands from the demands made of Jesus himself and from the demands that he in turn makes of his followers."

28. Segundo Galilea, *El Reino de Dios y la Liberacion del Hombre*, Coleccion Actualidades Teologicas (Bogota: Ediciones Paulinas, 1985), p. 19, my translation.

29. Elisabeth Schüssler Fiorenza, *In Memory of Her: A Feminist Theological Reconstruction of Christian Origins* (New York: Crossroad, 1983), pp. 121-28; Pope-Levison, *Evangelization from a Liberation Perspective*, p. 143.

30. Orlando Costas, *El Protestantismo En América Latina Hoy: Ensayos del camino (1972–1974)*, Coleccion "Iglesia y Mision" No. 3 (San José, Costa Rica: Publicaciones INDEF, 1975), p. 134.

31. Mortimer Arias, "Ministries of Hope in Latin America" in *International Review of Mission* Vol. 71 (January 1982), p. 7.

32. Valerie Saiving, "The Human Situation: A Feminine View" in Carol Christ and Judith Plaskow, eds., *Womanspirit Rising* (San Francisco: Harper & Row, Publishers, 1979), p. 35.

33. Ibid., p. 37.

34. Emilio Castro, *Hacia una Pastoral Latinoamericana*, Coleccion "Iglesia y Mision" No. 2 (San José, Costa Rica: INDEF, 1974), p. 88, my translation.

35. Leonardo Boff, *Jesus Christ Liberator*, pp. 286-87. Boff argues that conversion "is also concerned with human beings as concrete creatures involved in a whole network of living relationships and activities."

36. For a fuller discussion, see Pope-Levison and Levison, *Jesus in Global Contexts*, pp. 38-41.

37. Juan Luis Segundo, *The Historical Jesus of the Synoptics* (Maryknoll, N.Y.: Orbis Books, 1985), p. 141.

38. Ibid., p. 131.

39. Orlando Costas, *Christ Outside the Gate: Mission Beyond Christendom* (Maryknoll, N.Y.: Orbis Books, 1982), p. 37.

40. World Council of Churches, *Your Kingdom Come: Mission Perspectives—Report on the World Conference on Mission and Evangelism*, Melbourne, Australia, 12-25 May 1980 (Geneva: WCC, 1980), p. 229.

41. Alvaro Barreiro, *Basic Ecclesial Communities: The Evangelization of the Poor* (Maryknoll, N.Y.: Orbis Books, 1982), p. 68.

42. Leonardo Boff, *Desde El Lugar Del Pobre*, 2nd ed. (Bogota: Ediciones Paulinas, 1986), p. 41, my translation.

43. Such communities of women called "women-church" already exist. See Rosemary Ruether, *Women-Church: Theology and Practice of Feminist Liturgical Communities* (San Francisco: Harper & Row, 1985). Even though the

emphasis of these communities has not been on evangelism, they provide rich resources for a model of evangelism that puts women at the center.

44. Schüssler Fiorenza, *In Memory of Her*, pp. 136-38.

12: Crossbow Theology: Contextual Evangelism in Myanmar

1. There are Lisu in Laos, Thailand, Nepal, and Vietnam in addition to Myanmar and China.

2. Howard A. Snyder, *EarthCurrents: The Struggle for the World's Soul* (Nashville: Abingdon Press, 1995), p. 154.

3. Ibid., p. 153.

4. Quoted in Snyder, p. 153.

5. Walter J. Ong, "World as View and World as Event," *American Anthropologist* 71 (1969), p. 634.

6. John Wimber with Kevin Springer, *Power Evangelism* (San Francisco: Harper & Row, Publishers, 1986), p. 67.

7. Charles H. Kraft, *Christianity in Culture: A Study in Dynamic Biblical Theologizing in Cross-Cultural Perspective* (Maryknoll, N.Y.: Orbis Books, 1979), p. 53.

8. Ibid., pp. 54-56.

9. Paul G. Hiebert, *Anthropological Insights for Missionaries* (Grand Rapids, Mich.: Baker Book House, 1985), p. 48.

10. Snyder, *EarthCurrents*, p. 260.

11. James W. Sire, *The Universe Next Door* (Leicester, England: InterVarsity Press, 1977), pp. 26-42; quoted in David Burnett, *Unearthly Powers: A Christian's Handbook on Primal and Folk Religions* (Nashville: Oliver-Nelson Books, 1992), pp. 245-46.

12. Wimber, *Power Evangelism*, p. 72.

13. Ibid., p. 73.

14. From Jack Rogers's *Confessions of a Conservative Evangelical* (Philadelphia: Westminster, 1974), pp. 33-34; cited in Wimber, pp. 73-74.

15. Based on Charles H. Kraft, *Christianity with Power: Your Worldview and Your Experience of the Supernatural* (Ann Arbor, Mich.: Servant Publications, 1989), pp. 103-14.

16. Hiebert, *Anthropological Insights for Missionaries*, p. 66.

17. Based on Kraft, *Christianity with Power*, pp. 203-4.

18. Wimber, *Power Evangelism*, p. 75.

19. C. Peter Wagner, *The Third Wave of the Holy Spirit: Encountering the Power of Signs and Wonders Today* (Ann Arbor, Mich.: Servant Publications, 1988), p. 77.

20. Gailyn Van Rheenen, *Communicating Christ in Animistic Contexts* (Grand Rapids, Mich.: Baker Book House, 1991), p. 96.

21. Snyder, *EarthCurrents*, p. 249.

22. Ibid., p. 252.

23. Paul G. Hiebert, *Anthropological Reflections on Missiological Issues* (Grand Rapids, Mich.: Baker Books, 1994), p. 91.

24. David F. Wells, *God the Evangelist: How the Holy Spirit Works to Bring Men and Women to Faith* (Grand Rapids, Mich.: William B. Eerdmans Publishing Company, 1987), p. 67.

25. Snyder, *EarthCurrents*, p. 142.

26. Ibid., p. 293.

13: Evangelization and the Powers

1. Macumba is the generic name for witchcraft in Brazilian folk religion, which has been exported to other Latin American countries.

2. Edgard Silvoso, "Guerra Espiritual y el Plan Resistência," paper presented in the Spiritual Warfare Track at the 1989 Lausanne II in Manila conference.

3. Satan: from the Hebrew "satan," meaning enemy, adversary.

4. Gustav Aulén in *Cristus Victor* (New York: Macmillan, 1969) interprets the work of the cross, showing how it was both the victory of Christ and the defeat of Satan.

5. Jesse Penn-Lewis with Evan Roberts, *War on the Saints*, 6th ed. (New York: Thomas E. Lowe, Ltd., 1984), p. 2.

6. "Brasil, o maior país espírita," *Veja* Magazine, São Paulo (April 7, 1992).

7. Verbal report of Argentineans and personal confirmation of the author in Uruguay.

8. Bob Larson, *The Satanists* (Nashville: Thomas Nelson Publishers, 1989).

9. Ibid., p. 125.

10. Larry Keyes, *Letter to the Field Missionaries*, OC International, 1987.

11. Many people seek favors from the powers, and many become demonized in this way. The author is in contact with a number of such people through the ministry of deliverance.

12. Koissuke Koyama, *Mount Fuji and Mount Sinai* (Southampton, England: SCM, 1984), pp. 39-40.

13. C. René Padilla, *Mission Between the Times* (Grand Rapids, Mich.: Eerdmans, 1986), p. 50.

14. Michael Green, *I Believe in Satan's Downfall* (London: Hodder & Stoughton, 1981), p. 79.

15. Walter Wink, *Naming the Powers: The Language of Power in the New Testament* (Philadelphia: Fortress Press, 1984), p. 85.

16. See Walter Wink's trilogy on the powers: *Naming the Powers, Unmasking the Powers*, and *Engaging the Powers*.

17. John Dawson, *Taking the City for God* (Orlando, Fla.: Creation House, 1989), p. 152.

18. Ibid., p. 153.

19. Winkie Pratney, *Devil Take the Youngest: The War on Childhood* (Shreveport, La.: Huntington House Inc., 1985).

20. The following authors have written on the connection between Satanism and child sacrifice: Rebecca Brown, Mark Bulbeck, Duane Empey and Ted Schwartz, Jerry Johnson, Bob Larson, and Joan Michaelsen.

21. Authors who have written on the powers over geographical areas include Dick Bernal, Rita Cabezs, Richmond Chiundiza, Yonggi Cho, John Dawson, Steve Lawson, Arthur Mathews, David Sherman, Edgard Silvoso, Peter Wagner, Timothy Warner, Walter Wink, and Tim White.

22. C. Peter Wagner, ed., *Territorial Spirits: Insights on Strategic-Level Spiritual Warfare from Nineteen Christian Leaders* (Chichester, England: Sovereign World Limited, 1991), p. 44.

14: The Gospel as Global Good News

1. Tatiana Goricheva, *Talking About God Is Dangerous: The Diary of a Russian Dissident* (New York: Crossroad, 1986), p. 17.

2. Don Richardson, *Peace Child* (Glendale, Calif.: Regal Press, 1974). See the discussion in Robert A. Evans and Thomas D. Parker, eds., *Christian Theology: A Case Study Approach* (New York: Harper & Row, 1976), pp. 108-32.

3. Vincent J. Donovan, *Christianity Rediscovered*, 2nd ed. (Maryknoll, N.Y.: Orbis Books, 1981).

4. I have addressed this to some extent in *Models of the Kingdom* (Nashville: Abingdon Press, 1991), especially in chapters 1 and 11.

5. See David J. Bosch, *Transforming Mission: Paradigm Shifts in Theology of Mission* (Maryknoll, N.Y.: Orbis Books, 1991).

6. William Booth, "Salvation for Both Worlds," *All the World* 5:1 (January 1889), pp. 1-2.

7. Howard A. Snyder, *EarthCurrents: The Struggle for the World's Soul* (Nashville: Abingdon Press, 1995), pp. 97-101, 291-301.

8. Lesslie Newbigin, "Foreword" in J. Andrew Kirk, *Loosing the Chains: Religion as Opium and Liberation* (London: Hodder & Stoughton, 1992), p. vii.

9. Ibid. Newbigin, citing Harold Turner, refers to the first three of these "levels."

10. Kirk speaks of "the fatal flaw built into the notion of relativistic belief: it eliminates itself by its own arguments." Kirk, *Loosing the Chains*, p. 9.

11. Lesslie Newbigin, *Truth to Tell: The Gospel as Public Truth* (Grand Rapids, Mich.: William B. Eerdmans Publishing Company, 1991), p. 28.

12. Ibid., p. 47.

13. See Howard A. Snyder, *Liberating the Church: The Ecology of Church and Kingdom* (Eugene, Ore.: Wipf & Stock, 1996), chap. 10, "The Book of the Covenant."

14. Some biblical scholars raise the question of whether the Gospels give us the actual words of Jesus where we find these claims in the NT. My view is that the Gospel writers give us substantially the words of Jesus, and that he did indeed claim to be the Messiah.

15. See Howard A. Snyder, *Radical Renewal: The Problem of Wineskins Today* (Houston, Tex.: Touch Publications, 1996).

16. See especially the following twelve passages, which are either sermons or other summaries of the gospel message: Acts 1:1-3, 2:14-41, 3:11–4:4, 4:5-22, 5:29-32, 7:1-60, 10:23*b*-48, 13:13-43, 17:1-9, 17:16-34, 26:1-23, 28:17-29.

17. This is why phrases like "the Christ event" or "the resurrection event" are unhelpful and potentially misleading. See the insightful discussion in Robert Blaikie, *"Secular Christianity" and God Who Acts* (Grand Rapids, Mich.: William B. Eerdmans Publishing Company, 1970).

18. One of the best examples here is E. Stanley Jones and his use of Round Table conversations in the Orient. See Jones, *Christ at the Round Table* (New York: Abingdon Press, 1928).

19. A. H. Matthias Zahniser, "The Trinity: Paradigm for Mission in the Spirit," *Missiology* 17:1 (January 1989), pp. 69-82.

CONTRIBUTORS

Mortimer Arias has been a leading Methodist theologian and church-man in the Americas for many years. He has participated in several Latin American study conferences and served as a theological reflector in the Pilot Immersion Project for Globalization of Theological Education, coordinated by the Plowshares Institute, Simsbury, Connecticut. He and his wife Beatiz Ferrari currently reside in Uruguay.

Seth O. Asare served as the E. Stanley Jones Professor of Evangelism at the Boston University School of Theology, and is now engaged in pastoral ministry in The United Methodist Church. A native of Ghana, Asare has had extensive ministry experience both there and in the United States.

George G. Hunter III served as Dean of the E. Stanley Jones School of World Mission and Evangelism at Asbury Theological Seminary, Wilmore, Kentucky, from 1983 to 2001. He formerly taught at Perkins School of Theology at Southern Methodist University, and served as assistant general secretary for evangelism in The United Methodist Church. His books include *How to Reach Secular People* and *The Celtic Way of Evangelism*.

Neuza Itioka, a Brazilian of Japanese extraction, serves as a missionary in Brazil with OC International. After serving for several years as director of InterVarsity Christian Fellowship in Brazil, she completed a Ph.D. in Intercultural Studies at Fuller Theological Seminary.

J. Andrew Kirk is the Dean and Head of the School of Mission and World Christianity at the Selly Oak Colleges, Birmingham, England. Prior to that he was involved in "lay" education in London, and was theologian missioner with the Church Missionary Society, having been engaged in theological education in Argentina for twelve years. He has written ten books and many articles on mission and related themes.

Yishey Latt has served as General Secretary of the Lisu Baptist Convention in Myanmar and is a candidate for the Doctor of Missiology degree at United Theological Seminary, Dayton, Ohio. Latt has been an evangelist in his native Myanmar and has recorded a number of his own songs.

Gregory Leffel served on the leadership team of a rapidly growing evangelistic ministry with youth and young adults in Columbus, Ohio, which developed eventually into Xenos Christian Fellowship. He is currently a Ph.D. candidate in Intercultural Studies at Asbury Theological Seminary and is engaged in urban ministry in Lexington, Kentucky.

William R. O'Brien, a leading Southern Baptist missionary statesman, was the founding Director of the Global Center at the Beeson Divinity School, Samford University, in Birmingham, Alabama. He served as a missionary in Indonesia and as Executive Vice President and Director of the Global Desk of the Southern Baptist Foreign Mission Board. He lectures widely on global trends and their impact on mission.

Priscilla Pope-Levison teaches at The Divinity School, Duke University. She previously served as Assistant Professor of Contextual Theology at North Park Theological Seminary in Chicago. With her husband John Levison, she coauthored the books *Evangelism and Liberation* and *Return to Babel: Global Perspectives on the Bible.*

Luís Wesley de Souza is a Brazilian who has been a successful Methodist pastor and has also served as an interdenominational leader among evangelicals in Brazil. Currently he is pastoring in Brazil while completing doctoral studies in the E. Stanley Jones School of World Mission and Evangelism at Asbury Theological Seminary.

Howard A. Snyder served as Heisel Professor of Evangelization and Church Renewal at United Theological Seminary from 1992 to 1996. Previously he was a Free Methodist missionary in São Paulo, Brazil, and has pastored in Detroit and Chicago. Currently he is professor of the history and theology of mission at the E. Stanley Jones School of World Mission and Evangelism, Asbury Theological Seminary.

Norman E. Thomas is the compiler and editor of *Classical Texts in Mission and World Christianity* (Orbis Books, 1995). Until his recent retirement he was Heisel Professor of Evangelization at United Theological Seminary, Dayton, Ohio, and book review editor for

Missiology. He previously served as Professor of World Christianity at United. He and his wife Winnie, a midwife, were United Methodist missionaries in Zimbabwe for seventeen years.

Robert G. Tuttle, Jr. is Professor of Evangelism at Asbury Theological Seminary, teaching primarily at the Orlando, Florida, campus. He previously taught evangelism at Garrett-Evangelical Theological Seminary, Oral Roberts University, and Fuller Theological Seminary. His books include *John Wesley, His Life and Theology* and *Someone Out There Needs Me: A Practical Guide to Relational Evangelism.*

David Lowes Watson is Director of the Office of Pastoral Formation for the Nashville Episcopal Area of The United Methodist Church. He formerly taught at Perkins School of Theology in Dallas, Texas, and at Wesley Theological Seminary in Washington, D.C. He also served as an Executive Secretary with the General Board of Discipleship of The United Methodist Church. His books include *God Does Not Foreclose* (Abingdon Press) and *Forming Christian Disciples* (Discipleship Resources).

INDEX